W9-BLH-290

HORSE HOUSING

HOW TO PLAN, BUILD, AND REMODEL BARNS AND SHEDS

ALSO BY RICHARD KLIMESH:

Maximum Hoof Power (with Cherry Hill)

Horse Housing

How to Plan, Build, and Remodel Barns and Sheds

Richard Klimesh
and Cherry Hill

Illustrations by
Richard Klimesh

Photographs by
Richard Klimesh
and Cherry Hill

T

Trafalgar Square Publishing
North Pomfret, Vermont

First published in 2002 by
Trafalgar Square Publishing
North Pomfret, Vermont 05053

Copyright © 2002 Richard Klimesh

All rights reserved. No part of this book may be reproduced, by any means, without written permission of the publisher, except by a reviewer quoting brief excerpts for a review in a magazine, newspaper, or web site.

Disclaimer of Liability:
The authors and publisher shall have neither liability nor responsibility to any person or entity with respect to any loss or damage caused or alleged to be caused directly or indirectly by the information contained in this book. While the book is as accurate as the authors can make it, there may be errors, omissions, and inaccuracies.

Klimesh, Richard.
    Horse housing : how to plan, build, and remodel barns and sheds / Richard Klimesh and Cherry Hill.
        p. cm.
    Includes bibliographical references and index.
    ISBN-13:978-1-57076-216-1 (hardcover)
    ISBN-10:1-57076-216-3 (hardcover)
    1. Stables--Design and construction. 2. Horses—Housing--Design and construction.
    I. Hill, Cherry, 1947- II. Title.

    TH4930 .K49 2002
    636.1'0831--dc21   2002022646

Cover and book design by Lynne Walker Design Studio
www.lynnewalker.com
Typeface: Bembo and Copperplate

Printed in China

10 9 8 7 6

Dedication

To my wife Cherry Hill, the best friend a person
or a horse could ever have.

Acknowledgments

Thanks to the following individuals for assistance with various portions of this book: Detlef Juerss, Steinbau Konstruktion; Bonnie Manley, National Fire Protection Association; Wayne Millis, Carolina Electrical and Plumbing Company; and Mark Graham, National Roofing Contractors Association.

TABLE OF CONTENTS

PREFACE

When it comes to horsekeeping facilities, I am very particular. Not only do I want a safe and sturdy barn that is comfortable and healthy for my horses, but I also want the barn to run efficiently, be easy to maintain, and have that special ambiance. That's because I spend more time at my barn than in my house!

Before we settled in Colorado in 1983, my husband Richard Klimesh and I had owned and leased horse acreages in Canada and seven states from Alaska to Arizona and from Oregon to Illinois. During that time, we experienced quite a variety of weather and encountered topography and soil ranging from rocky mountains to desert to lush farmland to swampland. And we saw all kinds of horse barns—dank dungeons, luxurious people palaces, wind tunnels, ammonia factories, sweatboxes, flimsy ticky-tacks, chewed down and patched up shacks, and barns that rained inside when it wasn't raining outside. We also saw a handful of barns that were just right. We learned that there are certain things that just don't work well for horses, whereas other layouts and materials make horsekeeping sweet.

When we designed my current barn, we employed the good ideas we'd gathered over the years. Like many of our projects, the barn started on a napkin in a restaurant. From that, we honed the plan, inserting all of the necessary details. Then, Richard masterfully crafted a barn that suits my particular needs perfectly.

I usually have between six and eight horses (from foals to seniors) in various stages of training and management. With no children or employees to help, the "Klim Team" does it all. I'm responsible for the health care and training, and Richard heads up facilities' design and maintenance. In addition to that, we both are full-time photojournalists, book authors, and together work as a video production team. The term "spare time" just isn't in our vocabulary. That's why we both appreciate an efficient set up that facilitates daily chores and routine tasks.

Because all of my training and riding and the majority of our photo and video shoots start at the barn, my tack room functions as command central. Not only do I store

tack and equipment there, but veterinary supplies, horse records, film, daily shot lists, and storyboards are kept there as well. In addition, the tack room has a section where I clean, repair, and launder horse items. The wash rack and grooming area make up a full-service equine "beauty salon" complete with overhead infrared heater and a central vacuum for grooming horses and blankets. There are varied places to tie horses, which is a necessity for photo/video shoots when I need to have a few groomed and tacked horses ready at a moment's notice.

Where we live, we have a full spectrum of seasonal weather—from frigid winter winds to blazing summer sun at 7,000 feet in the foothills of the Colorado Rockies. So we designed the barn to provide comfortable shelter from both. In the last chapter of this book, I'll take you on a personal tour of my barn, which, I hope, will help you come up with some ideas that will work for you.

Building a horse barn is a big deal. It requires considerable space and lots of labor, money, and time. The more time you invest in the planning of your horse barn, the less redesigning and remodeling you'll have to do.

I know I'm somewhat biased because Richard is my best buddy and husband of over 25 years, but he has built me some great horse facilities and has practical ideas and suggestions for horse housing. That's why I'm so glad that he is sharing his knowledge and our collective horsekeeping experience with you.

Horse Housing is a tremendous resource whether you are planning a new barn, remodeling existing buildings, or are in the process of purchasing real estate with horse facilities. You'll know barns inside and out after reading this book.

As you research and plan, let those gray cells work as you design your own dream barn to fit your horse needs, your locale, and your lifestyle.

A poorly designed barn can make you gnash and gnarl on a daily basis—believe me, I've been there.

A well-designed barn, on the other hand, makes daily horse care and training flow like a peaceful Rocky Mountain stream.

Happy horsekeeping,
Cherry Hill

A NOTE TO THE READER

The author has provided a dictionary of Helpful
Building Terms in the book's Appendix 1. The terms
defined in this section appear throughout the book in
italicized type as an indication to readers that they may
refer to p. 163 for definitions.

INTRODUCTION

I wrote this book *to* horse owners but *for* horses. Taking proper care of horses is a noble, humbling, and rewarding experience, and, even with the best facilities it takes a lot of work and dedication. My goal is to help you make your barn safe and comfortable for horses but also pleasant and efficient for you to work in. I've corralled information, ideas, and resources that you can use to create an affordable and attractive barn that will serve your needs and those of your horses.

There are as many different barns as there are horse owners because everyone's horsekeeping situation is different. I saw this first hand during the seventeen years that I was a professional farrier. Traveling throughout many areas of the United States and Canada, I worked in barns of all shapes, sizes, and levels of comfort and efficiency. I realized that lighting, flooring, ventilation, and traffic patterns could affect safety, attitude, and quality of work. I also noticed how these factors affected the health, attitude, and behavior of the horses in the barns and of the people who cared for them.

Barns are often built to satisfy the needs of people, not the needs of horses. Indeed, I've seen many barns that once built are rarely inhabited by horses. Instead, they serve as repositories for horse feed, tack, and equipment. That's okay, since the myriad items required to care for horses have to go somewhere. And, in fact, horses are generally healthier and, we can suppose, happier, not living inside a barn, so long as they have adequate feed, water, and protection from wind.

But there are times when a barn is essential for providing proper horse care or for the attainment of your goals as a horse person. A stall can enable you to keep a horse clean when he is in regular work or being shown, or to keep an old, sick, or injured horse warm, dry, and confined. It can provide any horse with shelter during extreme weather, such as a blizzard. Using stalls, you can closely regulate the diets of horses by feeding them separately.

Having a clean, well-lit, sheltered place for you and your veterinarian and farrier to work is essential. People do better work when they're not squinting in the dark or battling the elements, so your horses will get better care. It would be difficult for a vet or farrier to see abnormalities or perform work, especially on limbs, in a dimly-lit or shadow-filled barn. These hard-working professionals appreciate barns that have pleasant facilities and shy away from those with unsafe, unsanitary, and dismal work spaces. Wouldn't you?

Before I became a farrier, I studied architecture at Iowa State University. Soon after, I began my first career as a carpenter and cabinetmaker. During that time, I found that there is usually more than one way to build something, and more than one material that will serve a given purpose. Since then, I've also seen that there are certain combinations of spaces and materials that have been proven to be safe and comfortable for horses. When it comes to horse facilities, if a method, material, or design works well, I suggest you think long and hard before changing it. Different does not necessarily mean better.

This book will provide information, or tell where to find it, that will help you determine what you need in a barn, sort through the options, and make decisions that will work best for your stable. (The words "barn" and "stable" are synonymous in this book and are used interchangeably.)

I've included Helpful Building Terms in Appendix 1 to help you better understand the processes and materials used in barn construction. A working vocabulary of construction terminology will help you communicate more knowledgeably and efficiently with barn designers and contractors in order to get the barn you want.

In Appendix 3, Resource Guide, you will find a list of web sites containing information applicable to barn design and construction, as well as contact information for manufacturers of materials and products mentioned in book. The World Wide Web forums and newsgroups listed there can be a useful source of answers, options, and opinions if you run into problems or have questions at any stage of your barn project.

In Chapter 7 you will find sample plans for barns designed for one to six horses. All the plans can be modified to accommodate more horses. The design and building principles that keep horses safe and make daily horsekeeping efficient apply to barns of all sizes. If you plan a large facility and need to hire an architect, you will also find a selection of architects and builders in the Resource Guide.

I've found that a seminar, clinic, magazine, or book is often worth its entire cost if I discover just one snippet of information that makes horsekeeping safer, easier, or more economical. I hope this book repays you many times over.

Richard Klimesh

SECTION I

PLANNING

CHAPTER ONE

LAW AND ORDER

The days are long gone when a horse owner could put up a barn without worrying what the neighbors or anyone else thought about it. As countryside becomes more populated today, to build horse facilities you have to deal with government building regulations, local *ordinances*, private land covenants, and builders' contracts. This first chapter will help smooth some of the early bumps on the road to your dream barn by explaining regulations and paperwork that could affect your project.

One important note before we start talking about buildings. A plentiful source of safe water is essential for keeping horses. In many states, water quality issues fall under the jurisdiction of the county health department. If the property you are considering buying has a domestic well, make certain the well has passed a county health department contamination test prior to the sale of the property. This is usually done at the seller's expense. Also, be certain that there are no restrictions on using the well to water livestock.

ZONING

Before you get carried away with the prospect of building your dream barn, determine if you can legally keep horses and build a horse barn on the property that you own or are purchasing (fig. 1.1). Zoning laws and ordinances (local laws enacted by a municipality such as a city or township) separate land into districts or zones according

to use and specify which types of buildings can be built where. Basic zones include residential, commercial, industrial, and agricultural. Each zone has permitted, conditionally permitted, and prohibited uses. Some *zoning* districts prohibit horses (ordinances are rarely written by horse people). Rather than relying on information from neighbors or realtors on how a piece of land is zoned and what uses are permitted, call the local zoning or planning department or building inspector with the address of the property.

Even if horses are allowed, regulations may exclude barns and stables. Zoning laws, county and city ordinances, and *building codes* often have specific development standards relating to the height, size, and placement of buildings on a site. This ensures, among other things, that buildings and corrals are set back a minimum distance from the road and property lines and that fences are a certain height. For example, stables might be required to be located in the rear yard (if there is also a residence) and at least 50 feet from the property lines.

To prevent overgrazing (fig. 1.2) and erosion some local ordinances dictate the minimum size of land needed to keep a horse, such as one acre of pasture per horse, and regulate the number of horses that can be kept in a given area, such as two horses per acre or one horse per five acres. Some districts require an environmental review, in part to ensure that the land is sloped and drained properly

1.1 *Check local zoning laws, regulations, and covenants to see if horses and barns are allowed in that area.*

1.2 *Too many horses cause overgrazing.*

so *runoff* from pens doesn't pollute neighboring properties and waterways. Other areas require a *permit* to keep horses, charge an annual fee (part of which might be used to maintain equestrian trails), require regular inspections of your facilities, or regulate how often manure must be disposed of to prevent offensive odors and the accumulation of flies from intruding onto adjacent properties.

Before buying property for horses, it pays to do your homework. It might be worthwhile to hire a lawyer to help uncover all the laws and ordinances that will affect your horse activities on that property. Look for horse ordinances, fencing ordinances, large animal ordinances, and farm animal ordinances, as well as ordinances that would affect any horse-related commercial uses you have in mind. Also, check if there are any plans to change existing laws or ordinances that might adversely affect your activities. In some cases, a lawyer can assist you in obtaining a *variance* for your property to exempt you from certain restrictive laws or ordinances.

This research is a lot of work and it will take time. One way to avoid losing a promising property to another buyer is to make an offer with a contingency stating that you must be satisfied with the results of your research regarding use of land for your horse activities or else the offer is withdrawn. (See the Resource Guide for sources of legal information regarding horse-friendly zoning).

COVENANTS

If zoning ordinances seem restrictive, wait until you experience covenants. Covenants, conditions, and restrictions (CC&Rs) are agreements among a group of land owners, such as communities, home owner associations (HOAs) or common interest developments (CIDs), that regulate land use and building types to keep property values up (for the lenders and realtors as much as for the residents). They are becoming more pervasive, and in many parts of the country it is difficult to find affordable horse property that is not in a HOA or CID.

When covenants conflict with zoning ordinances, the more restrictive rule applies. For example, you might buy land in a district zoned to allow horse barns but find that private property agreements prohibit them—sorry, no horses.

Private land groups are like little governments, and they strive to make life in their community better. They collect money from residents and use it to provide road and trail maintenance, security guards, trash collection, and street lighting. They pass rules designed to keep the development clean and tidy, preventing such things as junk car collections, unsightly fences, and overgrazed bare dirt lots. However, the law does not recognize these groups as actual governments, and the covenants they

1.3 *Landowner organizations can dictate if you can build a barn and what criteria it must follow.*

enact do not always comply with the Bill of Rights. Consequently, rules can be very restrictive to the lifestyles of residents, and particularly to horse owners—such as dictating where you can park your horse trailer, if you can build a barn (fig. 1.3), and what style and colors are acceptable. In many developments, your barn plans would have to be approved by an architectural review board before you could start building.

HOAs are often managed by a board of directors made up of residents of the association, some of whom take a hard line regarding enforcement. Since HOAs are private groups, police are not required to enforce their covenants. The rules are enforced either by residents themselves through the courts or by professional management companies and/or lawyers. Disputes over infractions can get ugly and very costly.

When you own or purchase property in a planned development, you automatically become a member and are required to pay monthly fees and abide by the covenants. Many buyers have little idea of what they are getting into, so many states now require the seller to disclose information regarding HOAs. To prevent surprises *after* closing, consider having an attorney search for and review covenants on the property that you are considering. Before you sign the purchase agreement, be absolutely certain the community's rules are compatible with your horsey lifestyle.

BUILDING CODES

Whereas zoning laws dictate what *types* of building may or may not be located in an area, building codes tell *where* it may be located on the property and *how* it should be constructed (fig. 1.4). Like other laws, building codes are intended to protect people. They provide minimum standards for building materials and construction methods to ensure safe buildings.

1.4 *Building codes ensure strong, safe buildings by regulating the materials used and how they are fastened together.*

HOW BUILDING CODES ARE WRITTEN

State and local building codes are most often based on a model code, which lays out requirements for all areas of construction including wiring, plumbing, and fire prevention. Model codes are based on *building standards* that detail the minimum design or the performance of a specific material. Standards are usually developed by independent nonprofit service organizations comprised of people involved in the construction and insurance industries, city and county building departments, and other companies and individuals familiar with construction methods and materials. Model codes are updated every year, with new editions published every three years.

The Uniform Building Code (UBC) is, by far, the most commonly used, followed by the BOCA (Building Officials Conference of America, used in the Northeast and Great Lakes region), SBCCI (Southern Building Code Congress International), and the National Building Code.

To buy a copy of the UBC, check your local building department, bookstore, or see the Resource Guide in Appendix 3.

For information on local codes, contact:
County: County Clerk, Council, or Commission.
City or Town: City Clerk or Council, Building and Zoning Department, Housing Department.

Building regulations in some form have been around for over 4,000 years. They were developed largely in response to losses of life and property from catastrophes such as fires, building collapses, earthquakes, and storms. European safety regulations came to America with the colonists. There is no national building *code* enforced by the federal government. The U.S. Constitution puts individual states in charge of ensuring safe buildings. Some states have mandatory statewide building codes, but regulation of building codes is typically left up to local governments. When no mandatory statewide code applies, counties or local jurisdictions may develop their own code, adopt or modify a *model code*, or choose to have no code at all. Only a few municipalities (mostly major cities) write and revise their own codes. Even if an area has no building code per se it may still have other specific codes such as fire, plumbing, and safety. Building regulations written by HOAs and other private developments must be at least as strict as the county or local building code that's in effect.

PERMITS

A *building permit* is a license to build or remodel your barn as long as it's done according to code. In areas where building codes are in force, you are required to buy a building permit before beginning construction. You can apply for the permit yourself or ask the barn company or *general contractor* to get it for you (see Chapter 2, Who's the Builder?).

A permit is issued for a specified period of time, often eighteen months. It can usually be renewed once for another 18 months. If you don't finish your barn within a certain time frame, say three years, you will likely have to pay for another permit. Permit fees are based on the total cost of the work being done and how many departments have to review the plans and inspect the project.

Part of the building permit is an inspection record card, a brightly colored poster board (often yellow) containing a checklist of construction stages (fig. 1.5). This card must be posted on the barn in plain view during construction for the building inspector to sign off on as inspections are completed.

Building a barn without a permit is illegal in most areas and can cost you a lot of time and money in fines, legal wrangling, and re-doing the work. And the building department doesn't need surveillance satellites to find you out. A neighbor could report you, a building inspector driving by to check other work in the area might notice construction activity and realize you haven't been calling for inspections, or the county assessor might discover during a periodic evaluation of your property that there was no permit issued on your new barn. In most parts of the country, an inspector can legally come onto private property to check on construction and code violations and the inspector is immune from civil or criminal prosecution for such entry.

When caught building without a permit, you will be required to apply for one and may also have to pay a fine. The inspector could make you hire an engineer to inspect the *foundation*, or poles of a pole building, to verify that the work already done is safe. This would mean expensive excavation. Furthermore, the engineer may need to design corrections to bring the construction up to code. You pay for design and corrections. Building a barn without a permit may exclude it from your homeowner's insurance. My advice? Get the permit.

GETTING A BUILDING PERMIT

To get a building permit you need to fill out a permit application and submit it along with the required plans to the Planning and Engineering Department. For some larger barns, such as when steel *beams* or specialized *concrete* are involved, plans must be prepared and sealed by a licensed engineer or architect. Plans for simple barns generally do not require a seal and can be drawn by anyone (see Understanding Plans, p. 44). Plans don't have to be fancy, but they do need to show that the barn will be built according to code.

The plans examiner will check the plans for accuracy and for compliance with zoning ordinances. If the plans are not up to code, the examiner will give instructions for necessary changes. If there is question of safety, you might be required to hire an engineer to check the plans. You may need to submit a revised set of plans before being issued a permit. In certain areas, approval may also be required from an Architectural Review Board if the barn will be in plain view. This process might take days or weeks, depending on the complexity of the project and how busy the examiner is. When the plans are approved, you'll be issued a permit.

Some areas require a separate permit for new electrical service or for a new septic system. Also, if your new property has no driveway, a County Road Access application may be required.

Check with your local building department to find out the exact plans you are required to submit with the building permit application. Most plans for a simple *pole barn* include a *plot plan* and a set of building plans (see Types of Plans, p. 45).

INSPECTIONS

The building inspector (code enforcement officer) will come to your building site and inspect the project for compliance with building codes and local ordinances.

1.5 *The inspection record card must be posted on the barn during construction.*

WHEN DO YOU NEED A BUILDING PERMIT?

A building permit is required for most construction activity, such as:

- new construction

- enlarging, altering, or moving a building

- repairing a building

- demolishing a building

Permits are generally not required for ordinary repairs you do yourself or for sheds under a certain size often 120 square feet (although you still might need approval by the local Planning Department or Architectural Review Board).

Because cities and counties can be held liable for injuries caused by poor construction, inspectors are usually diligent about enforcing codes. The building inspector is not the enemy. His job is to ensure that the barn you are building is safe for you and for future owners. Most inspectors have extensive building experience, and you can learn a lot by asking for and listening to their advice.

Some inspectors schedule specific areas of the county on certain days of the week. It's up to the builder in charge to call and arrange for inspections as the work progresses, although some *subcontractors* like to call for inspections themselves. It's a good idea to be clear on exactly who will call for an inspection or you may have to rip out *insulation* or stall paneling to show the inspector plumbing or wiring that wasn't checked.

Some inspectors require that a set of plans be available during inspections. As stages of construction pass inspection, the inspector will sign off on the inspection card. Information marked on the card is usually also entered into the building department's computer each day. If the work doesn't pass, the inspector will leave a Notice of Non-Compliance or a Correction Notice telling you what needs to be done. Building code violations are handled in the same manner as permit violations—if not corrected within a specified time you could be fined. There is usually an additional fee if the inspector has to return to the site for a recheck. At the end of the project, the inspector will sign off on the final inspection, at which time you can begin using the barn. ∪

COMMON INSPECTIONS FOR A POLE FRAME HORSE BARN
(varies depending on local codes)

TEMPORARY ELECTRICAL Also called "saw service." This provides power during construction.

SETBACK AND FOOTINGS (OR HOLES FOR POLE BUILDING) After holes are dug and concrete pads are poured.

CONCRETE SLAB Before pouring concrete, the following must be inspected:

- *forms* and ground preparation
- steel reinforcement
- any plumbing, electrical, waste, vent, and water lines that will be imbedded in concrete

TRADES All electrical, plumbing, mechanical, sprinkler, and fire alarm systems are inspected and tested before any concealing work or *framing* inspections.

FRAMING After the building is up but before insulation or interior covering is installed.

FINAL After all work is completed. Check electric, plumbing, concrete *slab, sheetrock,* and heating. Required before building can be used and sometimes before utility companies can provide service.

CHAPTER TWO

WHO'S THE BUILDER?

In the first chapter you saw how building codes are designed to ensure safe structures. A safe, legal building should top your list of priorities, but given the considerable sum of money you are investing, your horse barn should also look good and last a very long time. You want it built right—and that is up to the builder. Basically, you have four choices:

- Buy a modular or premanufactured barn and have the barn company put it up

- Hire a general contractor to take charge of all or part of the process

- Act as your own contractor and hire subcontractors to do all or some of the work

- Build it yourself

The method you choose will depend on how soon you need the barn, how much time you have to spend on the project, the extent of your building experience and carpentry expertise, and your budget.

MODULAR BARN BUILDERS

Buying a modular (premanufactured) barn can be the easiest, quickest, cheapest, and least time-consuming way to go (fig. 2.1). Most major barn companies have a network of representatives throughout the country. Many representatives are also builders or can suggest builders in your area who are familiar with the construction of their barns. They will usually work with the builder to coordinate building delivery and erection.

Barn companies have a variety of standard barn plans and variations to choose from. Most will design custom barns to fit your ideas and your budget and to comply with local zoning or CC&R restrictions. They will give you a price on the barn package, explain the financing process, and help you create and define your budget.

If you have little time to spend on the project, you'll probably be able to find a barn company that will do everything from getting the building permit to laying the stall mats. If you have more time than money, on the other hand, you can have the barn company deliver a barn package to your site and put it up yourself (fig. 2.2).

It pays to compare barns from several companies before ordering to become familiar with options available to you. Find out from each company if there is a completed barn you can look at and ask for names of local horse owners who have purchased their barns. Call several references to see if you can take a look at their barns. Ask how they like their barns and how the company was to deal with. Before you order a barn, be certain you know what you are getting and what you are not getting—in writing.

- Will the barn's dimensions, including door openings, suit your needs?

2.1 *Modular barns are available across the country and come in a wide variety of styles.*

2.2 *You can save money by having modular barn components delivered and assembling them yourself.*

- Will the barn satisfy local building codes?

- What is covered by warranty and for how long?

- Does the warranty depend on who erects the barn?

- Will the barn be insurable?

- Is foundation work included?

- What will you need that is not included?

- When will the barn be delivered?

- Are delivery charges included?

- When will the barn be completed?

- Who can you contact regarding questions and problems during construction?

- Who is responsible for clean up?

2.3 *A barn company or general contractor will have the tools and equipment to do the job right and stay on schedule. This tractor, for example, has a heavy duty auger for setting foundation posts, a front loader for moving materials, and a scaffolding on the roof for workers to stand on.*

GENERAL CONTRACTOR

The general contractor is a builder you hire to take charge of some or all aspects of your barn project. His duties can include finalizing building plans or blueprints, putting together cost estimates and material lists, getting permits, arranging for temporary services, hiring and paying competent subcontractors for various stages of construction (excavating, framing, wiring, and plumbing) and providing the equipment to get your barn built on time and within your budget (fig. 2.3). The general can also schedule delivery of materials and clean up the site when the job is completed. A good general contractor will promptly take care of problems you notice once the barn is built (called the *punch list*), such as a loose fastener or an ill-fitted door. For all this, you can expect to pay between 10 to 20 percent of the total cost of the barn, depending on how much responsibility you have him take on.

FINDING A CONTRACTOR

To get the barn you want, choose a general contractor that has standards of quality that are at least as high as your own. The best design in the world will never become a high-quality barn in the hands of a poor builder. Automatically giving the job to the lowest bidder can be a big mistake. In fact, don't even waste your time asking for bids until you've done some investigation on prospective builders.

Like good farriers and trainers, good builders are booked far in advance. Start looking for a builder early in the planning stage. The sooner you get on a builder's list the sooner he can schedule your barn. Above all, look for a builder that is familiar with horses and who specializes

in equine facilities. He'll be more likely than a non-horseman to spot things in your plans that will save you time, money, and headaches.

BEGINNING THE SEARCH

First of all, be sure you look for a general contractor. Subcontractors specialize only in certain aspects of building. Start making a list of potential builders by asking horsey friends, relatives, and coworkers for first-hand recommendations. You'll soon see whose name keeps coming to the top. To get a more comprehensive list of builders in your area check with:

- Local barn dealers. Even if you aren't buying a barn from them, most dealers will likely tell you of builders they recommend and those to avoid.

- Lumber suppliers. Check bulletin boards for ads and ask salesmen for recommendations.

- Yellow pages. Look under Barns, Building Contractors, Contractors-General, and Buildings – Post and Frame.

- Local newspaper and farm and ranch magazine ads.

- Bulletin boards at local building, farm, and feed stores.

- Local real estate agents that specialize in horse properties.

- Members of your local saddle club.

- Barn owners. Spend some time driving around your area to find barns you like.

WHAT TO LOOK FOR IN A BARN BUILDER

• Horse knowledge and experience

• Familiarity with materials and designs that are horse safe

• Knowledge of local building practices and codes

• Experience working with local zoning, planning, and building officials

• Established relationships with local subcontractors

• Effective methods of paying subcontractors and getting lien waivers

• Punctuality and the ability to develop a time schedule and stick to it

NARROWING THE FIELD

Don't waste time calling every contractor on your list. Concentrate on three or four. Find out if any claims are recorded against the builders on your short list by calling the Better Business Bureau and your state attorney general. Contact your state's department of professional regulation or licensing board to see what the licensing and insurance requirements are for builders. Some states have very specific requirements, whereas others do not. If your state requires contractors to be licensed, only consider hiring those that are licensed. You can check state requirements, search for a licensed contractor, and verify the state license of a contractor at www.contractorreferral.com.

Next, try to schedule appointments to meet the builders. Call each contractor and say you're building a barn and you'd like to discuss it with him. If he was referred by someone, tell him who gave you his name. If you don't get the contractor directly, leave an evening phone number where you can be reached. Note how long it takes for them to return your call.

When you meet with the builder, ask about his experience with horse barns. Take your *floor plan* or sketches and explain what you'd like added or changed. See how well the builder listens, if he can satisfactorily answer your questions, and if he offers helpful comments or suggestions.

Find out how long the contractor has been in business and how long his employees have worked for him. Find out if he has liability insurance and workers' compensation so you are not held liable for damages if one of his workers gets injured on your property. Ask the contractor if he is licensed or bonded.

Finally, ask each builder for several names of former barn clients. Take a tour of the barns with the builder, if possible, so he can point out important features. If you have a chance to meet the barn owners, try to find out more about the builder by asking these questions:

• Was the barn completed on schedule?

• Did it stay within the bid price?

• How did the builder handle changes to the original plan?

• Was the site kept clean during construction?

• Did the workers cause any problems?

• Was all debris hauled away after the job was done?

In some cases, it might be best to talk to the owner privately, so ask if you can stop back later or call.

Take accounts of building errors in perspective. Anyone can make mistakes. More important is how the contractor handled the mistakes. If a builder is mentioned repeatedly in regards to disappointing results or failure to follow through or fix things, cross him off your list.

GETTING ESTIMATES

Many good contractors don't like bidding, especially on a small barn that often means little profit and big headaches. They want work, not price shoppers. If you call up out of the blue and say you're "getting some bids," it tells the contractor that you're focused on price, not on quality. Instead, offer to stop by their office to discuss your plans and see photos of their work. This says you're looking for quality, not just the cheapest deal.

An estimate based on cost per square foot can give you a rough idea of cost, but it won't tell you much about the quality or completeness of

2.4 *Good construction includes covered wooden edges, protected light fixtures, and properly spaced grilles.*

the finished barn. To get the clearest, most precise bids, provide a list of exactly what types of materials, finishes, and *fixtures* you want included in your barn.

As you get estimates, check each one for a detailed description of the work to be done, materials, approximate starting and completion dates and payment procedures. Compare the bids for quality of materials and completeness of construction. If one builder's bid includes window *grilles* and rubber stall mats, make sure to take that into account when comparing it to other bids.

THE FINAL PICK
The estimates tell you which builder has the lowest price but not which one has the best deal. If one bid sounds too good to be true, it probably is. A contractor that submits a suspiciously low bid might be uninsured, use inferior material, and perform poor work. Now is the time to factor in what you learned talking with the contractor and his clients. Balance cost with professionalism and quality workmanship (fig. 2.5). Which of the builders returned your calls promptly? Which do you think is the most capable? The most honest? When all things have been

2.5 *Experienced subcontractors who specialize in horse barns might not submit the lowest bids, but they are more likely than inexperienced workers to get things right the first time.*

considered, listen to your gut feeling and go with the contractor you think will do the best job.

THE BUILDER'S CONTRACT
There are two ways to strike a deal with a barn builder: a verbal agreement based on trust and a written contract based on ink. Ink changes less than memory, so a written contract is a better choice for keeping both you and the builder on track and making sure you end up with the barn you paid for.

There are two types of building contracts: fixed bid and cost plus. With a fixed bid contract, the total costs are laid out before construction begins. With a cost plus contract, you pay the general contractor as you go for all materials and labor, plus a fixed percentage, usually around 10 to 15 percent. If the builder is also the barn dealer, you may need to sign two separate contracts, one for the barn materials package and another for construction of the barn.

Before work begins, go over the construction process with the builder. Make sure he understands what you expect from the barn and that you both are clear on what is to be done and when. Find out if there will be

---

GETTING THE MOST OUT OF A BARN TOUR

When looking at a barn to evaluate a builder's work, don't be "wowed" by irrelevant details like beautiful horses, high level of management, or fancy tack or embellishments. Concentrate on the quality and soundness of the construction. Here are some things to check for:

SAFE CONSTRUCTION Are there sharp edges, protruding latches, or loose nails or screws that could injure a horse, catch on mane and tail hair, or cause him to rub? Are there any small spaces where a horse could get his foot or head caught (fig. 2.4)?

APPROPRIATE USE OF MATERIALS Are there exposed wood edges that a horse could chew on? Is all glass or *fiberglass* out of a horse's reach or protected by steel grillwork? Are the floors solid and do they have good traction? Is metal *edging* heavy enough to prevent a horse from tearing it?

ADEQUATE LIGHTING Does the number and type of lights seem adequate? Are the lights and wiring protected from horse contact? Are the switches located where they are easy to use?

SOURCE OF WATER Are automatic waterers installed so a horse can't get injured on them? Are there hydrants and *faucets* within a hose reach of stalls?

QUALITY WORKMANSHIP Is the barn riddled with dents or hammer marks where the hammer missed the nail? Are there any loose or missing nails and screws? Is the paint or stain job neat? Are the roof edges straight? Do the doors fit and operate smoothly? Are the latches safe and easy to use?

TIDINESS Do you spot any scattered nails, screws, or other debris that could end up in a horse's foot?

additional charges for changes once construction is under way. Review the completion date and make a plan to keep informed if deadlines change due to unexpected delays. Don't be embarrassed of you don't understand the contract. There's nothing wrong with taking it home so you can look it over thoroughly at your own pace. Don't sign it until you do understand it.

SELF-CONTRACTOR

Self-contracting is about quality control and saving money. For a start, you save the 10 to 20 percent of the total construction bill you would pay a general contractor. In addition, you can save money by supplying all the materials yourself, rather than paying a markup on materials supplied by subcontractors. But this means you have to plan ahead, shop around, and take advantage of sales to get the best buys. And, of course, it helps to be familiar enough with construction to know which materials to buy.

Like everything else in life, self-contracting involves trade-offs. To save the money you would have paid a general contractor, you have to make time to perform all of his duties. If you are working a full-time job, this might be next to impossible. And along with the power to make all the decisions determining the quality of workmanship and materials that go into your barn, comes the cold fact that you have no one to blame but yourself for mistakes. And they can be expensive and have even been known to lead to divorce court!

Not everyone is cut out for self-contracting. It takes communication and organization skills and a basic understanding of the work being done by subcontractors.

BARN CONTRACT GUIDELINES

Including the following items on your contract will help everyone involved stay clear on the objectives, methods, and responsibilities.

- names of the contracting parties

- job location

- nature and scope of the work to be done

- starting date and a projected finish date

- responsibility for obtaining and paying for permits

- cost breakdown that includes contractor's total price and your payment schedule

- materials to be used, stating quantity and quality and specifying brand names where appropriate

- an assignment clause, which specifies that the contractor cannot hire another general contractor to do the work without your approval

- proof of insurance covering workers compensation, property damage, and personal liability (fig. 2.6)

- compliance with specified building codes or ordinances

- who is responsible for cleaning the building site and disposing of construction debris (fig. 2.7)

- warranties on workmanship

2.6 *Are you protected from liability if a worker gets injured?*

2.7 *Who is responsible for clean up?*

2.8 *Some owner-built barns move ahead in fits and starts, and may stall out for years.*

2.9 *Many horse owners hire a barn company or general contractor to at least do the walls and the roof.*

PAPERWORK

Building a barn is not all boards and nails. Before you begin, you need a set of plans to apply for permits and to guide construction. You can draw the plans yourself (see Understanding Plans, p. 44), hire an architect or engineer, or buy a set plans. With plans in hand, you can apply for necessary government permits (see Getting A Building Permit, p. 5). As work progresses, inspections will need to be scheduled and workers and suppliers have to be paid on time. Keep all of your agreements, schedules, payments, receipts, lists, and budget organized so you can refer to them as needed.

HIRING AND FIRING

Finding good workers and monitoring their work is a self-contractor's biggest challenge. The construction industry is like any other: there are workers with integrity and those without, some know what they are doing, and some only think they do. The more knowledgeable you are about a given trade, the better you'll be able to communicate with workers and subcontractors and separate the wheat from the chaff. You can learn a certain amount of "construction speak" by watching building shows, reading builder magazines and books, and, most importantly, by talking with builders, but there is no substitute for construction experience.

Hiring workers by the hour can be risky. They will likely be considered your employees and you will be liable for insurance, taxes, and government red tape that all employers must deal with. Subcontractors (subs), on the other hand, are not considered employees (unless paid by the hour). They work by contract for a predetermined amount to perform all or part of a larger contract. Although subs might charge more than hourly employees, they are generally a safer way to go.

Start by finding a carpenter subcontractor with horse barn experience. He'll likely be able to recommend the rest of the subs you'll need. The best place to begin looking for a sub is your local lumber store. Don't be surprised if some don't return your call or if they seem less than eager to work on your barn. Subs prefer working for general contractors rather than self-contractors because a general represents a steady stream of jobs where you provide only one. And that's one of the biggest advantages of hiring a general contractor—he has the connections to get good workers.

A difficult part about being the boss is holding subcontractors accountable for doing what you expect, such as showing up as promised, and firing them if you determine their performance is not satisfactory. Ask each subcontractor to supply you with a certificate of insurance to show that his employees are covered. This is a standard request and will ensure you are protected should a worker get injured while working on your barn.

Use a contract with all subs. Some supply their own or you can get forms from your lawyer or a stationery store.

FURNISHING SUPPLIES

Lumberyards should give you a contractor's discount on materials because that's what you are—a contractor. If you give them a copy of your plans, they will often work up a materials list and cost estimate for the project. By shopping around, you might find comparable deals at a large home or building center. Coordinate delivery of materials so they are on the site when workers are ready for them. Be aware that some of the subcontractors you hire might be adamant about only using materials they are familiar with. To prevent problems, discuss your choice of materials with prospective subs before hiring them or purchasing materials.

KEEP ON SCHEDULE

Think through your design carefully and make a written list of features before you begin. Once construction is under way, realize that each change you make means additional time and costs. Don't expect workers to finish according to the original schedule if you keep giving them more things to do.

QUALITY CONTROL

This may be the only barn you'll ever build, so take the time to see that things are done right. This means you have to be familiar enough with construction and design to know what *right* is. Plus, you need to be on-site during construction for several hours or more every day. Carry a pocket notebook to keep track of things that need attention. Communicate often with your subs and be assertive without being aggressive. Make sure you explain your expectations clearly so there are no misunderstandings.

KEEP IT TIDY

You and your family can help save money on your barn project by doing a lot of the clean-up work. A clean building site means workers don't have to constantly be walking over or around debris. Tools and materials are less likely to be lost and trampled if the construction site is picked up daily. And your finished barn will be a safer barn. Nails and other materials buried around the barn area have a way of reappearing as money in your vet's pocket.

BUILD IT YOURSELF

You could build the entire barn by yourself. This method will require the most of your time. Barn building is not rocket science, but it's not as easy as it looks either. You must be experienced in all aspects of building and have a good measure of "stick-to-it-iveness." It's not uncommon for an owner-built barn to linger in various stages of completion for several years or stall out altogether and never get finished (fig. 2.8). If you are not used to construction work, you'll find muscles you didn't know you had and will likely suffer cuts, scrapes, and blisters until your body gets accustomed to its new assignment.

You can build from scratch if you have the skills and confidence. You can order a *modular* barn and assemble it yourself. Or you can buy a ready-to-assemble barn in kit form, complete with instructions. Some barn kits contain everything but the foundation and the flooring and are designed to be assembled by persons with no building experience.

Another option is to contract a barn company to erect the *shell*—the walls and the roof (fig. 2.9). These are the most difficult parts to do alone. Then you can finish the inside as time and budget allow. Stall kits contain the metal framing and hardware—you typically provide all the wood components and labor (fig. 2.10). They are available in various stages of completion and to fit different types of construction. Even professional builders often utilize stall kits on custom barns. A *component stall* fits between posts within the barn and relies on them for

2.10 *Stall kits can save you time and money.*

2.11 *Some materials are too big and heavy for a person to handle alone.*

support. A *panel stall* is freestanding. It consists of completed wall panels that bolt together. It is the easiest kit to assemble and the most costly.

Certain components, such as roof *trusses*, are too big and heavy for one person to handle and may require lifting equipment to set in place (fig. 2.11). And you will likely need some help from family, friends, or neighbors with construction tasks that you are not capable of or comfortable doing alone, such as wiring or pouring concrete (fig. 2.12). But, if you enjoy building, aren't in a hurry, and have the necessary skills and experience to solve the problems you encounter, building your own barn can give you the final say on quality and a great feeling of accomplishment. ∪

2.12 *Be prepared to ask for help with stages of construction, such as pouring concrete, that are beyond your experience or ability.*

CHAPTER THREE

LOCATION AND ORIENTATION

It seemed like a logical spot for a barn: relatively flat, on solid bedrock, close to the hay shed, in view of the house, and facing south. I had drawn rough plans and was wrestling with how to pin a foundation to bedrock when my wife came up with another of her brilliant ideas—why not put the barn facing east on the hillside overlooking the arena south of the house? I could already hear the roar of huge, expensive earth moving equipment. I resisted. But she made a good case.

Although my location had merits, it also had serious drawbacks that I'd overlooked in my enthusiasm. For one thing, it turns out that during wet spells, runoff from a large meadow rushes right through the site. And even though a south-facing barn would have taken advantage of winter sun, the strong spring winds would have blown right into the stalls.

The cost of excavation paled in comparison to the daily problems confronting us at the "logical" site. We went with the wife's hillside plan, and it turned out great. I'm glad I came to my senses.

COMPROMISES

Finding the building site best suited for your barn plan and horsekeeping style can involve many compromises

3.1 *This barn gains wind protection and shade by being close to the woods but risks spread of fire and damage from falling trees during a storm. Note the south facing clerestory windows that take advantage of natural light.*

(fig. 3.1): scenic view vs. privacy, solar gain vs. wind protection, shade from trees vs. fire risk, morning light vs. evening light, view of horses vs. staring at pens. Discover the disadvantages of a prospective building site *before* the barn is built so you can make design adjustments or find another site. Once the barn is built, odds are you'll never move it. You'll learn to live with it, no matter how bad the location turns out to be.

SITE SKETCH

On many properties, especially five acres or less, the choice of a barn site will be limited and sometimes obvious. On larger properties you may have so many options that you'll have difficulty keeping track of them. To get a firm idea of what you are working with, hike the land with a pad and pencil and draw a bird's eye view of the property, called a *plot plan* (see Plot Plan, p. 45). Sketch the property boundaries and all objects that will affect the placement of your barn and use of the land, such as fences, large rocks, trees and water sources. Mark and number the locations of prospective building sites and make a list of pros and cons of each site on a separate paper. Later, you can use this field research to compare all possible sites and choose the best one.

THE NO ZONE

In some districts, you can't build a barn—period (see Zoning, p. 2). Building requirements vary from county to county and within land developments. Before anything else, check your local zoning codes and land covenants to avoid complications and disappointment.

Some portions of your property could be off limits for a barn because of regulations that dictate where utility lines can go and how close you can build to ponds and streams, neighboring buildings, property lines, and roadways. A 30-foot buffer zone is commonly required around the perimeter of acreage.

UTILITIES

How will you get water and electricity to your barn? A small barn could possibly tap into your house utilities, but most barns require a separate electric service. Check with your building department and electric utility before committing to a building site.

Electric wires can come to the barn overhead or underground. Water lines, however, must be buried below *frost line* to keep them from freezing and bursting. And the farther north you live the deeper they'll have to be. In some areas of the northeastern United States frost can go eight feet.

The longer and deeper the trench for utilities, the more it will cost, especially if you have to go through rock (fig. 3.2). And, the higher the barn is from the well, the larger the pump and the more electricity it will take to pump water to it.

3.2 *A trench for utilities can be expensive.*

SOIL

All soil is not created equal. Soil with high clay and silt content can shift and expand when it absorbs water and when it freezes. This can cause a barn to sink, shift, or heave with the frost, all of which can damage the structure and even cause it to collapse.

Generally, the less water soil holds, the better it is as a building site. Bedrock is most stable, but it can limit excavation and drainage options. Soil high in sand, gravel, and decomposed granite drains well and is generally preferred for building sites.

To determine the percolation rate of your soil (how well it drains), have it evaluated by an engineer (contact your state or county extension agent for recommendations; see Appendix 3). If the soil is very poorly drained, you can install drainage tiles, excavate and replace the soil, or choose another site.

A site with poorly drained soil could require excavation to ten feet to make it suitable for a barn. A layer of large rock is laid at the base of the excavation. Crushed rock of decreasing sizes is added in layers leaving about 1 foot for a top layer—a mixture of clay and sand, clean road base, decomposed granite or small gravel usually works well. (There should be no topsoil on the building footprint.) If a significant amount of fill is added, it should be compacted by heavy equipment in layers as it is added. Alternatively, let the site settle for a year before building.

DRAINAGE

Avoid low and wet areas. A constantly moist environment is bad for horses. It can lead to skin problems such as scratches, as well as thrush, cracks, and other hoof maladies. Wet pens are messy, difficult to clean, and provide breeding ground for many types of flies. Mud, rotting wood, rusting metal, mold, and fungi are all associated with high moisture areas.

More than one horse owner has built in the fall only to find the barn on a spring in the spring (fig. 3.3). A good time to check potential building sites is in late spring after the snow has melted and during or shortly after heavy rain. This is when runoff problems are least likely to be hidden by foliage.

Trouble is, some springs may be inactive for years and then pop up in the strangest places—even on hilltops. Ask previous owners or long-time resident neighbors if they know of intermittent springs or wet areas you should avoid.

Placing a barn on top of a hill can work well (fig. 3.4). But if you build on the side of steep hill it will be more difficult to access the barn, and runoff from the roof and pens could erode the soil (fig. 3.5). If the barn is on a hillside, extend the building pad well beyond the *eaves* on the uphill side and make a ditch to divert water around the barn. If the hillside covers a large drainage area, you might cut a second ditch higher up the hill to minimize the amount of water that reaches the lower ditch during gully washers.

Consider where water and the debris it carries from your barn site will end up. You (and others, like your neighbors) do not want runoff washing across the yard or contaminating water sources. Look for a portion of property that drains away from the nearest creek or

3.3 *Building over a spring or in a drainage area can put your barn and pens out of commission for weeks at a time during a wet spell.*

3.4 *The site of this concrete block barn, near the crest of a hill, drains well in all directions and overlooks a beautiful valley. The barn faces southeast so sun can dry the stalls and a solid back blocks cold northwest winds.*

3.6 *Try to envision how drifting snow and winter winds will affect your daily horsekeeping chores.*

3.5 *On a steep hillside it can be difficult to divert water from the hillside and the roof around the barn.*

3.7 *In cool climates, take advantage of the sun's warming winter rays by facing barn openings south or east.*

stream. Keep pens and manure storage areas at least 300 feet from ponds, streams, springs, and your well.

WIND

Determine the direction of the prevailing winds on your property. Hills, trees, and buildings all can have an effect on wind patterns, as could your excavation for the barn site. The wind on a specific site will often be different from the prevailing winds in the general area.

Consider carefully before building on an unprotected hilltop in windy country. The view might be terrific, but constant wind could make horsekeeping a chore instead of a pleasure.

Even though you want to protect your horses and facilities from unwanted wind, air should be able to move freely around the stable to remove dust and odors and to help dry things out after a wet spell. In very hot locations it's an especially good idea to position your barn to take advantage of summer breezes.

If you live in a snowy climate, plan for the worst (fig. 3.6). Imagine how a severe winter storm will affect the barn site—that's when you'll really need the barn. Avoid placing main entrances directly to the north where snow could block doors, and winds could create problems. Ask former owners or neighbors if they know of drifting patterns that you should be aware of. Check the local weather service, airport, newspapers, or your county extension agent for details on normal wind direction and speed. Also, some libraries have a copy of the *Architectural Graphic Standards* that tells about snowfall, wind direction, and the angle of the sun at any given time of year for a given location.

SUN

In winter climates, building on a south-facing slope will maximize solar gain and offer some protection from cold north winds. Even a slight slope will be warmer than a flat site because the more directly the sun strikes a surface, the more heat is absorbed. Locate stalls on the south side of the barn where the walls and horses will be warmed by the low winter sun (fig. 3.7). Pay attention to hills, trees, rocks, and buildings that could block the sun.

In hot climates you want to minimize solar gain, so consider a north-facing slope, take advantage of shade trees, and concentrate openings on the north wall of the barn.

SECURITY

The closer your barn is to the edge of your property, the easier it will be for trespassers to get to your barn unnoticed. If your stable is in plain view from the house you can keep an eye and an ear on the horses and activities around the barn. Live too close to the barn, however, and the smells and sounds you hold so dear might put off non-horsey family members. A compromise is to locate the barn in sight of, but downwind from, the house. To increase security, lay out your facilities so you have a clear view of driveway approaches to the barn.

ACCESS

If your barn catches fire, will firefighters be able to get to it? If you need to rush a horse to the vet, can you pull a trailer up to the barn, load your horse, and drive away quickly without having a wreck?

Plan barn access for the largest vehicle that will ever use it: fire truck, hay truck, long-bed pickup with six-horse trailer, or tractor trailer rig hauling equipment. It's always risky to back a truck and trailer and it can take a lot of room to jockey a big rig around. A circular drive is best because it allows vehicles to drive to and from the barn without turning around. If you have room, make one.

Allow at least 75 feet between buildings for emergency equipment and to prevent fires from spreading. This will also provide room to maneuver a tractor, manure spreader, hay trailer, and other equipment.

Provide adequate space for maneuvering a horse trailer to where you plan to load, for lowering ramps on both sides and rear, and for clear access straight to the loading doors.

Plan parking areas so vehicles don't block the drive and have room to maneuver when arriving and leaving.

WOODS

Building deep in the forest can increase your sense of privacy, and woodland creatures can add another dimension to your horsekeeping experience: twittering birds, chirping squirrels, and sightings of deer and other wildlife. But skunk and possum can carry diseases and parasites, squirrels and raccoons can pillage your feed, and horse flies and deer flies (which spend idle time in trees and brush) will feast on your horses.

Tree branches touching the roof will scratch and gouge the roof material as they are blown back and forth by the wind. Falling branches from overhanging trees can damage—or even puncture—shingles and other roof materials or crush the building. Leaves on the roof surface retain moisture and cause rot, and leaves in the gutters block drainage and are a fire hazard. Furthermore, some nuts, leaves, needles, and bark are toxic to horses.

For safety and comfort, you'd be wise to clear a defensible space 30 feet or more around the barn site, even though this could be costly. If possible, place the barn downwind and 30 feet or more from the edge of the woods. This will take advantage of the windbreak without stifling airflow in and around the barn. A buffer zone between the barn and woods will minimize fire danger, prevent branches and trees falling on your barn during storms, and minimize wild animal intrusion. Create a no-fly zone by installing fly traps in the buffer to intercept flies on their way from the woods and to draw flies away from the barn and your horses.

OTHER FACILITIES

If you're planning to attach runs to the barn be sure to allow ample room when preparing the building site.

Consider where training pens and riding areas are or will be located. For safety, try to keep them in view of the house and barn so a horse mishap is likely to be noticed (see fig. 12.2, p. 153).

If you plan on composting manure, locate the compost heap downhill and downwind from the barn and house. This will make moving full handcarts to the pile easier and help keep flies and odors from drifting into the barn. Allow room around the compost so a tractor and spreader can maneuver.

For fire safety, it's smart to store the bulk of your hay and bedding in a separate storage building. Keep it at least 75 feet from the barn to prevent fire from spreading between the buildings. ᘔ

DESIGN

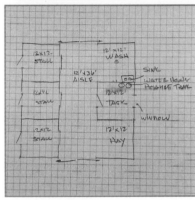

CHAPTER FOUR

LAYOUT AND FEATURES

The style of your barn is an expression of your personality and horsekeeping philosophy. It is defined primarily by the shape of the building and by the materials you choose for the visible parts, such as *siding* and *roofing*. Material selection will be covered in depth in Chapter 6.

City ordinances or homeowner covenants might dictate materials and style making your choice of style considerably quicker (see Covenants, p. 3). Climate will influence function and shape. Will you need a steep roof to shed snow or a wide low *overhang* for shade? Will you insulate and heat a room or the entire barn or is air conditioning more of a possibility? Will you rely on windows and doors for *ventilation* or use roof vents, *gable* vents, or cupolas?

How the barn will be used will determine the sizes of spaces within the barn and how they are laid out. Will the horses live in stalls and be turned out or live outside and be brought in as necessary? Will the barn have a loft? Where will the bulk of your hay and bedding be stored, and how much storage will you need to allow for in the barn? Will there be an apartment or full-fledged house incorporated in the barn or an attached arena?

Unfortunately, like other products of human design, some barns look great but do not work. Don't sacrifice your horses' comfort, health, and safety for making a fashion statement. Take the axiom "form follows function" (by American architect Louis Henri Sullivan) to heart, and consider the purpose of the barn as the starting point in your design. Combine your knowledge of what works for horses with the picture-perfect barn in your imagination. Don't feel you have to do what everyone else has done, but don't ignore the time tested ideas of experienced horse people either. Keep the needs of your horses uppermost, and let the style of your barn flow from there.

FLOOR PLAN

The floor plan of a barn affects style by determining the overall shape of the building. Most barns are rectangular and single story, but L- or U-shaped layouts, some with a second floor, are not uncommon and may suit your purpose better.

COMMON BARN LAYOUTS

RUN-IN SHED   Not a barn per se, the ubiquitous run-in shed, or *loafing shed*, is the simplest shelter to build, having three sides and either a single-slope roof *(shed roof)* or an *offset gable roof* (fig. 4.1, see figs. 7.1 and 7.2, pp. 50–51). The open side allows a horse to enter and leave the shed at will. It is often one room for a single horse but it can be made as long as desired and divided into many compartments to separate horses.

4.1 *The run-in shed.*

4.2 *A shed row barn is a single row of stalls that open directly to the outdoors. It usually has an overhang to provide shelter over an open aisle. Photo courtesy of Barnmaster.*

4.3 *A raised center aisle (RCA) barn.*

4.4 *A mare motel is basically a barn with no walls used to provide shade for horses in hot climates.*

SHED ROW Put a front wall on a run-in shed and you have a shed row barn with stalls open on one side (fig. 4.2). A gable roof often replaces a shed roof in order to gain an overhang for more protection from sun and rain. The shed row is popular in warm climates where it's not critical to have inside aisles in which to work. It is not practical for areas with snow, where more protection is needed.

BACK-TO-BACK OR RACETRACK Attach two shed row barns back to back for a racetrack barn. Since the stalls share a common back wall a racetrack barn is an economical way to house a large number of horse. Like the shed row, it is not practical for snowy areas.

CENTER AISLE Two facing rows of stalls with an aisle between is the most common enclosed barn configuration (see fig. 7.7, p. 55). It offers complete protection from weather so horses can be fed, groomed, and tacked without having to leave the barn.

TRAINER This is like two center-aisle barns side by side and covered by a gable roof (see figs. 7.23 and 7.24, pp. 70–71). There is a double row of stalls down the center of the barn (like a racetrack barn), an aisle on each side, and then another row of stalls along each outer wall. Often an indoor arena is attached to the end of the trainer barn.

BREEZEWAY Any barn with a large door at each end of the aisle, which can be opened to allow a breeze to blow through the barn.

RAISED CENTER AISLE (RCA) This term refers to the roof style, *monitor,* rather than the floor plan. It is a center aisle barn that has a raised roof over the aisle (fig. 4.3, see fig. 7.35, p. 80). Clerestories, short walls with windows between the roof levels, let light into the center aisle. In hot climates, the clerestories are left open for ventilation.

MARE MOTEL A series of pens, usually of steel pipe panels, covered by a roof. Used in hot climates to maximize airflow and provide shade (fig. 4.4).

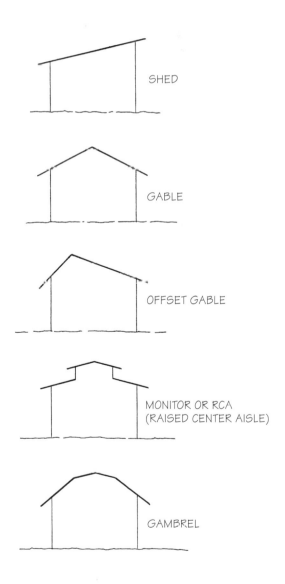

SHED

GABLE

OFFSET GABLE

MONITOR OR RCA
(RAISED CENTER AISLE)

GAMBREL

4.5 ROOF TYPES. *Top to bottom: shed, gable, offset gable, monitor (raised center aisle), gambrel.*

ROOF SHAPE AND OVERHANG

Roof shape determines the appearance of a barn, the volume of air inside the barn, and how well the roof sheds rain and snow (fig. 4.5).

COMMON ROOF SHAPES

SHED ROOF Also called a pitched flat roof. The shed roof is all one plane and is often used for three-sided shelters or small stables. It is also commonly attached to the eaves of an existing gable roof or to the wall of a barn.

GABLE AND OFFSET GABLE Also called saltbox. The gable roof is a roof with two planes. If one side is longer than the other it is an offset gable. It is perhaps the most popular roof style. It often extends past the barn walls to provide additional shelter for horses or equipment.

MONITOR Also called raised center aisle or RCA. Lets in light to center aisle, and the added height increases airflow. The monitor is essentially two shed roofs with a gable in the middle. This is good for long rows of stalls. The area under the upper gable roof can be windows, vents, or clear panels.

GAMBREL A double-pitched roof popular on two story barns having a second floor because of the increased headroom and useable floor space it allows. Gambrel trusses eliminate the need for interior *post and beam* supports, which allows you to create any floor plan you wish (see fig. 7.10, p. 58).

RAFTERS AND TRUSSES

Rafters extend from the top of the walls to join in pairs at a ridge board along the top of the roof. They exert a downward and outward force on the walls. To contain this force and prevent the walls from spreading, a ceiling *joist* or collar tie connects two opposing rafters to make a joist in place. In wide barns, *rafters* often require support from posts and beams on the inside of the building, which can limit floor plan flexibility.

Trusses are engineered to transfer lateral forces directly downward onto perimeter walls with no outward pressure. This *clear span (free span)* design eliminates the need for support posts and beams within the structure itself, and allows you to place non-*load bearing* interior walls anywhere you like.

LOFT

Two-story barns with hayloft storage were popular when horses were used to power agriculture and hay was put up loose. They are still used for dairy and other livestock operations. It can be tempting to consider adding a loft—when considering all that wasted space that could

4.6 ROOF TERMS

SLOPE Roof slope is commonly expressed as *rise* over run, i.e., how much a roof rises for every foot it measures horizontally—run is a constant 12 inches. A 4/12 slope means the slope rises 4 inches for every 12 inches of run. A steeper slope makes snow slide off the roof more readily and creates a larger air volume inside the barn. It also uses more material.

PITCH Roof *pitch* is often confused with slope, but it is a different way of describing the angle of a roof. It is the ratio of the total rise of the roof to the total *span*, expressed as a fraction. For example if the rise of a roof is 4 feet and the span is 24 feet, the roof has a pitch of 4/24 or 1/6.

PROJECTION This is the distance the roof extends past the building, measured horizontally from the wall to the eaves, or edge of the roof.

OVERHANG This is also a measurement of roof extension past the building, but it is measured along the slope of the roof from the top of the wall to the eaves. It is commonly used to refer to any extension of the roof past the side or end of a building. A 2-foot overhang at the eaves should be plenty to keep water away from the foundation, even without gutters. A larger overhang can provide shelter for horses. But keep in mind that as the overhang increases the eaves get lower. For a long overhang you may need to build higher walls or change the slope of the roof to end up with enough head clearance at the eaves.

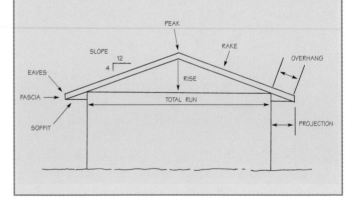

be used for storing hay, bedding, equipment, and general overflow (fig. 4.7). But consider this option carefully.

In the first place, potential fire hazard alone should be enough to clear the loft idea from your head. Facilities experts all agree that the bulk of hay should be stored in a building separate from the stable.

4.7 *It is tempting to add a loft for storing hay and other items, but it is generally not a good idea.*

4.9 *Combining living quarters with the barn enables you to keep close tabs on your horses or provides accommodations for a horse sitter or guests.*

Second, that huge volume of space overhead is not wasted. Quite the contrary, it is serving to keep your horse healthy (see Ventilation, p. 26). A large volume of air helps dissipate stale, humid air, that should be allowed to rise and escape through roof vents to be replaced by fresh air drawn in through lower openings (fig. 4.8). A loft drastically reduces air volume and traps dank air in stalls and aisles, necessitating the use of electric fans for ventilation. Hay stored overhead adds dust, mold and fungal spores, and other pollutants to the air, especially when hay is thrown down for feeding. Make your barn two stories high then leave out the second floor.

LIVE-IN

A stable/apartment combination can offer permanent living quarters for a stable owner, worker, or broodmare manager, a place for a barn sitter to stay while you're away or a retreat for visitors wanting a horsey experience (fig. 4.9). Living in close proximity to your horses enables you to keep close watch on them to nip trouble in the bud. This arrangement could allow you to sleep better at night, knowing you'll hear if a horse gets in trouble, but constant night-time horse sounds could keep you or family members awake. (see Chapter 8, Sample Plans).

FRAMING TYPE

Framing is the skeleton of the barn to which the inside and outside coverings are attached. The type of framing you choose can affect the shape and appearance of the finished barn.

POLE BARN (POST FRAME)

Pole framing utilizes posts and beams to minimize the number of framing elements in walls. It is economical,

4.8 *A large air volume improves ventilation by dissipating stale air. Photo courtesy of Hearthstone, Inc.*

4.10 *Post framing such as used in pole barns is the most common framing for barns.*

4.11 *Timber frame barn under construction. Photo courtesy of Cabin Creek Timberframes.*

4.13 *Stucco and other types of masonry barns are popular in hot climates.*

4.12 *The exposed joinery of traditional timber framing can add class and drama to a barn's interior. Photo courtesy of Hearthstone, Inc.*

strong, and relatively simple to build, making it the most popular framing method for custom barns (fig. 4.10). A pole barn frame consists of 6- to 8-inch round or rectangular *pressure-treated* wood posts set 3 to 6 feet below the ground. Poles are typically set at 8- to 12-foot intervals and rest on a pad of concrete at the bottom of each hole (see fig. 10.9, p. 124). Poles and trusses or rafters are generally visible inside the barn. Pole barns are easy to build in part because they require no trench work for a foundation, only holes, and these can be dug using a tractor auger or a hand posthole digger.

TIMBER FRAME (POST AND BEAM)

Timber framing is another type of post and beam construction, but rather than plugging into the ground like a pole barn, a timber frame barn sets on a concrete foundation (fig. 4.11). A properly constructed timber frame is incredibly sturdy—some have lasted for hundreds of years. It is typically comprised of 8- and 10-inch square timbers for main *members* and smaller timbers for roof *purlins* and floor joists. Major joints are traditionally *dovetails* and *mortise and tenon*, often hand cut, and secured with wooden pins, like fine furniture construction on a larger scale (fig. 4.12). Craftsmen using traditional timber frame methods don't use nails or other metal fasteners unless they are required by local codes. Timber frame barns are sometimes built in or near the builder's shop and shipped to the site to be erected by the builder, a local contractor, or the owner. Timber-frame kits are available that use metal connectors to secure joints.

WOOD FRAME AND MASONRY

Wood frame construction is the most popular style for houses but is not widely used for barns. It is generally not as strong as either pole or timber framing and requires more material to build.

Masonry barns are especially popular in desert climates because the thermal mass of the walls tends to keep the inside of the building cool during the day and radiates heat at night (fig. 4.13). A masonry barn typically consists of *concrete block* or wood-framed walls faced with brick or *stucco*. The advantages of concrete block walls are that little or no inside finish treatment is required, and they are generally impervious to damage from chewing or kicking horses.

Like timber framing, wood frame and masonry buildings require footings and foundation walls to transfer the load of the structure to solid soil and to elevate the walls from the ground. Concrete footings are formed and poured in a trench where the outer walls of the building will be. The trench must be dug to below the frost line or according to local building codes. Foundation walls, either poured concrete or concrete block, set on the footings and extend approximately 16 inches above *grade*. The wood framing or masonry portion of the barn sets on the foundation walls.

MODULAR

Modular barns generally consist of a steel framework with steel-framed panels fitted in between (fig. 4.14). The panels are typically comprised of a plywood or *OSB* (oriented strand board) core with sheet steel *laminated* to the inside surface and steel, wood or other siding material laminated to the outside surface. An advantage of this framing is that damaged panels can be replaced relatively easily. Some modular barns have a "warehouse" appearance, but many manufacturers offer a variety of styles, siding, and roofing materials. If you don't see a plan you like, most manufacturers will modify an existing plan to suit your needs. Modular barns generally go up quicker and with less expense than custom barns. They are especially fire resistant because of the steel framing and steel-skinned wall panels.

HEATING

If you live where it gets cold in the winter, you'll have to decide how much of the barn to heat if any. Ask yourself: "Is the barn primarily for my comfort or my horse's health." You may want to do winter chores in your shirtsleeves, but your horses dress for winter in the fall and don't take off their coats until spring. Horses are generally more comfortable and much healthier living outside or in an unheated barn. It has been found that horses living in a stable rather than outside have higher antibody titers, meaning they have been fighting infectious agents likely caused by bad air and dirty bedding. If you can, build a variety of paddocks, runs, and sheds so horses can live outside most of the time. Not only will they be healthier and happier, but also your daily chores will be simpler and there will be less wear and tear on the barn.

All but very young foals and sick horses will do fine in an unheated barn as long as they are protected from drafts (wind that blows directly on them). When it gets really cold, below 0°F, it is healthier for a horse to wear a blanket and have plenty of fresh air than to close the barn up tight and blast him with a heater. When a horse does require additional warmth, because of sickness or

injury, you can use an infrared (radiant) heater (see fig. 12.5, p. 155) or a well-protected heat lamp. A radiant heater can also be used to prevent a wet horse from chilling as he dries after a workout or bath and to warm a newborn foal.

Most barns only require heating in one or two rooms, commonly the tack room and utility room (see Heaters, p. 107). A warm tack room will provide a place to prevent freezing of medications and grooming products and give you a place to warm between chores or horses. A heated utility room will keep your washing machine, pressure tank, water heater, or other water appliances from freezing (see Utility Room, p. 39). An exception is a show barn where horses are kept with a short hair coat year round. A temperature of 50°F is comfortable for people to work and is healthy for horses. Raising the temperature above this will only increase heating costs.

Any space that is heated, whether one room or the entire barn, needs to be insulated and have a *vapor barrier* on all sides, ceiling, walls, and floor to prevent damage from *condensation* and to make efficient use of energy.

CONDENSATION

Damp air contributes to respiratory ailments, stiffness, and bacterial and fungal growth. It also promotes condensation, which can drip down onto your horses, tack, and feed; rot framing; rust metal siding and roofing; ruin insulation; and cause ice to form on ceilings and walls.

Condensation occurs because warm air can hold water in suspension, but as it cools, it loses as much as one half of its water carrying capacity. When warmer, moist warm air inside a building contacts a cooler ceiling or wall, water is "squeezed" out of the air and collects on the surface. An example of this phenomenon is the formation of "sweat" on a cold beverage can—warm, moist air releases water as it is cooled by the metal surface of the can. The same event fogs your glasses when you enter a warm, humid house on a cold day.

Condensation problems occur mostly in climates where temperatures dip below 35°F for an extended period of time. Barns in the desert and uninsulated barns where the inside and outside temperatures are about the same seldom have condensation problems.

You can prevent or minimize condensation by:

- keeping humidity low: no moisture, no condensation.

- providing plenty of ventilation: in a heated barn this will allow humid air to escape; in an unheated barn it can keep inside air temperature close to outside temperature. With no cooler surface, there is no condensation.

4.14 *Modular barn.*

4.15 *Large doors can admit air and sunlight into the barn.*

- installing insulation: it can keep the inside surfaces of the barn close to the inside air temperature; again, with no cooler surface, there is no condensation.

HUMIDITY

Humidity fuels condensation, and be assured that respiring horses and wet stalls supply plenty of moist air. Respiration from a 1,000-pound horse puts two gallons of moisture into the air each day. Four horses supply eight gallons of humidity per day, and that's not counting moisture from evaporation of urine and manure. A good humidity level for horses is 50 to 75 percent, with 60 percent being optimum; however, too dry is better than too humid.

A dehumidifier, although suitable for an enclosed room, is impractical for an entire barn. Better to eliminate the primary source of moisture by using stalls only when necessary and by removing wet bedding as often as possible when horses are in stalls.

VENTILATION

Good ventilation begins with good design. Ventilation designs (or lack thereof) that work for animals like cows, pigs, and chickens are seldom ideal or even adequate for horses. Horses typically spend many more years in a barn than other animals. Plus, they are usually required to perform as athletes and so require a plentiful supply of clean air for optimum health and fitness.

Besides contributing to condensation, poor ventilation prevents stalls from drying out and leads to moldy bedding. And it can make air downright unhealthy. Contamination by ammonia fumes from decomposing urine and dung, dust from hay and bedding, bacteria, and mold and fungal spores all can contribute to allergy and respiratory problems in horses and humans. Foals are especially vulnerable to high levels of ammonia and are unfortunately subjected to higher concentrations because they live close to the ground where ammonia

tends to layer. Respiratory infections often set in once a foal's developing immune system has been weakened by ammonia fumes. The goal of ventilation is to exchange stale inside air with fresh outdoor air without chilling horses in the process.

AIR MOVEMENT

Air moves through a barn in three ways. *Convection* causes a cycle called the "stack effect" where warm air rises and flows out through roof or high wall vents, drawing in cool air through openings lower in the barn. Aspiration is when wind blowing across the roof creates a low-pressure area, a vacuum, which pulls air out of the barn through vents or any other openings. Perflatation is when air moves through a barn by passing through openings (windows, doors, and vents) located on opposite walls. Locating a barn to take advantage of breezes can facilitate ventilation by aspiration and perflatation. You can use the smoke from a stick of incense to help you evaluate *air changes*, how fast the smoke dissipates, and airflow—where the smoke goes.

VENTS

Windows and doors that open will allow air to move through the barn, especially when they are placed on opposite sides of the barn and there are few solid walls between them (fig. 4.15, see fig. 5.1, p. 32). Drafts at the height of a horse's or foal's body should be avoided. Drafts can have an unhealthy chilling effect, especially if a horse is wet. Stall windows that open inward and slope upward will direct air over a horse, rather than causing drafts to blow on him. Inward opening windows, however, do present installation and safety problems, (see Chapter 5, Spaces).

A *vent* on the outer wall of each box stall, just under the roof, will encourage airflow by letting warm air out so fresh air can move upward. High-placed windows serve the same function, with the added advantage of letting in sunlight but they can be difficult to reach for opening and closing. Vents

4.16 *Dutch doors enable a horse to stick his head out for a breath of fresh air and let air flow through the barn.*

placed low in walls admit fresh cool air into the barn (see Farm Tek in the Resource Guide). Be careful about placing a low vent in a stall where drafts could blow on a horse or where a horse might be injured on the vent or damage it.

Dutch doors on outer stall walls can allow the top door to be latched open to admit outside air and to let a horse put his head out directly into fresh air (fig. 4.16). An open top door generally provides adequate ventilation for a stall.

Grillwork on the top portion of stall walls and using walls that stop short of the ceiling will enable air to flow throughout the barn more freely than having solid walls from floor to ceiling. Using stall guards (straps or chains) across open stall doors also encourages airflow but can lead to safety and behavioral problems and will allow bedding to spill into the aisle.

While large doors at the ends of a barn can provide good ventilation, they will also admit birds, insects, and other unwanted animals. A solution is to install giant sliding screens (see the Resource Guide) to keep out pests and strong wind while still admitting gentle airflow.

There are many ways to let warm air escape through the roof. A pot vent is a simple metal dome that covers a hole in the roof. A cupola is a short and usually square tower with louvers on all sides built over a hole in the roof ridge (fig. 4.17). One or more cupolas can serve as large vents and add character to your barn in the bargain.

Continuous ridge vents are perhaps the easiest and most effective roof vents to install. Some are concealed by shingles, while others serve as a ready-made ridge cap to finish off steel and other roofing (fig. 4.18).

4.18 *Ridge vent.*
Photo courtesy of MWI Components.

4.17 *A cupola can be functional as well as stylish.*

FANS

If your barn is sheltered from natural airflow, for example, by trees or land formations, or if you keep it closed tight, you'll need to install exhaust fans and intake vents to move air through the barn. Exhaust fans are rated in cubic feet per minute (CFM), how many cubic feet per minute of air they move.

When researching an exhaust system, figure 1 square foot of vent or inlet space for every 750 CFM fan capacity. More than this will create a draft and less than this simply will not ventilate adequately.

Ceiling fans that draw air up toward roof vents are one solution. Make sure they are at least 11-feet high to prevent horse contact. Portable fans mounted on stands or fastened to the walls or trusses can also be used to move air through the barn and can be focused on stalls to cool horses and to dry bedding and on grooming areas to keep flies away.

Vents with integral fans placed high on the outside walls in each stall are another option. Use screened vents with louvers or downward pointing hoods on the outside to cut down on drafts and to keep out insects, birds, rain, and snow.

HOW MUCH VENTING

There should be sufficient air intake and exhaust openings, with or without fans, to ensure six to eight air changes per hour (one air change is the time it takes for all of the interior air to be replaced with fresh air). A large air volume and good airflow is important for distributing fresh air throughout the barn without drafts and for minimizing concentration of bad air around the horses. The air volume inside a barn can be increased by having higher walls or a gambrel, monitor, or steeper-pitched roof.

Vents are rated by "net free area," which refers to the size of the opening and taking into account blockage from insect screen or other obstructions that interfere with free airflow. A typical pot vent has a net free ventilating area of around 50 square inches, while most continuous ridge ventilation products have a net free ventilation area of 18 square inches per lineal foot of vent.

There are two rules of thumb for calculating vent requirements:

- allow 1 square foot of vent for every 300 square feet of floor space.

- 60 percent of the venting area should be lower intake vents, and 40 percent should be higher exhaust vents.

For example, if your barn is 40-feet wide by 60-feet long you have 2,400 square feet of space. Divide 2,400 by 300 to get 8 square feet, or 1,152 square inches, of vent. Sixty percent of 1,152 equals 691 square inches of lower vent required, leaving 461 square inches of upper vents. A standard ridge vent supplies 18 square inches per lineal foot: $461 \div 18 = 25$ feet of continuous roof vent will fulfill the thumb rule and installing vent the entire 60-feet length will more than double it.

A normal unheated barn could leak enough air around doors and through siding to satisfy the 691 square inch requirement for lower venting without adding vents. The open top of a Dutch door would provide 1,728 square inches, almost three times the required area, but all of the air would enter at one place and wouldn't serve to mix with stale air as well as more numerous openings throughout the barn would.

BATHROOM VENT

For bathrooms up to 100 square feet in area, HVI (Home Ventilating Institute, see the Resource Guide) recommends an exhaust fan that provides 1 CFM per square foot to properly ventilate the bathroom.

For example, an eight foot by five foot bathroom has 40 square feet of area so would require a fan rated at 40 CFM.

A timer switch set to turn off after twenty minutes will make sure the room is vented after use and that the fan is not left running.

Generally, bathroom doors are undercut to allow air to enter the room and replace air exhausted by the vent. But in a barn, it might be a good idea to have doors fit snug to a door *sill* to keep out rodents. Use a screened vent near the bottom of the door or low in a wall to let in air.

FLOOR VENTS

For a wood floor, such as in a tack room, that has space between the floor and the ground, foundation vents will remove humidity that migrates up from the earth, and prolong the life of the floor. The total vent area should equal 2 square feet for each 100 lineal feet of foundation perimeter, plus one half percent of the *crawl space* area. A vent fan controlled by a humidistat will turn on and off according to a preset humidity level. It can be mounted in the foundation or connected to the crawl space by ducting.

ICE DAMS

Ice dams are often the result of poor ventilation and insulation. They occur when snow melts on a warm part of a roof then runs down the roof and refreezes along the eaves. Ice dams can build up many inches thick and water backed up behind them can run under shingles ruining the roof and even leaking into the building. Ice dams are exacerbated by poor insulation in heated barns and by poor ventilation between roofing and insulation. Good airflow under a roof ensures that the roofing stays cool from the peak to the eaves. Building codes of many northern states require an extra waterproofing membrane at the eaves to prevent damage from ice dams.

Gutters can also cause increased ice buildup. Make sure gutters slope correctly and are cleaned out each fall so they can drain properly.

VAPOR BARRIER

A vapor barrier keeps moist air from migrating through walls and ceilings and into the insulation. If moisture should collect within the insulation, the insulating value is greatly reduced. If moisture moves through the insulation, it will condense on the back of the siding or the underside of the roof and lead to rot and rust. A vapor barrier is always installed on the warm side of insulation. Putting a vapor barrier on the cold side will trap moisture within the insulation. Only one vapor barrier is needed or recommended. A vapor barrier on both sides of the insulation is asking for trouble because if any moisture should get between them it would be trapped and could lead to rot, mold, and mildew.

A vapor barrier can consist of almost any waterproof membrane, including special paints, plastic sheeting, laminated paper, Kraft-backed aluminum foil, foil-backed *gypsum board*, and spray foam.

INSULATION

Insulation keeps heat in your barn during the winter, out during the summer, and it also absorbs sound. If you are planning a steel roof, think seriously about insulating under the roofing to make the barn quieter during rain and hail. Insulating a barn but not heating it will still result in a slightly higher inside temperature. Our barn in Colorado, for example, has as its only insulation ½-inch thick fiberboard under the steel roofing for absorbing sound of rain and hail. On winter mornings the inside is 5 to 10°F warmer than the outside temperature, and it rarely drops below freezing inside. At midday during summer it is approximately 5 to 10°F cooler than outside.

Insulation is classified according to form: *loose fill*, flexible, rigid, reflective, and foamed-in-place. The three types of insulation most commonly used for barns are flexible, rigid, and reflective. Loose fill cellulose insulation is made primarily of ground-up or shredded newspaper, which is flammable even when treated with fire retardant chemicals; it is not recommended for a horse barn.

HEAT MOVEMENT

Heat always moves to cooler areas and is transferred in three ways. *Conduction* is direct heat exchange through an object like paneling or *studs*. Convection is the transfer of heat through air. *Radiation* is the movement of heat across open spaces (such as the sun warming the earth and a woodstove heating a house).

Conductive heat loss through walls and ceilings is slowed down by mass fiber insulation (*batts*, rigid board). Convection heat loss through walls and the roof caused by air infiltration can be prevented by sealing all holes through which air can move. Radiant heat loss can be reduced by using a reflective barrier.

R-VALUE

The *R-value* of insulation refers to its resistance to heat transfer. A higher R-value means higher insulating capability. R-values are printed on the insulation itself, on the packaging, or attached on labels.

The amount of insulation a barn requires depends on where it is located and how it is built. For information on insulation recommendations for your area, contact the local building department or gas or electric utility. A chart by the U.S. Department of Energy that shows recommended insulation levels based on geographic zones can be seen on the website of the North American Insulation Manufacturers, www.naima.org.

DOORS

Give some thought to where doors are located and how they will affect surrounding activities when they are opened. Doors that you will be carrying tack through should be easy to open with one hand or an elbow and be wide enough so you don't crash your saddle or arm into the doorjamb. Doors that horses will pass through should be easy to open with one hand, and while wearing gloves in cold country, and be at least 4-feet wide with no sharp edges or protrusions that could injure a horse or catch tack or blankets.

HINGED DOORS

Hinged doors are commonly used on tack rooms, feed rooms, utility rooms, and exterior stall openings. They can be installed to open either inward or outward. To order a door so it swings the correct way, you need to specify if it is right or left-handed. Face the door opening on the side the door opens toward you. If the knob is on the left, it's a left-hand door; if the knob is on the right, it's a right-hand door.

Panel doors have inset panels that add to the character as well as to the cost. Flush doors are smooth-surfaced, less expensive than panel doors, and are easier to keep clean in a barn environment.

Solid wood doors are all wood and can be of flush or panel construction. Solid-core doors are generally made of particleboard covered by a wood, fiberglass, or steel *veneer*. Both types are suitable for barns. Hollow-core doors have cardboard honeycomb centers covered by a thin veneer. They are too light duty for use in a barn anywhere a horse might contact them. They could be used, however, for a closet or lavatory located within another room.

Unassembled doors come without *jamb* or trim, which you must provide and install. *Pre-hung doors* are much easier to install because they come already hinged and hung on a fully assembled set of side and top jambs (plus a threshold along the bottom if it's an exterior door) and are ready to be nailed into the opening. Plus, door *casing* (trim) is often installed on one side of the jambs.

SLIDING DOORS

Sliding doors take little space to operate and are the most common stall and barn aisle door (see fig. 12.8, p. 156). You can build a sliding stall door from scratch, from a kit, or buy them completely assembled with grillwork on the top half. They are commonly comprised of 2-inch thick *tongue and groove* lumber exterior with a smooth inner surface (facing the inside of the stall) of sheet steel, plywood, or OSB to minimize chewing.

Two or more sets of rollers (small wheels) are attached to the top of the door. The rollers fit into an overhead track (trolley) fastened to the wall above the doorway. The door is suspended from the track and rolls along it to open and close. The roller assemblies can be adjusted to raise and lower the door so it slides level and clears the ground. Inexpensive steel rollers can be noisy and prone to inconsistent movement. Rubber or nylon rollers are more costly, but generally provide quieter, smoother operation.

OVERHEAD DOORS

Overhead garage doors made of hinged sections are sometimes used at the ends of barn aisles (fig. 4.19) (see Aisle, p. 32). They roll on tracks, like sliding doors, but in this case a track is mounted on each side of the door opening and the track is curved to extend horizontally above the door on the inside. Overhead doors don't take any lateral space to operate.

Manually operated garage doors use huge springs and cables to assist opening and closing. These can be troublesome to operate, especially when leading a horse. Doors opened by an electric door opener are better for a barn because they enable you to enter the barn without touching the door. An electric opener is mounted between the tracks overhead that uses a chain to help springs raise and lower the door. It can be activated by a remote controller or by a switch on the wall. Some openers even turn on a light. Mount the control button at least 5 feet above the floor to discourage small children from playing with the door.

Like anything else, the more moving parts the greater chance of malfunction, and a sectioned overhead garage door has many more moving parts than a sliding door or swinging hinged door. Also, they require periodic maintenance and the hinges between the sections, rollers, pulleys, cables, and such are subject to wear every time the door is operated. Overhead doors have been known to crash down during operation. If you decide to go with a sectioned overhead door, be sure that it is installed correctly and maintained regularly. It is essential that the opener be equipped with a sensing device that stops or raises the door if it touches or detects a person or object beneath the door as it is closing. Most doors made since 1993 have such safety devices.

WINDOWS

Any window a horse can contact must be protected from the horse by heavy screen or grillwork. Windows in a tack room should likewise be protected with grillwork, usually on the outside to discourage burglary. Grillwork can interfere with opening and closing windows, so choose your styles carefully and decide on which side the grillwork should be installed.

TYPE OF WINDOW OPERATION

FIXED Does not open. Often used in clerestories and other areas where windows are difficult to access to open and close.

DOUBLE-HUNG Consists of two *sashes* (framed panes of glass), one or both of which slide vertically. Good for use anywhere in a barn. In a stall, a person should be able to reach through grillwork to open a double hung window. Opening the top sash will be less likely to cause drafts on a horse than opening the bottom sash. Dirt can accumulate on the top rail of the lower sash.

SLIDER (SLIDE-BY) Operate like double-hung windows turned sideways. Commonly used in modular barns. Sliders in stalls are more easily opened by reaching through grillwork if the grillwork is horizontal, rather than vertical.

CASEMENT Consists of one or two sashes that hinge at the side and open outward by means of a crank handle

4.19 *Electric overhead doors operate at the touch of a button and take up no lateral space.*

or slider. Not appropriate for a stall because the opening mechanism could be difficult to operate through grillwork and it also could be adversely affected by dirt.

AWNING Consists of one or more sashes hinged at the top and usually opening outward by means of a crank handle or slider. Good for a tack room because it can be opened and still keep out rain. Not good for a stall for the same reasons as for a casement window.

HOPPER Like an upside down awning, hinged at the bottom and usually opening inward. Although I've seen hopper windows used in stalls they are not appropriate. The protective grillwork must protrude into the stall to allow the window to open and this reduces stall size and invites horse to rub on the grill.

MATERIALS

Since all windows in your barn should be completely protected from contact by horses, choose window materials as you would for your house or other building.

Solid wood can be ordered raw, primed, or finished; painting trim is usually required every five to seven years; can rot and warp if not properly installed and cared for. Not recommended for a barn because of the high maintenance required.

Windows made of aluminum or vinyl don't require painting and will last indefinitely with very little maintenance. Some are made of solid aluminum or vinyl while other use a layer of aluminum or vinyl over a wood core.

CONSTRUCTION

Glazing refers to the glass portion of a window. Single glazing, one layer of glass, is sufficient for all uninsulated rooms of a barn.

DOUBLE-GLAZED Consists of two layers of glass joined together with a space between them; the space is filled with argon or another inert gas to increase insulation value.

TRIPLE-GLAZED Consists of three layers of glass and two insulating air spaces; better insulation value than double glazed, but heavier and more expensive.

SAFETY GLASS (TEMPERED GLASS) Required by code in certain applications, like in bathrooms; a good option for any window in a barn. Even if you choose safety glass, if the window can be contacted by horses it must be protected by steel grillwork.

COMBINATION STORM Has a built-in screen to keep insects out when the glass sash is opened to let fresh air in.

ENERGY RATING

Knowing which type of window to buy can be confusing enough, but it gets worse when you consider energy performance for windows in a heated room like a tack room.

The National Fenestration Rating Council (NFRC) (see the Resouce Guide) is the country's only independent source of window, door, and skylight energy performance information (*fenestration* refers to the openings in a structure). It is a voluntary, non-profit organization created by the window, door and *skylight* industry. It is comprised of manufacturers, suppliers, builders, architects and designers, specifiers, code officials, utilities, and government agencies. The NFRC provides consumers with ratings on window, door, and skylight products. The NFRC label rates:

- **U-FACTOR** How well a window keeps heat inside a building. This refers to not just the glass, but also to the frame and sash components. A lower *U-factor* means better insulating ability. An efficient window should have a U-factor of 0.35 or less. Less efficient units have higher U-factors.

- **SOLAR GAIN** A window's ability to keep out heat from sunlight. For a tack room especially, look for windows with a coating called low-E (low-emissivity), which reduces heat transfer and ultraviolet (UV) penetration. Both heat and UV can damage leather tack.

- **VISIBLE LIGHT TRANSMITTANCE** How much light gets through.

- **AIR LEAKAGE** Heat loss and gain by infiltration through cracks in the window assembly. ∪

CHAPTER FIVE

SPACES AND OPENINGS

The first step in laying out a horse barn is to determine the overall outer dimensions of the building, the size and location of spaces inside, and the size and location of doors and windows.

You can design a barn from the outside in or inside out. If the building site is limited by rocks, trees, buildings, or budget, start with a barn size that fits the parameters and divide the space inside to suit your needs. If there are no restrictions on size, you'll have more design freedom and you'll be able to lay out whatever spaces you need and add them to get the barn's outer dimensions. Remember, the barn will not be the only thing on the building site. Allow room for pens, tie areas, drainage areas, walkways, driveway approaches, and parking.

AISLE

The width and height of aisles will affect what size equipment can enter the barn and how easy it is to move horses and equipment through the barn. If the aisle is going to be used as a storage area, such as for tack trunks, allow extra space when you're designing the barn.

A 10-foot-wide aisle is sufficient if stalls are cleaned into a handcart and no more than one horse is being led down the aisle at a time. This allows enough room to safely turn a horse around or groom a horse in aisle cross-ties.

An 11-foot aisle will allow a small tractor (60 hp) or pickup to drive through but is tight for a full-size pickup. (Some local building codes require firewalls in a barn when access is included for motorized vehicles.)

A 12-foot aisle will let a larger tractor and full-size pickup through and will allow two persons leading horses to pass comfortably (fig. 5.1). If there will be several persons using the barn at the same time make the aisles at least 12-feet wide.

A 14- to 16-foot aisle is required to comfortably open doors on both sides of a pickup in the aisle. This width

5.1 A 12-foot aisle like this one allows ample clearance for vehicles. The large door at the end of the aisle offers good ventilation.

will also allow for tack trunks in the aisle and blanket rods on stall doors with room for two persons leading horses to pass.

Overhead clearance in the aisle should be at least 11 feet. Any lower and a rearing horse is likely to break light fixtures or injure his head. Ceiling height is usually determined by the height of the walls supporting trusses and joists.

Design aisle doors for the largest piece of equipment you'll ever need in the barn. A 12-foot door will allow a vehicle to drive in for delivering feed or for cleaning stalls. Hinged doors are appropriate for openings under 8-feet wide but they can be difficult to operate when leading a horse and especially when a wind is blowing. Sliding doors are more popular for openings wider than 8-feet—either one large door or two doors that latch together at the center. Beware of extending a sliding door past the end of the roof because wind could catch it and blow it off the track. Electric overhead doors (garage doors) take up only headroom and offer hands free operation once they are activated (see fig. 4.19, p. 30). The noise and movement can startle horses at first, but most soon get used to it. Unlike a hinged or a sliding door, the operation of an overhead door is affected very little by snow buildup against the door.

STALLS

Long periods of confinement in dark stalls where horses have little visual contact with other horses or with people lead to bored horses, and bored horses are likely to develop behavioral problems referred to as vices. Wood chewing, cribbing, weaving, pawing, and kicking can all begin out of boredom. Minimize vices by keeping horses inside only as necessary and providing visual stimulus by means of open windows and doors and grillwork in stall partitions. Some horse owners have found that mounting a plastic shatterproof mirror securely to a stall wall helps alleviate boredom in their horse.

TIE STALL

The tie stall (standing or straight stall) is a narrow compartment where a horse is tied. It was a common stalling method years ago when horses served as the backbone of our work force and had ample daily exercise. Today, a tie stall can be useful for feeding horses separately, letting a horse cool out after exercise, or "storing" tacked up horses for short periods. They can be used to keep a horse overnight, providing the horse has plenty of exercise during the day. If you plan to use tie stalls regularly, make at least one more than the number of horses. Then you can rotate horses between the stalls and let the empty one dry and air out.

Walls or partitions between tie stalls should be at least 54-inches high along the sides and 72-inches high near the head area to prevent horses from fighting or putting their heads over the partitions.

A tie stall for a pony should be at least 36-inches wide and 72 inches total length, with 54 inches from manger to butt bar. For a riding horse, it should be at least 60-inches wide and 108 inches total length, with 86 inches from manger to butt bar. A warmblood or draft horse stall should be 60-inches wide and 120 inches total length, 98 inches standing room from manger to butt bar. Extra width will allow you to move around the horse easier for grooming or tacking, but making the stall too wide invites some horses to try to turn around. Ceilings should be at least 11-feet high over a tie stall so that if the tie rope is tied long or comes loose and the horse rears up he will not be injured.

A tie stall typically has a manger at the front for feeding hay and grain. A standard manger is the full width of the stall with the top opening 22 inches from front to back. The front face of the manger is 32-inches high and extends straight to the floor or at an angle away from the horse's front legs. A grain tray can be built into the manger or a bucket or dish can be used. Water that is provided in a tie stall is soon fouled by feed. If a horse is in a stall for more than a few hours, it is generally better to carry a bucket of water to him and remove it after he drinks.

A horse should always be tied in a tie stall and a butt bar, rope, or covered chain should be fastened across the

5.2 *12-foot by 12-foot stalls with at least 11 feet of headroom are the standard for riding horses.*

rear of the stall to prevent the horse from backing up and pulling on the tie rope. If a horse is left loose in a tie stall with the butt bar attached, he could be injured trying to turn around in the stall. The tie rail or ring should be securely attached so it cannot be pulled loose. One option is to fasten a 2-inch diameter or larger pipe to the top edge of the manger and to the wall at both ends. The pipe also prevents chewing on the manger edge.

BOX STALL

The box stall (loose stall), in which a horse is free, is the most common type of stall used today (fig. 5.2). It is more suitable than a tie stall for long periods of confinement because the horse can get a certain amount of exercise by walking around. Nevertheless, a horse in a box stall requires daily exercise out of the stall.

The number of stalls you need will depend on how many horses will require stabling at one time. If your horses live mainly outdoors, in pens or on pastures, you might need only one or two stalls for those horses you want to bring in during stormy weather, to keep clean for riding, or for recuperation from injury or sickness. If you plan on keeping all your horses stalled full time, plan one or two extra stalls so you can rotate horses among the stalls and allow empty stalls to thoroughly dry between uses. An extra stall can also be used as a buffer when you need to isolate a horse from the others or to store equipment, feed, and extra bedding. Later, you might want to convert an extra stall into a utility room, grooming area, bathroom, waiting room, or extra tack room. Better too many stalls than not enough.

A box stall should be large enough to allow a horse to turn around freely and lie down and get up without difficulty. A stall that is larger than needed will require more bedding. Some horses will churn if the stall is too large or too small, which also wastes bedding. The optimum stall size will allow the horse to create and maintain separate eating, resting, and defecating areas (of course, that doesn't mean he will). 11 feet is the minimum ideal height for stall ceilings, same as aisles. Lights, heaters, and fans should not project below ceiling framing (see fig. 12.5, p. 155).

Stall doorways should be a minimum of 8-feet high and 4-feet wide to allow a horse to pass without banging against the doorway and to allow a handcart to pass through for stall cleaning. To minimize injury to people

RECOMMENDED STALL SIZES

MINIATURE HORSES: 6-feet by 8-feet.

PONIES and horses weighing less than 900 pounds: 10-feet by 10-feet. But if you have the room, you might want to make the stalls 10-feet by 12-feet or 12-feet by 12-feet to make the barn more versatile and more appealing to future buyers who might have larger horses.

HORSES weighing 900 to 1300 pounds: 12-feet by 12-feet is the industry standard (fig. 5.2). To conserve space, 10-feet by 12-feet will work as long as a horse is not kept in the stall continually.

WARMBLOODS and small draft horses: from 12-feet by 14-feet to 14-feet by 14-feet.

DRAFT HORSES such as Clydesdales: 16-feet by 16-feet.

A FOALING STALL should be at least twice the size as a single stall for that size horse.

AN ISOLATION STALL is used to keep a horse separate from others for health or behavior reasons. It should be the size of a foaling stall when used to keep a horse in for extended periods, such as when recuperating from an injury, so the horse has more room to move about. If possible, the isolation stall should be apart from yet within view of other horses.

5.3 *A latch at the bottom of this Dutch door prevents a horse from pushing the door out and getting his foot caught between the door and the sill.*

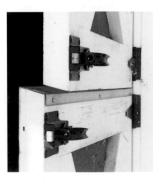

5.4 *Dutch door with beveled edges where the top and bottom meet.*

and horses and damage to clothing and blankets, round the corners of boards and posts in doorways using a *router* or a hoof rasp.

If possible, have two doors on every stall. One door opening to the aisle and the other to the outside. This will enable you to enter the stall to help a horse that is cast (has laid down and is unable to get up) against one door or to get a horse out quickly in case of a fire.

Hinged doors need room to swing either into the stall or into the aisle. An inward swinging door is sturdier because it is backed up by the doorstop when a horse leans or pushes on it (see fig. 12.9, p. 156). But bedding often impedes the door unless the door is cut off at the bottom. Then a high doorsill, such as a 2 x 6 on edge, is sometimes added to keep bedding from spilling into the aisle, and this can make it more difficult to roll a cart through the doorway.

An outward-swinging door, on the other hand, can impede traffic in the aisle when it is opened. And when a horse leans on the door the latches and hinges take all the stress and often come loose. In some instances, a pawing horse can force the bottom of a hinged door open just far enough to get a foot caught between the door and the sill, and a second latch at the bottom of the door is required for safety (fig. 5.3).

Dutch doors are comprised of a top and bottom portion that hinge and latch separately. The top is commonly latched open to provide light and ventilation and to let a horse look out. Many Dutch doors are *beveled* where they meet so the top door overlaps the bottom door when they close (fig. 5.4). This makes a door more weather-tight but prevents the bottom door from opening independently. When weather is not a concern (for example, a roof overhang protects the doorway) consider Dutch doors that don't overlap. One benefit of being able to open just the lower door is that a person can duck through while not allowing a horse to pass, such as when taking feed from the barn to a horse in the pen. It can also serve as a creep feeder, allowing a foal to pass through the open bottom to eat foal ration or lay down in stall bedding while the top door blocks the mare from entering the stall (fig. 5.5).

A sliding door is generally preferred for the aisle door of a stall because even though rollers and track cost more than hinges, it takes much less space to operate (see Sliding Doors, p. 29). Plus, it can usually be forced opened even if a horse is lying against it. It's important that both sides of the bottom of the door are secured close to the jamb when the door is closed so that a horse can't push the door out and get a foot wedged between the door and the jamb (fig. 5.6). Stops should be installed to keep the door from coming off the track.

5.5 *A Dutch door that allows the lower door to open separately.*

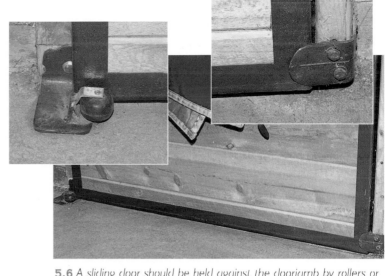

5.6 *A sliding door should be held against the doorjamb by rollers or guides to prevent a horse from pushing the door out and getting a foot caught between the door and the frame.*

Latches should be horse-proof and horse-safe. With some latches, an auxiliary snap is needed to lock the latch and prevent a horse from opening it. A latch should not have protrusions on which a halter could be caught or sharp edges that would encourage a horse to rub. Slide bolts with horseshoe or other loop type handles should not be used where horses can reach them because a horse could get his lower jaw caught in the loop and suffer severe injury. Keeping stalls locked, such as with padlocks, might discourage theft or prevent unauthorized access to your horses, but the locks can also prevent someone from saving a horse in the event of a fire or from aiding a cast horse.

Windows add light and ventilation to stalls but must be designed carefully to avoid damage and injury. Glass is easily broken and must be protected by guards made of heavy screen or metal grillwork having spaces no wider than three inches (fig. 5.7). A drawback is that such guards can make it difficult to open windows from inside a stall. Whatever type of window guard you choose, they must be designed and installed so there are no sharp edges or protrusions that could injure a horse or encourage him to rub. Window guards also help keep windows clean. Unprotected heavy-duty Plexiglas might withstand abuse from a horse, but it would soon become smudged and smeared to near opacity by nosey horses.

Windows that slide or open outward are generally safer and easier to protect with grillwork than windows that open inward (see Windows, p. 30). Many barn designs dispense with stall windows altogether and instead use Dutch doors or glassless window openings that are covered by shutters or doors that open outward and fasten against the barn siding. Grilles to keep a horse from extending his head through the window opening may or may not be used.

It's most natural and healthy for horses to eat from ground level. But feeding on the floor can result in the feed being mixed with fouled bedding, which is wasteful and can promote parasite infestation. One solution is to attach a deep bin to one corner of the stall. This will keep most of the hay contained and catch the leaf in the bottom (see fig. 12.5, p. 155). Affix the feeder at least 4 inches off the floor so you can get a broom under it.

A small door in the wall or grillwork enables a person to drop feed in the stall feeder without entering the stall. This is especially handy and safe for non-horse people who might be doing chores for you. Wall-mounted

5.7 *Stall windows like the one in this Dutch door must be protected by a steel grille or heavy screen.*

MAKING A DOUBLE STALL

To conserve space, it is common to have a hinged or removable partition between two stalls to create a double stall for foaling, lay-up, or other purpose.

To make a removable wall it is common to fasten steel U-channel to two opposing walls or make channels out of wood. Slide 2-inch-thick boards down between the channels from the top, stacking them to make a wall. Tongue and groove boards lock together and make a solid wall. Boards that are not tongue and grooved require a wall stiffener to keep the boards flush and to prevent them from flexing. You can purchase metal wall stiffeners for this purpose or screw a 2 × 6 vertically to the center of the boards once they are in place. To protect the mare and foal from the sharp channel edges when the wall is removed, cut a board to fit into the each channel and project past the edges about ⅛ inch. Fasten these safety boards in place with several screws.

To make a hinged wall is initially more difficult but it is ultimately more convenient for dividing two stalls (see fig. 12.6, p. 155). Weld a steel frame from 2-inch U-channel (for rough-cut lumber) slightly smaller than the size of the opening (hold off welding the top channel in place until the boards have been inserted into the frame). Add a diagonal steel strap on each side for stability. Use wet cloths to prevent the boards from burning when you weld the top channel. Purchase or have made three extra heavy duty hinges rated for at least 600 pounds. Those in the photo are welded from ¾-inch pipe and ¼-inch thick steel strap. Make sure that there is a solid vertical framing member behind where the hinges fasten to the wall and use bolts long enough to go 2 inches into this member. Set a metal foot, or plate, in the floor for the end of the door to set on—one at the closed position and one at the open position. That way the hinges carry the door only as it swings. Cut a 2-inch by 6-inch slot in the edge of one of the boards about waist high at the end opposite the hinges to serve as a handle when moving the wall. Install a slide bolt latch at the top and the bottom to hold the wall open or closed.

5.8 *Swing-out hay and grain feeder.*

combination feeders have a heavy wire rack for hay and a tray or bin beneath the rack for grain and to catch hay particles. Some can be swung out into the aisle for filling, like a "lazy Susan" (fig. 5.8). The unnatural position a horse must assume to eat hay from this type of feeder, however, can adversely affect neck muscles. But worse, this type of feeder tends to deposit hay dust and flake in the horse's nostrils, eyes, and face. It's better for the horse to feed him on a clean floor or in a low bin.

Steel grilles on stall fronts promote airflow through the stall, let a horse see what's going on, and let a person see into the stall. Solid steel bars are stronger than tubing and will last longer without bending. While grilles between stalls promote airflow and allow horses to see one another, familiarity sometimes leads to playing, fighting, kicking, and injury. Solid walls between stalls, especially where feeders are adjacent to one another, can reduce fractious behavior. Try to avoid having Dutch doors or any doors with open top portions next to one another. This arrangement encourages horses to play and fight around the doors, leading to injury and damaged facilities.

Cover all wood edges that a horse can reach with steel angle trim at least 16-gauge thick (fig. 5.9). Several manufactures of stall components and accessories sell ready-made chew-guard edging. I had a local metal fabricator custom-bend extra wide edging (2 inches on a side) from 14-gauge steel (see fig. 12.7, p. 155). I cut the pieces to length and drilled and painted them before installation. Lightweight metal corners such as drywall edging are worse than no protection at all. A horse can rip thin metal to shreds and suffer lacerations from the resulting sharp edges.

WAITING ROOM

A waiting room is a room adjoining the foaling stall that has an unbreakable or shielded transparent panel or a sliding shutter in the common wall so a person can observe the stall unobtrusively (fig. 5.10). This is not only

5.9 *Metal chew-guard edging protects wood and prevents injury.*

5.10 *This waiting room doubles as a lounge and has windows looking into two separate stalls.*

useful around foaling time, but it also lets you keep an eye on an injured horse or study horse behavior without being seen. Unless you plan to have many foals, a dedicated waiting room might seem extravagant, but the room could also serve other purposes, such as lounge or bathroom/dressing room. Alternatively, you could install a viewing window in a tack room that adjoins a stall.

An 8-foot by 10-foot waiting room will accommodate a chair, cot, table, small refrigerator, and hot plate.

TACK ROOM

The tack room is the center of activity and the most personalized room in your barn (fig. 5.11). How well it is designed and organized will determine to a large degree how smoothly your barn operates.

The size of the tack room will depend on how many horses you have and what you will use the tack room for besides storing tack. Things you might consider for your tack room:

- hangers for halters and bridles
- a sink for washing your hands and tack
- a small desk area to keep records organized (fig. 5.12)
- a chest of drawers for storing clippers, brushes, wraps, and other small items
- a counter or table for repairing tack
- shelves for folded blankets or boxes of stuff
- cabinets for supplies
- washer and dryer (see fig. 12.22, p. 158)
- small refrigerator for vaccines and beverages

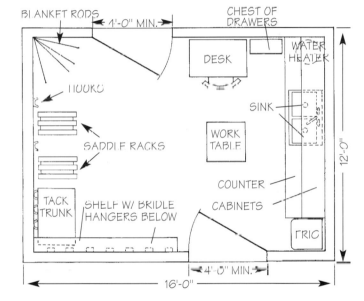

5.11 TACK ROOM.

- tack trunk for seasonal blankets, boots, and extra gear
- swivel blanket rods for drying and storing blankets

A 12-foot by 12-foot tack room, the size of an average stall, is the smallest you should consider. Build it twice as big as you think you will ever need—no one has ever complained that their tack room was too big. If the tack room will double as a utility room be sure to allow room for appliances—refrigerator, washer, and dryer—and make the door large enough to fit them through.

Consider 9-foot ceilings to allow room for shelves along the upper portion of walls. You'll be glad you did.

Plus, a high ceiling will allow space for vertical storage units for blankets and saddles.

5.12 *The corner of this tack room is set up for paperwork and communication: it has a counter for writing, a small shelf for phone and intercom, and a high shelf and lower cabinet for notebooks and records.*

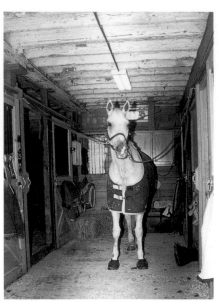

5.13 *The aisle serves as the grooming area in this remodeled dairy barn. Note that the 8-foot, 6-inch ceiling is too low for safety and that the light fixtures would be less likely to be struck by a rearing horse if they were located along the sides of the ceiling rather than in the center.*

GROOMING AREA

In a small barn, and even in many large barns, grooming and tacking up commonly take place in the aisle (fig. 5.13). A single tie ring or cross-ties that attach on either side of the aisle are used to keep the horse in place. This is fine if one person is using the barn, but problems can arise when another person with a cart or leading a horse needs to get by. A grooming area off the main aisle leaves the aisle open for traffic, which is safer for everyone.

The grooming area should be at least 8-feet wide and 12-feet long to allow a person to move all around the horse when grooming and tacking (see fig. 12.13, p. 157). A wider space, for example 11 feet, will allow room for a grooming kit, vacuum, stepstool, and other items without crowding. CAUTION: If the cross-tie area is wider than 11 feet, a horse can turn around in the cross-ties and face the wrong direction. This will cause most horses to panic and result in severe injuries to the horse's face from the twisted cross-tie ropes.

Tie rings should be secured with bolts that extend at least 2 inches into a framing member. Fastening to just a board or paneling is asking for trouble. If a horse pulled back, the ring or board could break loose and be swung around on the end of the tie rope by the panic-stricken horse, causing injury to the horse or nearby persons.

One way to get the most from a small space is to build shelves into the wall (see fig. 12.14, p. 157) to hold grooming tools and supplies. That way everything you need is close at hand yet not underfoot where a person or horse could step on or trip over them.

WASH RACK

A wash rack (wash stall) is a waterproof area where a horse can be bathed without hosing down the entire barn (fig. 5.14). It might seem like a luxury to some people, but if thought is given to its design and location it can be useful for activities besides bathing horses, such as a grooming and tacking up, and a place for your farrier and vet to work.

A wash rack is typically a large open space or is enclosed only on two or three sides, having no doors or windows. The minimum size for a wash rack to be safe and useful is 8-feet wide by 12-feet long. An arrangement I've found useful is to start with a wider area, like

Plan for two doors. A door directly to the outside near a driveway will make loading your trailer for horse shows or trail rides much easier. More importantly, in case of fire, it may save your life and allow you to evacuate your tack. A door directly to the grooming area where you will tack up will save steps. This door should swing inward so as not to crowd the grooming area. Stick with hinged doors; sliding doors takes up less room, but are more difficult to seal against cold and insects. Make doors at least 4-feet wide so a person can easily pass while carrying a saddle. Standard commercial 4-foot doors generally have a smooth steel face so you may have to order custom doors if that look doesn't appeal to you. Doors should have secure locks to discourage theft.

There are pros and cons to having windows in a tack room. Although they offer a view and provide ventilation, they also are a possible entry for burglars. They let in sunlight, which is damaging to tack, and they take up valuable wall space, which never seems to be in abundance in a tack room. Consider installing vents and fans for ventilation instead of windows (see Vent and Fans, p. 26). If you do install windows, cover them with sturdy steel grilles on the outside for security.

5.14 *Concrete block wash rack with rubber mats over concrete floor. Note that rubber brick aisle in the foreground is level with the adjoining concrete floor.*

5.15 *This 10-foot by 10-foot outdoor wash rack makes it easy to lead a horse in and back him out but is too small to easily turn a large horse around. Water drains out the front onto the surrounding ground.*

11 feet or 12 feet, and set pipe railings in the floor approximately 1½ feet from the walls (see fig. 12.18, p. 158). This makes an 8-foot-wide work area in the center and the railings allow buckets and other equipment to be set on the floor or on shelves along the walls without them being stepped on by the horse.

A wash rack requires cold water, and the addition of hot water is preferable. Faucets or hydrants need to be protected by a rail, as mentioned above, or by other means to prevent damage to the faucets and injury should a horse knock against them. In a winter climate in an unheated barn, locate the wash rack next to a heated room, like the tack room, so freeze-proof faucets can be installed in the common wall.

An indoor wash rack is located where overspray won't cause problems. The floor typically slopes to a drain in the center of the floor (see fig. 12.19, p. 158).

An outdoor wash rack may not need a drain if the location permits water to run onto the surrounding ground (fig. 5.15). A concrete floor is always best to ensure a mud-free work place. There are several types of pre-made pipe wash racks available that are set into a concrete pad, usually outdoors, when it is poured.

FARRIER/VET AREA

One of the most overlooked areas of barn design is providing a suitable place for a farrier and veterinarian to work. The space should be sheltered from sun, wind, and precipitation and have a solid, level floor. (A sure way to lose favor with these professionals is to ask them to work in mud.) Concrete works well and when covered by rubber mats is even better. The wash rack or grooming area often doubles as the farrier/vet work space. A wash rack is particularly nice for vets because their work often involves washing parts of the horse and washing equipment when they are through. It's not always the best place for a farrier to work, however, because the floor often slopes toward a drain, making assessing hoof balance more difficult, and the drain can become clogged with hoof trimmings and raspings.

The area should be large enough for the practitioner to get around the horse, yet small enough to help contain the horse so it is not dancing all over the place. A space 8 feet to 12 feet wide and 10 feet to 12 feet long works well for most situations.

Both the farrier and vet require good lighting to do their best work (see Lights, p. 99). Plan for plenty of electric lights, located at the sides of the workspace, not just overhead, to minimize shadows. Also, install several outlets nearby for portable plug-in lights and tools.

UTILITY ROOM

A dedicated utility room can consolidate your cleaning and laundry supplies and help prevent congestion in the tack room and wash rack, which otherwise would share the duties of the utility room (figs. 5.16 and 5.17). Plan the utility room close to the grooming area so dirty tack can be taken from the horse directly to the laundry.

A 4-foot by 6-foot utility room would be sufficient for a water heater and a sink but not much else. The plan shown in figure 5.17 is for a 12-foot by 12-foot room with 2 x 6 walls, so the inside dimensions are 11 feet 6 inches by 11 feet 6 inches.

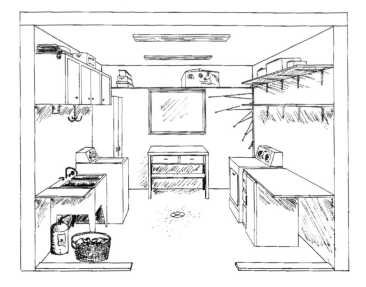

5.16 UTILITY ROOM, *perspective view.*

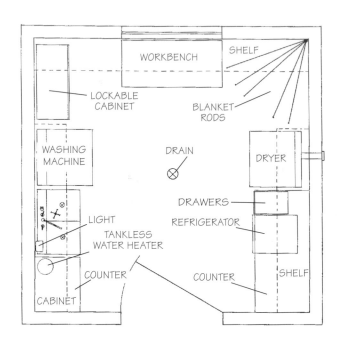

5.17 UTILITY ROOM, *plan view.*

- 2 x 6 walls allow ample space for running wiring and plumbing through the studs and also for a generous thickness of insulation if the room needs to be heated.

- A 9-foot-high ceiling gives plenty of head room and allows for storage over cabinets and on high shelves.

- Two 4-foot fluorescent ceiling light fixtures provide economical illumination.

- Concrete floor sloping to a central drain makes cleanup easy.

- A 4-foot-wide door gives a person room to carry horse blankets to and from the laundry without getting hung up on the doorway.

- A counter just inside the doorway to the left provides a place to pop in and set things to be washed or stored. The countertop can also hold a drain board for the double-basin utility sink that has hot and cold water, a spray nozzle, and ample room to wash tack and scrub grooming tools.

- A sink is conveniently located just a step to the left inside the door.

- There is a small fluorescent light over the sink.

- A tack hook hanging from the cabinet over the sink holds bridles for cleaning.

- A washing machine next to the sink is just a couple steps from the door, so it's easy to pull a blanket off your horse and pop it in the wash.

- A tankless (instant-heat) water heater is located under the counter with enough room left over for a basket near the door for accumulating wraps and other small laundry items.

- All plumbing items are within 5 feet of one another to simplify installation and maintenance.

- In the corner next to the washer is a 3-foot-wide by 6-foot-high lockable steel storage cabinet. This is for medications, fly sprays, solvents, and other products, especially those you want to keep away from children.

- A cabinet is mounted on the left wall above the counter, sink, and washer. It is for laundry supplies, leather cleaning products, and general storage. Boxes and other supplies can be stowed over the cabinet.

- Against the center of the back wall, beneath a 4-foot by 3-foot window, is a work bench for repairing tack and for servicing equipment such as clippers and vacuums. Drawers under the bench hold small tools and repair supplies like rivets and leather straps.

- A shelf over the window extends the width of the room for storing supplies, blankets, and other items.

- In the far right corner is a blanket rack with 42-inch-long swivel rods for hanging blankets, saddle blankets, and other items to dry or to store.

- Next to the blanket rod system is a clothes dryer. It is situated directly across from the washer to make shuffling laundry from the washer to the dryer most efficient. The dryer vents through the wall to the outdoors or, in a climate with very low humidity, to a tool room or wash rack next door. If the adjoining room is not suitable for venting into, the vent can be run along the wall to exit the back wall to the outdoors or up the wall to exit the ceiling into the barn or through the roof.

- Next to the dryer is a 24-inch-wide by 5-foot-long counter that's fastened to the wall. This counter is handy for laying out blankets and pads to vacuum before washing and for folding dry horse laundry.

- Under the counter and next to the dryer is a stack of drawers for storing tools such as clippers and supplies like snaps and braiding bands.

- A compact refrigerator sets next to the drawers under the counter. It holds temperature sensitive medications, pharmaceuticals, and supplements as well as cold beverages.

- The remaining space under the counter can be used to store large items such as a vacuum for pre-cleaning blankets or a step stool for reaching shelves.

FEED ROOM

The feed room is used for daily feeding and for storing feed to protect it from, heat, moisture, and vermin. A well-organized 8-foot by 10-foot or 6-foot by 12-foot feed room is a practical size for a two- to six-stall barn and allows space to move around and reach the various feeds and supplements without straining. Extra space can be used for storing tools or tack.

The room should be close to the stalls for daily feeding and easy to access with a truck for deliveries. One door should be at least 4-feet wide to allow a person to carry grain bags through without banging into the doorway. A second door to the outside will allow grain delivery without driving into the barn.

There should be enough light so the notations on the feed board and the ingredients on feed containers and labels can be read. Although a window can provide natural light and ventilation, a feed room is generally small and you might opt to use the wall space for shelves or hooks. In humid climates, a dehumidifier can help keep feed from spoiling.

Storage containers should be able to be emptied completely and cleaned on a regular basis. This will minimize mold and damage from forage mites, which damage feeds and can cause skin problems and gut upsets in horses.

Following are comments on feed rooms in general and our present feed room in particular (fig. 5.18, see fig. 12.27, p. 160).

- A feed room should at least be made of 2 x 4 studs placed 16 inches on center—12 inches on center would be stronger. This 8-foot by 10-foot room has 2 x 6 studs, 16 inches on center. To keep rodents out, walls should fit tightly to the floor, and there should be no holes or gaps in the walls or at the corners where the walls meet.

- The outside of the walls should be covered with paneling a minimum of ⅝ inch thick. We used T-111 siding. Two corners of the walls project into the traffic area, so we covered them with steel anti-chew guards to protect the corners from damage from carts and other equipment.

- The walls are bolted to the concrete floor. There's always a chance a horse might get loose in the barn when no one is around, and the walls and door of the feed room must be constructed so as not to break or move on the floor if a horse collides with them. If a horse gains access to large amounts of grain he could founder and die or be left permanently lame.

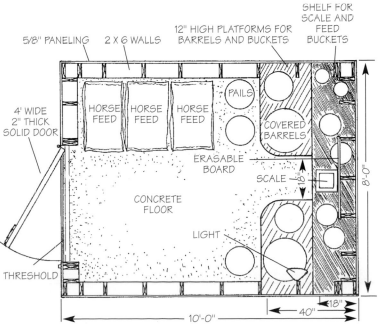

5.18 FEED ROOM.

- The feed room door should be solid wood or a solid core covered with wood veneer or metal. A hollow-core door, like that used for closets inside houses, is not strong enough for a feed room. The door should fit closely in its frame and there should be a threshold to seal the space between the bottom of the door and the floor.

- The latch needs to be horse-proof. With a standard door latch, use an auxiliary lock such as a hasp with a snap or a padlock.

- The ceiling is 2 x 8 joists topped by ¾-inch oriented strand board (*OSB*), which provides a loft floor for storage.

- The smooth concrete floor is easy to sweep clean, rodent-proof, and durable. In our dry climate, sacks of feed can be stacked directly on the concrete floor. In humid climates sacks of feed should be stacked on wooden pallets to prevent condensation on the floor from ruining the feed. When adding a feed room to an existing barn that has a history of rainwater draining into the barn, make the floor of the feed room 4 to 6 inches higher than the main floor.

- Setting feed barrels on low platforms makes scooping feed from the bottom half of tall barrels less difficult.

- A shelf holds a scale, feed buckets, and measuring cans to make serving up the rations more convenient.

- An erasable board mounted on the wall over the shelf helps ensure that feed changes are kept current and that the horses are fed a consistent ration when more than one person does the feeding.

- A light fixture with two 100-*watt* incandescent bulbs is located on the wall to the right of the shelf, where the shadow of the person dishing up grain will not fall on the work area.

- There is no window in this feed room. The top portion of the siding is translucent fiberglass, which eliminates the need for electric lights during daylight hours.

HAY STORAGE

It is safer in terms of fire hazard to store the bulk of your hay in a separate building that doesn't house horses and to move only smaller quantities of hay into the horse barn as needed (see fig. 12.28, p. 160). As mentioned in Chapter 4, loft storage of hay is not a good idea for a horse barn; it is a fire hazard, it encourages vermin, it impedes ventilation by limiting the ceiling height over the stalls, and it creates dust when hay is thrown down from the loft.

Limited quantities of hay that are stored in the barn should be close to the feed room for convenience at feeding time. Hay should be protected from ground moisture, if necessary, by stacking it on pallets or boards. The size of the area depends on how much you plan to store in the barn. The size of a normal stall, 12 feet by 12 feet, should be sufficient for most barns. Two normal hay bales cover an area 3 feet by 3 feet (9 square feet), and with five bales stacked high, this space will store ten bales. So, an area 6 feet by 12 feet, can store up to 80 bales, enough to feed four horses for two months. This leaves an area six feet by twelve feet for handling bales, filling hay nets, and loading and parking a hay cart.

BEDDING STORAGE

Like hay, the bulk of your bedding should be stored in a separate building to reduce fire risk. Bulk bedding is commonly stored in a bunker and brought to the barn as needed. For straw bales or bagged bedding, a 6-foot by 6-foot space is sufficient to store 50 bales or bags. It is commonly stored in the same area as the hay (see fig. 12.28, p. 160). If you must store loose bedding in the barn, locate it away from the stalls so horses are not continually exposed to irritating dust particles. Likewise, locate outdoor hay and bedding storage where prevailing winds will not be blowing dust toward the barn.

FIREWALLS

You might consider installing (or be required by code to install) *firewalls* between the hay storage area and the rest of the barn. The purpose of a firewall is to slow down the progress of a fire. It is constructed so that during a fire one side can collapse without the entire wall coming down. The walls can extend from the floor to the underside of the roof or through and above the roof. A firewall is rated as to how long it will withstand a fire, usually one or two hours.

Construction varies and can consist of masonry, steel, or wood framing with a fireproof material, commonly drywall rated X, on each side. Windows and doors in a firewall, and sealer used to fill holes and gaps in a firewall, must be rated the same as the firewall. Consult a fire protection engineer for design help. (For more on firewall design see www.usg.com.)

BATHROOM/DRESSING ROOM

A combination bathroom and dressing room will enable you to clean up and change clothes between sessions at the barn or before you return to the house. A bathroom needs to be a minimum of 8 feet by 6 feet to comfortably accommodate a sink and toilet and a few hooks on the wall for a change of clothes. A 12-foot by 12-foot room would allow space for a shower and clothes closet as well.

If you are planning a bathroom (fig. 5.19), locate it near the utility room to minimize plumbing installation.

INDOOR ARENA

An indoor arena (see figs. 7.25 and 7.26, pp. 72–73) is a large, free-span building used for ground training and riding. Build the largest arena you can afford and make it at least large enough to practice your event. An ideal size would be 100 feet by 200 feet or larger.

Good drainage is of utmost importance so locate the arena on high ground or build up the arena site with fill dirt to prevent flooding during wet cycles. On hilly or sloping terrain, dig ditches or *swales* around the site to direct runoff away from the arena.

Lots of airflow is essential for a pleasant and healthy riding environment (see Ventilation, p. 26). Plan large

5.19 *A bathroom can save you and your guests a trip to the house and provide a place to wash up and change clothes.*

doors at both ends of the arena that can be opened for cross ventilation. In hot climates orient the doors toward the prevailing breeze; in cold climates away from the prevailing wind. Consider installing large hinged panels in the sidewalls to enhance airflow. Roof vents allow rising warm air to escape, and the movement will draw cooler air in through doors and lower vents.

Dust is harmful to both horses and riders. Many footing materials, including sawdust, dirt, and some rubber products, are pulverized into fine powder by horses' hooves. Overhead sprinkler systems can be used to dampen the footing and hold the dust down. Another option is to use a tractor-mounted spray unit to treat arena footing with water or arena additives. Watering the footing can make an arena very humid and stuffy unless adequate ventilation is provided.

DRIVEWAYS

If your horse is injured, you won't want to waste an hour or more trying to get a trailer close to the barn to take the horse to a vet. And if your barn catches fire, you'll want firefighters to be able to get to the fire quickly and safely and have room to set up their equipment.

- Provide access for emergency vehicles that is at least 12 feet wide with overhead clearance of at least 14½ feet across the entire width.

- Grade the driveway to slope at least 0.5% to prevent pooling of water on the traveled surface.

- Avoid steep driveways—keep grades below 15%.

- Make curves and corners wide enough to accommodate a large truck or trailer, and the largest fire emergency vehicle likely to use the driveway.

- If possible, build a driveway on the windward side of your barn to act as a firebreak.

- Make gates 2 feet wider than the roadway and have them open inward.

- Make sure fire personnel have ready access to gate lock combinations or keys.

- Dead end driveways should be clearly marked and should have a turnaround with a minimum radius of 50 feet or a "T" turnaround for emergency vehicles.

- Make separate parking areas for trailers and equipment so roads are kept clear. ᵿ

CHAPTER SIX

UNDERSTANDING PLANS

Clear and accurate plans are a critical link between the picture in your mind and the barn at the end of your budget. I am not going to go into great detail on plans, but I do want to give you a basic understanding so you are not totally confused when confronted with a plan. When you look over various barn plans, such as from barn companies, contractors, catalogs, and the Internet, you'll be better able to compare features and tell a builder or architect what changes you would like.

Working drawings, also called building plans, contain all the drawings needed to build a barn from start to finish. Reproductions of working drawings are called blueprints, no matter what color they are. Some contractors require a set of working drawings for a custom barn to provide an accurate bid. All drawings are to exact scale so a person reading them can tell the relationship between the parts of the barn. There are basically three ways to obtain plans for a barn: draw plans yourself, hire someone to draw them, or buy plans that are already drawn.

DRAW PLANS YOURSELF

Plans can be as simple as a sketch on a napkin. In fact, that's how most of the barns I've built started out (fig. 6.1). Start by sketching the number of stalls and other spaces you want and move them around until you

find an arrangement you think will work. Graph paper is ideal for working out ideas because it keeps spaces in scale. A ¼-inch grid size is most useful and is available at office supply stores. Using a scale of ¼ inch = 1 foot (each square represents 1 foot) you can quickly sketch in stalls, aisles, and rooms and fit a barn up to 80 feet by 100 feet on one sheet of paper (fig. 6.2). For larger barns have each ¼-inch square equal 2 feet. On a separate piece of paper, show more detail, for example of a utility room, by having two or more squares equal one foot.

If you will do the construction yourself, graph paper drawings might be all you'll need. Whether the local building department will accept them with your permit application is another story. The drawings will need to convince them that the barn will comply with zoning ordinances and building code. Most building departments supply handouts stating the drawings you need and what needs to be included on them.

One of the most difficult parts of designing a barn is figuring the sizes of *beams, joists, girders, headers,* and *rafters*. Maximum span depends on the load the member must carry, the size of material, and the species of wood you are using. The maximum span for a yellow pine joist, for example, is longer than for a white pine, fir, or hemlock joist. Load calculations take into account snow, wind, and

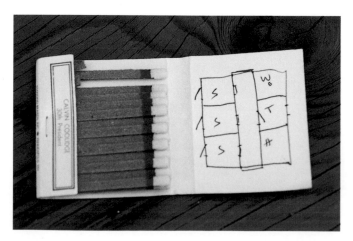

6.1 *Initial sketches can be very rough and made almost anywhere.*

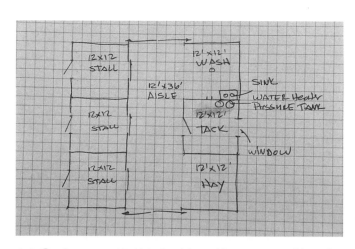

6.2 *Graph paper with ¼-inch grids enables you to quickly make sketches that are in proportion.*

use of the building. Most state and local codes include standard tables or will reference another publication that might be available at your public library. Several websites offer online calculators for figuring spans and material sizes (see the Resource Guide). If you are using trusses, don't attempt to design them yourself unless you have engineering capabilities. The building inspector will likely require your trusses to be certified on site by a licensed engineer at your expense. Truss suppliers will often design trusses at no extra charge using the barn dimensions you give them.

If you will hire one or more contractors to do all or part of the construction, they will need a professional set of plans drawn up either by a contractor or an architect.

HIRE AN ARCHITECT

An architect or contractor experienced in designing horse facilities should be able to tell you about materials appropriate for a horse barn, explain details to you, and solve any problems the plan might have regarding horse health, safety, and comfort. For an additional fee, the architect can make a scale model of the barn, which makes the plan easier to visualize. It's best if the architect visits the site before starting on your plans to make best use of topographical features of your property. If that's not possible, provide photos of the site from all vantage points, pointing out trees, ponds, and other features of the site relevant to the plan, especially those you don't want disturbed.

BUY PLANS

A less expensive option than hiring an architect is to purchase a set of plans through a catalog or the Internet. There are many detailed plans available for barns already designed and built; so many of the bugs have been worked out. You will likely want to make modifications, but at least you'll have a starting point. Look for plans on which critical spans and dimensions have been checked by an engineer to ensure compliance with national building codes. When looking at modular barns, make sure the final plans will comply with your local building codes.

TYPES OF PLANS

The number and types of plans you will need depends on the requirements of the building department and the complexity of the barn. A plot plan, floor plan, and two elevation views are typically mandatory and often all that are required for a simple horse barn.

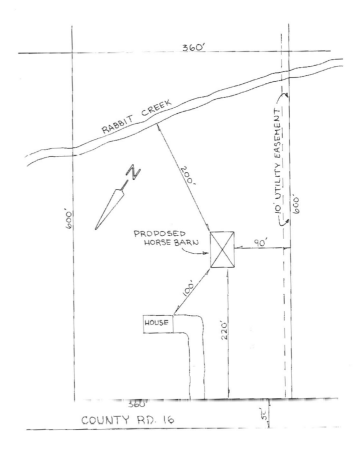

6.3 *Plot Plan.*

PLOT PLAN

This is an accurately scaled bird's-eye view of your property that shows the size and shape of the proposed building in relation to existing buildings, property lines, ponds, creeks, roads, and buried and overhead utilities (fig. 6.3). You may also need to show the location of and distances from well, septic system, and buildings on adjacent properties and across roads.

Start by drawing your property lines, use a compass to find north on your property and indicate it on the drawing. Then fill in details. Measurements don't have to be dead on but they should be in proportion. An easy way to measure long distances is to pace them off. A full stride, left foot to left foot, is usually around 5 feet. Measure your own stride and adjust accordingly. Use graph paper or use a ruler to scale the drawing to fit blank paper. You may be able to obtain an aerial map of your land from your local zoning office or on the web, which will save you some hiking and measuring. Also, your county courthouse may have area maps you can trace to get a scale outline of your property.

A plot plan typically includes:

- Owner's name

- Section, township, and range

- Subdivision name, lot, and block number

- Statement of scale (the minimum might be 1 inch = 20 feet or ¹⁄₁₆ inch = 1 foot)

- Indication of north by an arrow

- Dimensions of all property lines

- Driveways and adjacent roads, with names

- *Easements* for utilities

- Parking areas

- Existing structures labeled according to use (e. g., "house," "shop")

- Proposed structure labeled according to use (e.g., "horse barn")

- *Setbacks:* the distance from the proposed barn to all property lines and to centerline of adjacent roads and existing structures

- Creek, pond, or body of water within 100 feet of structure, noting distance from structure to water

FLOOR PLAN

A floor plan shows width and length dimensions, use of each room, and locations and sizes of doors and windows (fig. 6.4). Minimum scale is typically ¼ inch = 1 foot. A separate plan is required for each level. This plan usually receives the most emphasis and is almost always drawn first, because it determines the overall size of the barn and the arrangement and size of spaces inside. It is a view looking straight down from above. It is actually a horizontal *section view*, as if the barn were sliced off halfway up the walls, so you see the thickness of the walls and the locations of doors and windows. If a wash rack or toilet and sinks are planned, drain lines for wastewater might be shown on the floor plan.

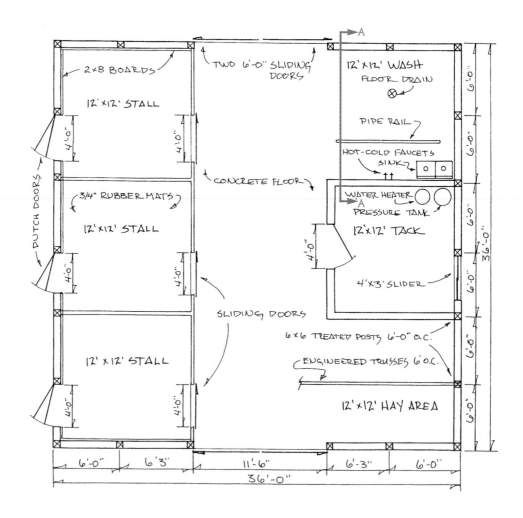

6.4 *Floor Plan.*

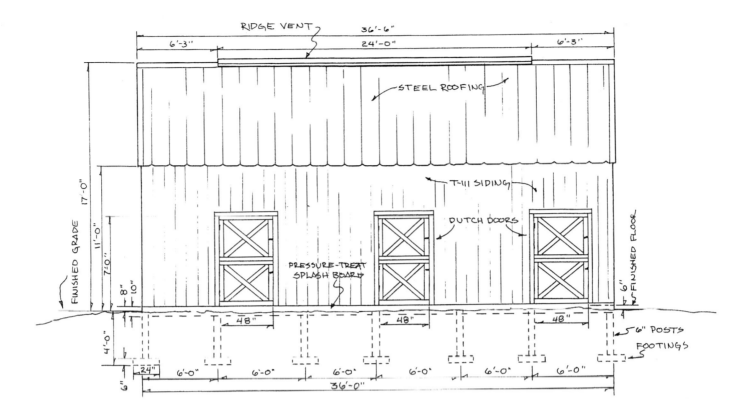

6.5 *Side Elevation.*

FRAMING PLAN

This drawing shows direction, size, and spacing of the roof system, girders, *columns*, and *piers*. It is sometimes omitted if the same information is found on a section view and foundation or floor plan as in figure 6.4.

FOUNDATION

A foundation plan shows location, size, and materials of footings or poles. It is often combined with the floor plan or elevation plan, or both, as in figures 6.4 and 6.5.

GRADING AND DRAINAGE PLAN

This may be required for properties located in a flood plain. Also, certain ordinances and covenants require a *grading* and drainage plan to ensure runoff from your horse operation won't pollute neighboring properties or waterways. A drainage plan usually includes a topographic map of the area and proposed clearing and grading, cuts and fills, and final contours at 2-foot intervals. This plan is beyond the capabilities of most horse owners and is usually prepared by an engineer or landscape architect.

ELEVATIONS

Elevation views show what the barn will look like from the front, back, and sides (fig. 6.5). They typically include:

- finished grade line (ground level)

- all vertical dimensions above and below grade

- finished floor lines

- sizes and types of doors and windows and where they are located vertically as well as horizontally in a wall

- type and slope of roof, roofing materials, and locations of vents and overhangs

- type of siding

- exterior electrical fixtures and outlets

- *gutters* and *downspouts*

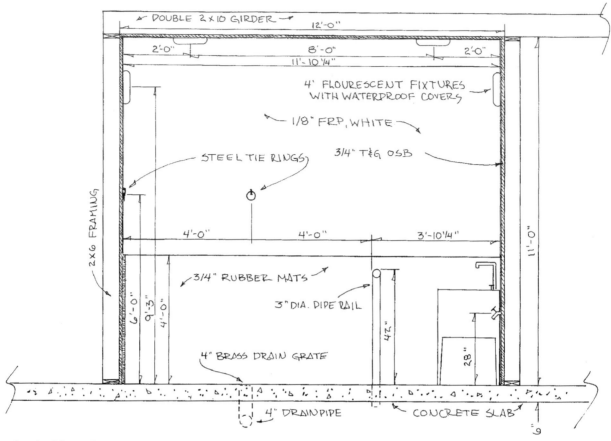

6.6 *Section A – A of figure 6.4.*

SECTIONS

A section view is used to show details about floor levels and how interior features relate to ground level (fig. 6.6, see also figs. 7.25, p. 72, and 7.28, p. 74, and fig. 10.9. p. 124). They show what it would be like looking at a vertical slice through the barn from roof to footings. Most simple horse barns do not require section views.

DETAILS

A detail view is used when a special feature, such as a foaling window, needs more explanation. It is often a portion of a section view drawn to a larger scale than the other drawings.

PERSPECTIVE

A *perspective* drawing best shows you what the barn will look like (see fig. 7.6, p. 54). It is more like a photograph than other drawings are, and it is drawn from a vantage point that shows the most interesting features of the barn. With only a perspective drawing and the floor plan, you can get a pretty good idea of what a barn will be like.

SPECIFICATION SHEET

This is a list that describes materials, fasteners, and details not explained in other views.

RESUBMITS

To avoid extra costs and delays, have a firm idea of the barn's design and location before submitting plans for a building permit. If you make significant changes, such as moving beams or headers, or changing floor joist size, after the plans have been approved, you may need to resubmit your plans. If you change the square footage or the location of the barn; a new plot plan will likely be required as well. There is often an additional fee to recheck plans.

VISUALIZE THE PLAN

When looking at barn floor plans, picture yourself as being very small (or the plan very large) and visualize what you would see as you walked through every portion of the barn. Picture each and every aspect of caring for and interacting with your horse. Pay particular attention to traffic patterns, especially if there will be more than one person moving horses around at the same time.

- Is there a clear path from where you enter the barn to the stalls or the tack room?

- When you lead a horse from a stall or pen to the grooming/tacking area will you have to detour around another horse that is cross-tied in the aisle?

- Will it be convenient to carry tack from the tack room to the horse and back?

- Where will you store hay and grain and how much?

- How will you get hay and grain into the feed room?

- Will it be convenient to distribute feed to the horses?

- How will you fill horses' water containers?

- How will you get dirty bedding out of the stalls and out of the barn?

- Are there doors, windows, and vents to allow plenty of airflow?

- Are light switches conveniently located so you can reach them while leading a horse?

If you see something on a plan that you don't think will work, now is the time to speak up. The longer you wait, the more expensive changes become. ∪

CHAPTER SEVEN

SAMPLE PLANS

The horse barn plans in this chapter are intended to spark your imagination and show you various ways spaces can be utilized. They are not working drawings; however, an experienced draftsman or builder could make a set of building plans using these drawings.

Each barn is represented by a perspective drawing to show style, and a floor plan to show layout. All barns are pole-frame construction unless otherwise noted. I will point out interesting features of each plan and explain advantages of certain space arrangements and other details. I will also point out occasional disadvantages so you can learn to spot them in other plans and make modifications accordingly. Most plans can be expanded to accommodate more horses by simply extending the length of the barn and adding more stalls.

1. LOAFING SHED

A three-sided pole-frame shed, commonly called a loafing shed (figs. 7.1 and 7.2), is useful in any climate for providing shelter from sun, wind, and wet weather. It can be made as long as desired and divided into partitions to keep horses separate at feeding time.

DIMENSIONS
- 12 feet by 48 feet
- 3/12 roof slope
- 8 feet high at eaves, 10 feet high at peak

FEATURES
- 4-foot-high kick-boards (2-inch thick lumber or double thickness ¾-inch plywood supported every 4 feet by posts) on the inside of the shed prevent a horse from kicking through the siding.
- *Partition walls* are solid kick-wall below and heavy screen above.

OPTIONS
- Enclose one or more partitions with metal panels and a gate (as shown here) to confine a horse or to keep horses away from stored hay or equipment.
- Use siding to completely enclose one or more partitions for feed room or tack room or both.

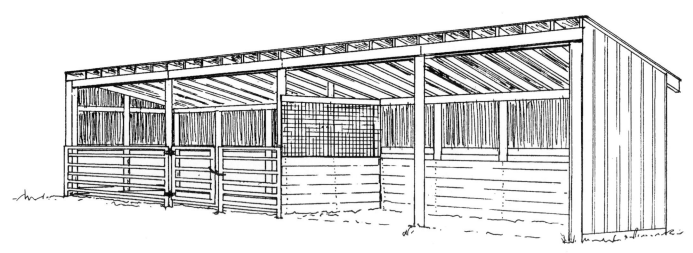

7.1 LOAFING SHED *Perspective view.*

- Add a short roof on the front for added protection from rain, snow, and sun.

- Cover the floor with rubber mats to prevent horses from ingesting sand and dirt with their feed (this will reduce the risk of sand colic). Set railroad ties or pressure treated timbers across the opening to help keep the mats in place and to minimize the amount of mud and dirt dragged onto them.

- If the shed were oriented on a fence line, you could put 2-foot by 2-foot window doors in the back wall to allow a person to drop hay into both stalls without entering the shed or the pen.

- This simple building can also serve as the first stage of a larger barn. Flip the floor plan and, as time and money allow, build an identical structure 10 or 12 feet away from and facing the original shed. Extend the two roofs to meet at a ridge over what is now the center aisle of a gable-roofed barn (fig. 7.3).

- For temporary protection while you build the other half of the barn, enclose the top 4 feet of the open wall with siding.

TIPS

- Locate the shed on high ground or build up the site to ensure drainage away from the shed. If the shed is located in a low spot or on poorly drained soil, the horses might have shelter from the storm but will end up standing in mud, which can be very bad for their hooves.

- Orient the shed with the back wall to the wind to give horses a protected place to eat their hay without it blowing away.

- Treat exposed wooden edges with an anti-chew product or cover them with steel angle trim to prevent chewing damage.

- The bottom edge of the siding, especially steel siding, should be securely attached to a *skirting* board to prevent a horse from cutting a foot on it.

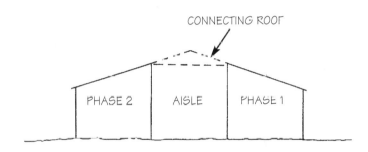

7.3 **LOAFING SHED** *end view of expansion.*

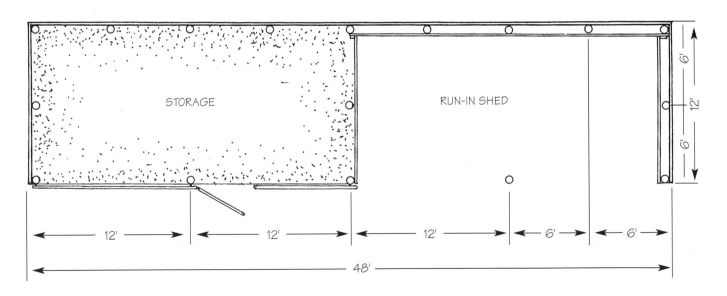

7.2 **LOAFING SHED** *Floor plan.*

7.4 **ONE-STALL EFFICIENCY,** *perspective view.*

2. ONE-STALL EFFICIENCY BARN

This compact design is well suited for the horse owner with one or two horses (figs. 7.4 and 7.5). The main structure is relatively inexpensive and easy to build, consisting of only twelve 6-inch posts, six walls, and a roof.

DIMENSIONS

- 12 feet by 28 feet

- The steel roof overhangs the main structure by 4 feet on both sides for protection from rain and snow.

- 3/12 roof slope

- 7 feet high at eaves, 9 feet 6 inches high at peak

FEATURES

- The 12-foot by 12-foot covered pen has a pea gravel floor and two solid walls. The walls are covered on both sides with ⅝-inch thick T-111 wood siding, with a double layer on the lower half of the inside of the stall. The walls protect the horse from wind and protect items stored at the back of the barn from the horse.

- Metal panels are attached to the building to make a pen or a run.

- The floor of the 10-foot by 12-foot *breezeway* is covered with five standard-size 4-foot by 6-foot rubber mats to make a tidy grooming area.

- Rafter framing allows more headroom inside the building than trusses would.

- The floor slopes toward the rear of the building for drainage when washing a horse.

- Location of the cross-ties results in the horse's near side being toward the tack room to make grooming and tacking of the horse more efficient.

- Usher ropes or chains connect across the openings at both ends of the aisle to discourage a horse from moving too far forward or backward in the cross-ties.

- The water hydrant is located safely away from the grooming area.

- A hose for filling the water tub in the pen and for washing a horse in the grooming area hangs next to the hydrant on the tack room wall.

- The 6-foot by 12-foot enclosed tack/feed room is covered on the outside with T-111 siding and has a wooden floor for cleanliness and to prevent rodent invasion.

- A sliding door is used for convenience and to conserve space.

- The door is fitted with a hasp so a padlock can be used to discourage unauthorized persons and loose horses from entering.

- In a dry climate the covered space at the rear of the barn can be used for storing hay, tack trunks, and feed barrels.

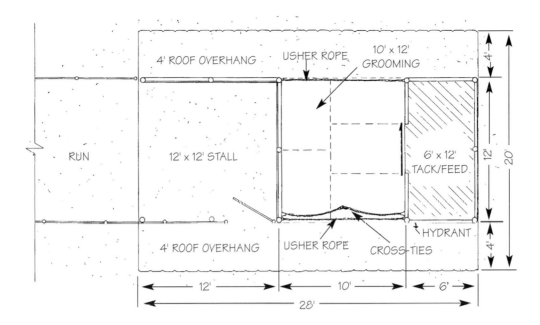

7.5 **ONE-STALL EFFICIENCY**, *plan view.*

DISADVANTAGES

- 7-foot eaves are too low for safety.

- The 4-foot overhang provides limited hay storage so hay must be hauled in frequently or stored nearby in a larger quantity.

OPTIONS

- Make the walls at least one foot higher for safer clearance.

- Close in and/or extend the overhang at the rear of the barn to provide more protection from the elements.

- Add another metal panel and gate between the covered pen and the run so the horse can be locked in or out of the covered pen.

- Extend the barn on one or both ends for more stalls or rooms.

TIPS

- If a horse chews the wood siding, coat it with a clear anti-chew product.

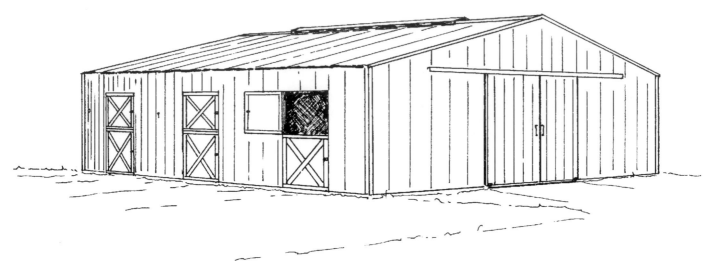

7.6 SQUARE BARN, *perspective view.*

3. SQUARE BARN

This simple, yet effective, design is relatively inexpensive to build and can also be used to remodel an existing pole building (figs. 7.6 and 7.7). It is based on a grid of poles set 12 feet apart resulting in nine equal squares. Three of the squares along one side are stalls. Three middle squares make the aisle. And three squares along the other side provide a wash area, tack room, and hay/bedding storage.

DIMENSIONS

- 36 feet by 36 feet

- The side walls are 9 feet high, roof peak 13 feet 6 inches.

- 4/12 roof slope

- 9 feet high at eaves, 15 feet high at peak

FEATURES

- Pole construction, steel siding and roof, and minimal use of concrete keep the cost of the building to a minimum.

- Concrete is used for the tack room and wash rack floors. The remainder of the barn floor can be crushed limestone, decomposed granite, or other native base.

- Interior and exterior stall doors are 4 feet wide by 7 feet high and located opposite one another for ease of leading a horse through, for cleaning and bedding the stalls, and for drying stall floors.

- Dutch doors on the exterior wall of the stalls provide light and ventilation for horses in the stalls.

- A 12-foot-wide center aisle with 9-feet-high by 6-feet-wide sliding doors on each end provide room to drive a truck or tractor through for barn cleaning and delivery of feed and bedding.

- Tack room is insulated and heated to protect tack and prevent pressure tank, water heater, and other plumbing from freezing.

- A tack room window provides light and ventilation.

- Loft over tack room provides storage area for seldom-used items.

- The wash rack has hot and cold water, cross-ties, and a deep utility sink for washing buckets and tack. A 4-foot-high pipe rail keeps the horse away from the sink and hose hook-ups. The rail also provides a place to hang blankets and other tack for washing and drying.

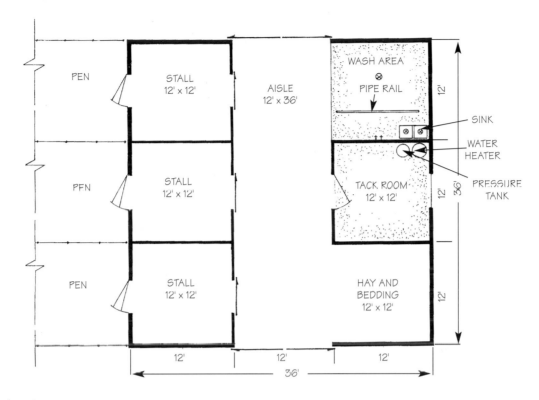

7.7 SQUARE BARN, *plan view.*

DISADVANTAGES

- Limestone and other crushed rock floors can be very dusty and hard to clean.

- Steel roofing, unless insulated, can be deafening during rain or hail storms.

- Lack of roof overhang means rain and snow will accumulate right next to the building. This can be especially messy by the stall doors, and, since the doors swing outward, snow can prevent them from opening.

- Tack room window is a security risk and could allow sunlight to damage leather tack.

OPTIONS

- Cover stall floors with rubber mats to prevent holes from moisture and pawing.

- To minimize dust, replace the limestone floor in the aisle and storage area floor with concrete or cover with rubber mats.

- Cover the window in the tack room with a sturdy iron grille for security. Install a shade or drape to control the amount of sunlight reaching leather tack.

- Make the barn walls 2 feet higher for more headroom.

- Extend the roof or attach a roof overhang to the stall side of barn to provide outdoor shelter and to divert roof runoff away from the doors.

- For natural illumination, install skylights in the roof or replace some or all of the steel panels in the top of the gable walls with translucent fiberglass panels.

- Add roof vents to improve ventilation.

- Add pens off the stalls to allow easy turnout (as shown on floor plan in fig. 7.7).

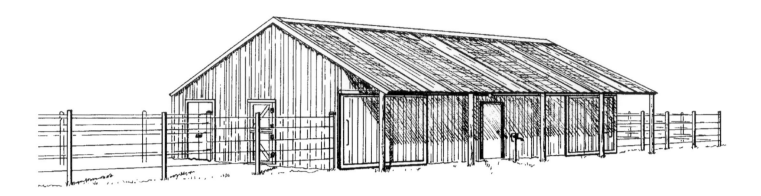

7.8 **2-STALL REMODELED POLE BUILDING,** *perspective view.*

4. TWO-STALL REMODELED POLE BUILDING
This design is based on an existing empty 24-foot by 48-foot pole building (figs. 7.8 and 7.9). Expense is minimal, since the basic structure is already there.

DIMENSIONS AFTER REMODELING
- 40 feet by 48 feet
- 4/12 roof slope
- 8 feet high at front eaves, 6 feet high at back eaves, 16 feet at peak

INITIAL FEATURES
- Steel roof and siding
- Two 12-foot-wide by 9-foot-high sliding doors on one long wall
- One 3-foot by 6-foot door between the sliding doors
- Dirt floor
- Freeze-proof hydrant near small door

REMODELED FEATURES
- Roof and walls are extended 10 feet on one side for hay storage (400-bale capacity). 4-foot-wide doors provide access from both ends of this addition.
- Small feed doors are added into each stall to allow feeding directly from hay storage area.
- A 6-foot overhang is added on the front of the building to keep the entrance areas free of rain and snow.
- Translucent fiberglass panels replace four sections of steel roofing on each side of the roof for natural light.
- A 12-foot by 16-foot insulated tack room is built in the center of the building across from the small door. The floor over the tack room provides storage for seldom-used items. The tack room floor is insulated and covered with ¾-inch OSB.
- A 3-foot by 6-foot 6-inch door is added between the tack room and hay storage addition.
- Stalls are lined to a height of 54 inches with 2-inch-thick rough sawn boards.
- Dutch doors are installed in exterior stall walls and lead to pens on each end of the barn.
- The remaining half of the original building is used as a grooming and tacking area. Two sets of cross-ties, which can also serve as four individual tie rings, are installed from each end of the tack room to the outside wall. This allows space for two horses to be tied for grooming.

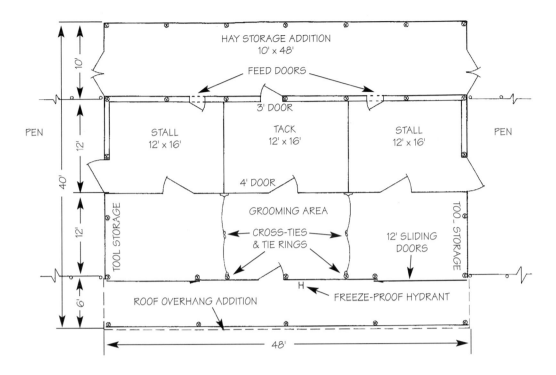

7.9 *2-STALL REMODELED POLE BUILDING, plan view.*

DISADVANTAGES

- Dirt floors are uneven and dusty.

- Stalls receive no direct sunlight and very little cross-ventilation to aid in drying.

- Steel roofing can be deafening during heavy rain or hail.

- Storing hay adjacent to the stalls is a safety hazard in case of fire.

OPTIONS

- Pour concrete or install another type of flooring to keep the floor level and the barn cleaner.

- Add gravel and rubber mats to stalls for easier maintenance and better sanitation.

- Add windows to stalls for more light and ventilation.

- Move the bulk of hay to another building and use the hay addition for equipment storage.

- Omit the hay addition altogether and install Dutch doors in the back wall rather than in the end walls.

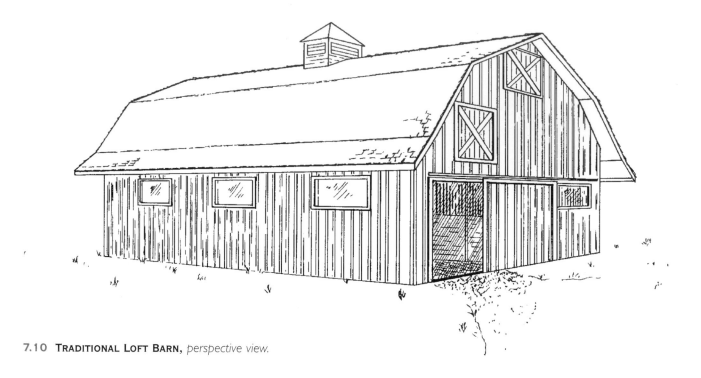

7.10 TRADITIONAL LOFT BARN, *perspective view.*

5. TRADITIONAL LOFT BARN

As mentioned in Chapter 4, lofts can often present more problems than they are worth. I include a traditional loft barn for those of you who have your hearts set on this design (figs. 7.10 and 7.11).

DIMENSIONS
- 24 feet by 48 feet
- *Gambrel roof*
- 8 feet at eaves, 21 feet at peak
- ceiling below loft 9 feet

FEATURES
- Gambrel roof, fiber *cement* shakes, and *board and batten siding* give this barn an old-time flavor.

- A brick floor in the aisle and wooden floor in the stalls add to the old-time feel and sound of the barn. The aisle floor slopes to a centrally located drain so the grooming area can serve as a wash area as well.

- The 8-foot-high by 10-foot-wide sliding door allows a truck or tractor into the barn for stall cleaning and feed delivery.

- A 4-foot-wide by 7-foot-high door on the other end provides another entrance and cross-ventilation with the other door and windows.

- 6-foot-wide awning windows in stalls, feed room, and grooming area are a modern touch that provide light and ventilation. For security, there is no window in the tack room.

- Feeders and water buckets are located on the aisle wall of each stall for easy access.

- A freeze-proof hydrant located at the corner of the feed room provides water for stalls and bathing.

- Cross-ties are located to facilitate grooming, tacking, and bathing.

- The gambrel roof provides enough loft space to store a year's supply of hay for three horses.

- A loft floor of tongue and groove plywood minimizes dust trickling through to the lower level.

- A two-week supply of hay can be dropped through the trap door and scooted into the adjoining "hay bay," making daily climbs into the loft unnecessary.

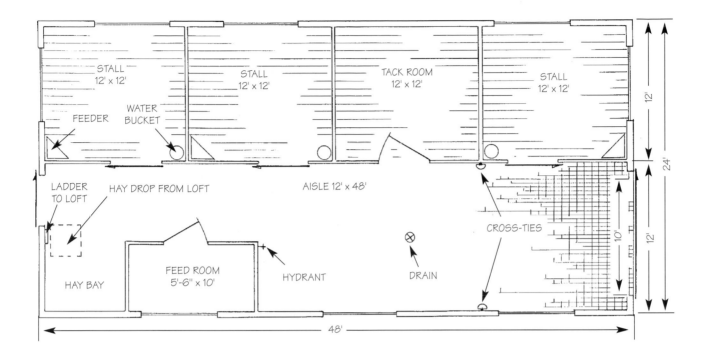

7.11 TRADITIONAL LOFT BARN, *plan view.*

DISADVANTAGES

- Storing a large quantity of hay in the same building as horses is a big risk in case of fire and can cause a dusty environment below.

- A 9-foot ceiling is too low for safe stabling and inhibits ventilation, creating an unhealthy atmosphere.

- Wood siding is also a fire hazard.

- Having only one door in each stall could prevent horse rescue in case of a fire.

- Wood floor in stalls is difficult to clean and sanitize.

OPTIONS

- Use loft for an apartment, and store the bulk of hay in another building.

- Build lower level 11 feet high instead of 9 feet for more headroom.

- Eliminate loft altogether so the barn is one open space and install skylights in roof

- Use a more fire resistant siding, such as fiber cement or steel.

- Replace wooden stall floors with interlocking rubber mats.

- Install doors in exterior walls of stalls.

- Install automatic waterers and swing-out feeders.

- Replace solid partition between two stalls with a moveable partition to make a double stall for foaling, recovery, or a large horse.

- Install water heater in feed room; in cold climates, insulate, and heat feed room to keep plumbing from freezing.

7.12 **FRESH AIR BARN,** *perspective view.*

6. FRESH AIR BARN

This design would be suitable for a hot, dry climate since it is only partially enclosed (figs. 7.12–7.14). The floor plan, which is basically a gridwork of posts, is very versatile. By installing walls between various posts, the space can be divided into spaces for horses, equipment, storage, and work areas as desired.

DIMENSIONS
- 32 feet by 45 feet
- 6/12 upper roof slope
- 4/12 lower roof slope
- 8 feet high at eaves
- 12 feet high under loft
- 20 feet to peak

FEATURES
- As with the expanded loafing shed (fig. 7.3), this barn can be built in stages: first the central structure, then the wings, then interior details.
- Open walls cut down on construction expense and allow plenty of air and light into the barn. This helps keep the floor dry and reduces the need for electric lights.
- The central section and wings are long enough to park a truck and trailer or tractor and spreader.
- The loft has room for 400 bales of hay or bedding, equipment, etc.

DISADVANTAGES
- Dust from the dirt floors will cover everything in the barn.
- Open walls allow dust, rain, and snow to blow into the barn.
- Horses in the run-in shed portions could reach over or through the board fence to chew on equipment or whatever is in the center section of the barn.
- Loft storage means getting whatever is being stored up and into the loft via a ladder, hay elevator, tractor bucket or other means, and down again when you need it.

OPTIONS
- Make the center section as tall as needed, to park an RV, for example.
- Enclose entire barn and install overhead doors or hinged doors on the end of the center section.
- Pour a concrete floor in the center section and especially under a feed and tack room if they are added.
- Use the wings for run-in sheds or hay storage (fig. 7.14).
- Build a feed room, tack room, grooming area.
- Make the walls of the loft area taller to allow more headroom, say for an apartment or more storage.

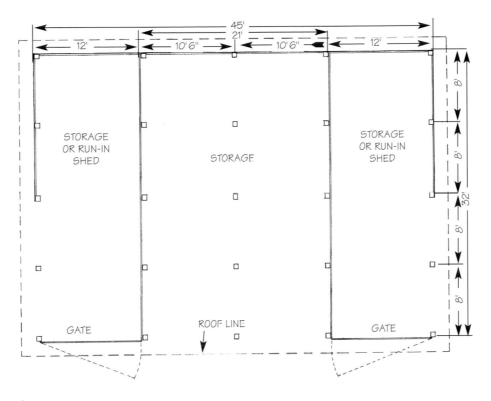

7.13 FRESH AIR BARN, *plan view.*

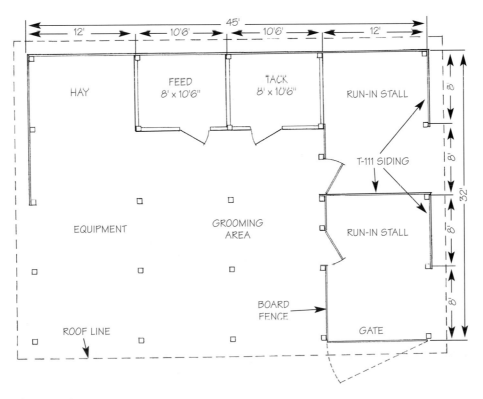

7.14 FRESH AIR BARN, *alternate plan view.*

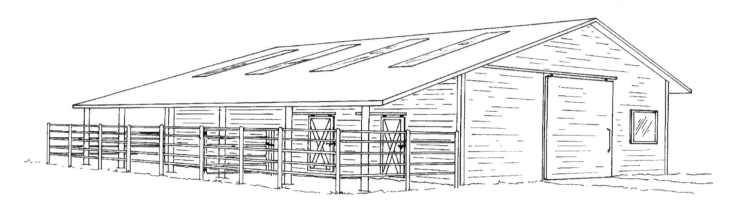

7.15 TWO-STALL RV BARN, *perspective view.*

7. TWO-STALL RV BARN

If you have a large recreational vehicle (RV) or camper trailer, this design might give you some ideas (figs. 7.15 and 7.16). The 14-foot-high walls of this barn offer many advantages. Two side-by-side sliding doors the full height of the walls allow plenty of headroom for driving in even the largest RV for storage or for delivery of a truckload of hay.

DIMENSIONS

- 60 feet by 36 feet building; 64 feet by 59 feet roof coverage
- 4/12 roof slope
- 8 feet high at eaves over pens
- 14-foot-high walls and doors

FEATURES

- The 12-foot by 24-foot multi-use area can be utilized for additional stalls, wash rack, feed room, vehicle storage, or hay storage (when stacked ten high, more than 600 bales will fit in this area).

- The tall walls mean plenty of headroom for storage over the tack room and the tool room.

- The entire floor is concrete.

- Rubber mats are used over the concrete in the stalls and in the aisle between the stalls and the tack room.

- An open tool room is handy for storing barn tools as well as tools for vehicle maintenance.

- The 12-foot-wide center aisle can double as shop space for working on a tractor or other equipment.

- Skylights provide daytime illumination.

- A hydrant at the corner of the tack room is out of the grooming and traffic area, yet close enough for filling water buckets in stalls using a hose.

- Each roomy stall has two 4-foot-wide sliding doors, one leading to the aisle and one to the covered pens.

- The spacious 12-foot by 24-foot tack room, with two 4-foot by 6-foot windows, can double as a lounge or office.

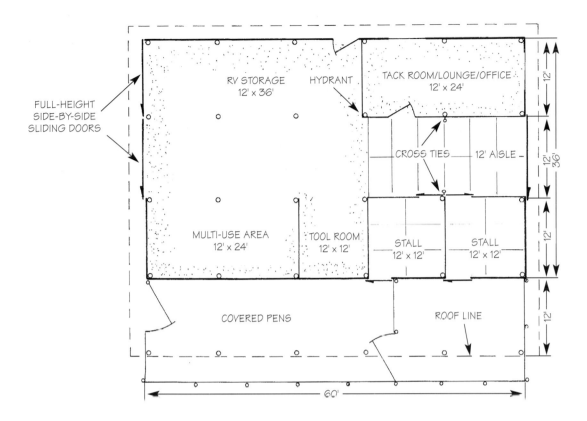

FULL-HEIGHT
SIDE-BY-SIDE
SLIDING DOORS

RV STORAGE
12' x 36'

HYDRANT

TACK ROOM/LOUNGE/OFFICE
12' x 24'

12'

CROSS TIES   12' AISLE

12' 36'

MULTI-USE AREA
12' x 24'

TOOL ROOM
12' x 12'

STALL
12' x 12'

STALL
12' x 12'

12'

COVERED PENS

ROOF LINE

12'

60'

7.16 **Two-Stall RV Barn,** *plan view.*

DISADVANTAGES

- There is no floor drain for washing a horse, rinsing buckets or cleaning tack.

- Urine can accumulate between the rubber mats and the non-draining concrete floor in the stalls leading to an odor problem.

- Windows in the tack room are a security risk.

- Grain will have to be stored in rodent- and horse-proof containers in the hay storage area or tool room.

OPTIONS

- A dirt/gravel floor for most of the barn, with rubber mats in stalls and grooming area of the aisle and a wooden floor in the tack room.

- Install automatic waterers in the stalls (and pens) instead of using a hose from the hydrant.

- Make a wash rack, complete with floor drain and sink, in the area near the hydrant.

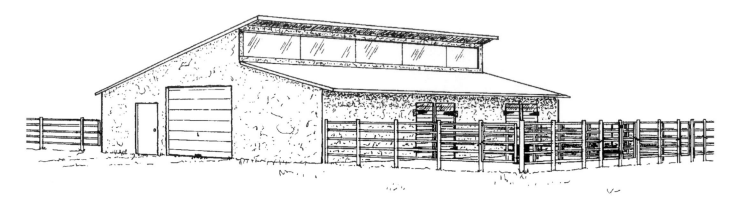

7.17 FOUR-STALL YEARLING/PONY BARN, *perspective view.*

8. FOUR-STALL YEARLING/PONY BARN

This design has four 10-foot by 12-foot stalls that are an efficient size for yearling horses and ponies (figs. 7.17 and 7.18). It is a pole frame building with a stucco finish that is very low maintenance, wind-proof, and horse-proof. Stucco can be colored to blend with the natural terrain or to match other buildings.

DIMENSIONS

- 50 feet by 60 feet
- 4/12 roof slope
- 12 feet high at eaves
- 15 feet to top of lower roof
- 20 feet to peak

FEATURES

- Plexiglas light panels in the *clerestory* between the two roof levels provide daylight illumination for the aisle, feed area, and stalls.

- Aisle doorways are 11 feet wide to allow easy drive-through access for feed delivery and stall cleaning.

- Overhead garage doors on each end of the barn are conveniently operated by electric door openers. Opening both doors provides plenty of cross-ventilation.

- A walk-through door lets you enter the barn without having to open a large overhead door.

- Sliding doors on the stalls and tack room conserve room in aisle and are easy to operate. 4-foot-wide doorways provide plenty of room for maneuvering a manure cart and for carrying a saddle through.

- A concrete floor in the aisle, feed storage area, and tack room helps keep dust to a minimum and provides a smooth clean surface on which to work.

- Wooden floors in the stalls are warmer and have more cushion than concrete, and provide a drier more level surface than dirt. Wood also provides the romantic clomp of hoof on wood.

- The open hay and grain area can store up to 375 bales of hay and several grain barrels. It's close to a large door for deliveries and only a few steps from the stalls for feeding.

- Automatic waterers provide a continuous supply of fresh water to stalls and pens.

- Having runs adjoining the stalls makes turning the horses out easy since you don't have to halter and lead them.

- Hinged doors leading from the stalls to the runs can be latched open to allow the horses to go in and out at will.

- A run-in shed on the wall opposite the stalls provides shelter for horses that are turned out.

- The 4-foot-wide door leading from the barn to the shed is convenient for leading horses through and for feeding.

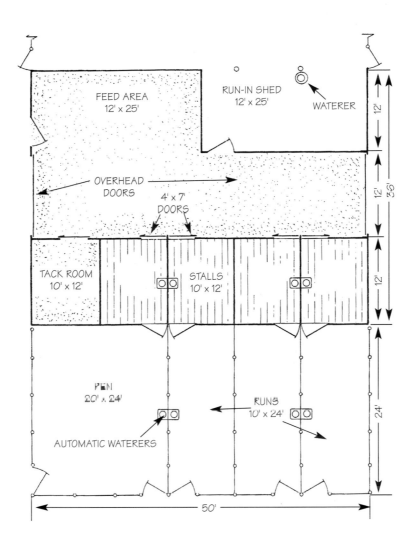

7.18 Four-Stall Yearling/Pony Barn, *plan view.*

DISADVANTAGES

- Overhead doors can be noisy and slow to operate.

- Wood floors absorb urine, can be smelly, and are difficult to clean and disinfect.

- Stalls are too small for most full size horses.

- Storing hay in the barn can be a fire hazard.

- Most automatic waterers don't allow you to know how much water your horses are drinking or if they are drinking at all.

- There are no hydrants for grooming or veterinary purposes.

OPTIONS

- Use sliding doors instead of electric overhead doors.

- Use rubber mats over gravel instead of wood flooring in stalls.

- Install a hydrant and use buckets and troughs for watering horses; this would be cheaper but would require more labor.

- Enclose the run-in shed to make large stall, such as for foaling, or a stall and a feed room.

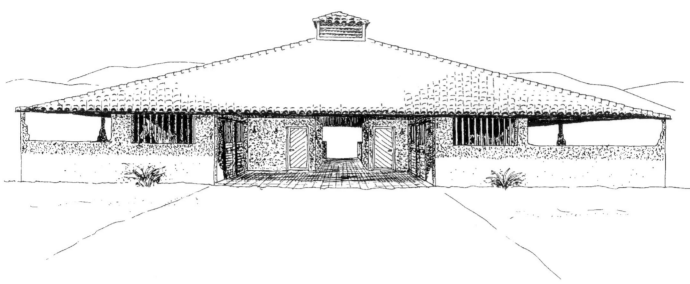

7.19 DESERT BARN, *perspective view.*

9. DESERT BARN

This four-stall stucco barn has a concrete foundation and concrete block walls (figs. 7.19 and 7.20). The large concrete tile roof area and open design maximize both shade and airflow in hot climates. Flooring is rubber tile over concrete, except for the stalls, which have rubber mats over compacted gravel.

DIMENSIONS
- 44 feet by 80 feet
- 3/12 slope roof
- 9 feet to eaves
- 22 feet to top of cupola

FEATURES
- Main entrance is an open 18-foot by 28-foot grooming area that allows plenty of room for grooming several horses at once (every wall has tie rings), maneuvering stall-cleaning carts, and delivering feed.

- The entrance on the opposite side of the barn is adjacent to a 12-foot by 12-foot washing/grooming area.

- An 8-foot-wide aisle connecting the two open areas encourages breezes to move freely through the barn.

- A vented cupola at the peak of the tiled *mansard roof* allows hot air to continually escape from inside the barn.

- A misting system dispenses measured amounts of insecticide at regular intervals to ensure that the barn remains free of flies.

- A 12-foot by 14-foot tack room forms one side of the aisle and has two doors, one opening to each work area. This allows two people to be working on horses at the same time without getting in each other's way.

- An 8-foot by 10-foot rodent-proof feed room is across the aisle from the tack room.

- Each half of the barn has one 12-foot by 12-foot and one 12-foot by 16-foot stall. The larger stalls are roomy enough for an average-sized horse to foal in.

- Each stall has a sliding door that opens onto the grooming area.

- There are large steel grilles between stalls and in the outer walls of each stall to promote airflow. In case of severe winds, the grilles can be covered on the inside by metal covered shutters (similar to the "sandwich" panels used for walls in modular barns). The shutters hinge at the top and swing up against the ceiling when not in use.

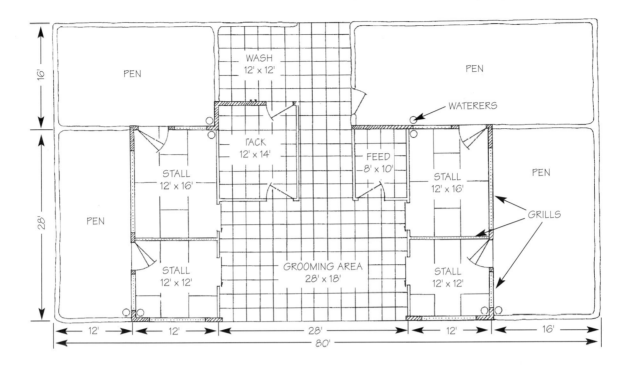

7.20 DESERT BARN, *plan view.*

- Each stall has a Dutch door that leads to a covered pen enclosed by a 5-foot-high stucco wall. The doors hinge inward and can be fastened open against the stall wall. Alternatively, just the top half of the door can be opened to keep the horse either in the stall or pen, yet maximize airflow.

- Automatic waterers in each stall and pen ensure that horses always have access to fresh water. Waterers are located in pairs, on either side of the stall walls, to minimize plumbing installation.

DISADVANTAGES

- There is no permanent place to store stall cleaning tools or more than a few days worth of hay.

- Given the barn's open design, bird nests and droppings could be a problem.

- The solid walls of the pens decrease airflow and have no "give" if a horse kicks or collides with them.

- The large tile roof, stucco walls, rubber tile floors, and multiple waterers make this barn relatively expensive to build.

OPTIONS

- Make walls 11 feet high instead of 9 feet for more headroom.

- If three or fewer horses are housed in the barn, one stall could be utilized for storage of tools and hay.

- Make pens larger for a better exercise area or have gates in the pens that lead to larger runs or paddocks.

- Make pens of metal panels or *PVC* post and board fencing instead of block and stucco.

- Install a sliding screen across the large opening of the grooming area to keep out wind and birds.

7.21 **WYOMING BARN,** *perspective view.*

10. WYOMING BARN

This barn was designed for the wide-open spaces, where horses spend most of their time turned out on pastures or in large pens (figs. 7.21 and 7.22). The arrangement of gates and panels provides both indoor and outdoor shelter for up to six horses with minimum effort. (See fig. 8.1, p. 83; it shows a log variation of this design.)

DIMENSIONS
- 56 feet by 60 feet
- 4/12 roof slope
- 9 feet to eaves
- 19 feet to peak

FEATURES
- Steel roofing to encourage snow to slide off.
- A 12-foot roof overhang on three sides of the barn provides shelter for horses without having to bring them inside the barn. The overhang is supported by 8-inch diameter round wood posts spaced 8 feet apart.
- Gates leading to pastures or runs allow horses to come and go at will.
- Gates and panels between the posts and the barn divide the sheltered areas and allow individual horses or groups of horses to be separated when necessary, such as for feeding.
- A 12-foot by 20-foot tack room keeps tack, records, and vet supplies clean and accessible.
- The ceiling, walls, and wooden floor are insulated for efficient heating in winter.

- Concrete floor in the feed room, tool area, and aisle provides a durable maintenance-free surface that minimizes dust.
- A 8-foot by 12-foot tool alcove keeps tools such as carts and forks from cluttering the aisle.
- A lockable 12-foot by 12-foot feed room keeps grains and supplements safe from rodents and accidentally loose horses.
- A 12-foot-wide aisle with cross-ties and rubber mats provides a safe, clean area for grooming and for farrier and vet work.
- Two 12-foot by 16-foot stalls can be used for lay-up of injured or ill horses, to keep horses clean that are in work, and to provide individual shelter during severe weather.
- The stalls are covered with solid rubber mats for efficient cleaning and to minimize floor maintenance.
- Doors leading from the stall to the runs allow easy turn-out.
- The 20-foot by 36-foot enclosed run-in area on the end of the barn provides a shady in/out shelter for summer and a place out of the wind and snow in winter.
- The four doorways in the run-in shed have both gates and solid sliding doors. The gates can be used to contain horses while maximizing airflow, and the sliding doors can be used to shut out severe weather and to completely separate horses that are inside the shed from those outside.

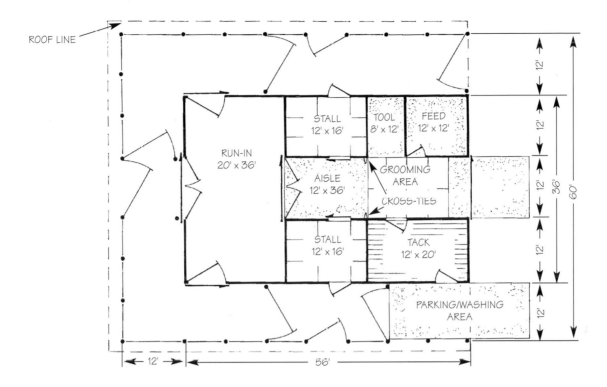

ROOF LINE

STALL 12' x 16'
TOOL 8' x 12'
FEED 12' x 12'
RUN-IN 20' x 36'
GROOMING AREA
AISLE 12' x 36'
CROSS-TIES
STALL 12' x 16'
TACK 12' x 20'
PARKING/WASHING AREA

12' 12' 12' 36' 60' 12' 12'

12' 56'

7.22 **WYOMING BARN,** *plan view.*

- The stalls and run-in area are lined to 4 feet high with 2-inch-thick lumber or two layers of ⅝-inch-thick plywood to prevent damage to the barn's outer skin from horses that might kick the inside walls.

- Three 12-foot-wide by 11-foot-high sliding doors allow a truck or tractor to drive straight through the barn for delivering feed and bedding and for removing old bedding from the stalls and run-in area. During hot weather all three doors can be opened for a cooling airflow.

- Translucent fiberglass panels on the upper walls allow natural illumination of the interior and reduces the need for electric lights.

- T-111 plywood siding where horses will not contact the walls.

- Smooth ¾-inch stained plywood siding over ¾-inch sheathing, on the lower 6 feet of walls in pens to minimize horses' chewing and rubbing.

DISADVANTAGES
- Wood support posts for the roof overhang may require regular treatment with an anti-chew product to prevent chewing by horses.

- Sliding doors can be hampered by drifting snow.

OPTIONS
- Use all or part of the run-in area for storage of hay or equipment. Divide the area with metal panels to separate horses or keep them away from stored items.

- Replace sliding doors with electric overhead doors.

- Make stalls larger or smaller depending on intended use.

- Use insulation board beneath the steel roofing to reduce the roar of rain and hail.

- Apply steel siding instead of T-111.

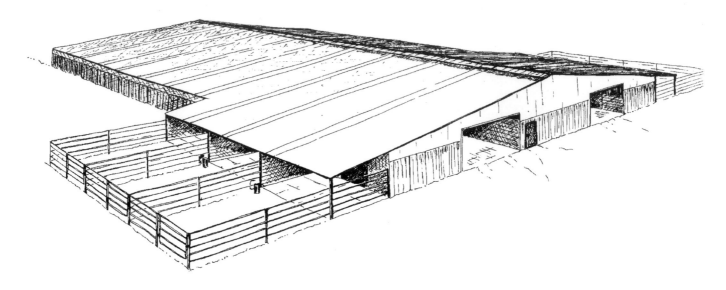

7.23 TRAINING BARN, *perspective view.*

11. TRAINING BARN

To keep horses on a steady work schedule, you need a place to work that's protected from the weather. This small training barn with attached arena provides maximum sun protection; so it is ideal for hot, dry climates (figs. 7.23 and 7.24). The large, relatively flat roof would need to sustain a very heavy snow load in snowy climates. The basic pole barn structure is sided and roofed with panels of steel and fiberglass.

DIMENSIONS

- 36-foot by 68-foot barn
- 72-foot by 72-foot arena
- 3/12 roof slope
- 8 feet to eaves
- 22 feet to peak

FEATURES

- Translucent fiberglass panels at the top of the walls, the gable ends, and at regular intervals in the roof for daylight illumination.
- A continuous ridge vent promotes airflow.
- The 72-foot by 72-foot arena is large enough to ride at all gaits and to longe or drive a horse in a beneficial and low stress 66-foot diameter (20-meter) circle.
- Arena provides all-weather turnout, such as when cleaning stalls.

- Corners of the arena can be closed off by short walls and gates for storage areas: the two corners farthest from the barn for cavaletti, cones, barrels, harrow, and other arena equipment; one corner near the barn for carts, forks, shovels, and other barn cleaning tools and supplies; one corner left open for training purposes. Use portable panels to determine the size and shape of spaces that work best before building permanent partitions.

- One of the six 12-foot by 12-foot stalls can be used to store several weeks worth of hay. Main hay storage is in a separate building.

- The centrally located 12-foot by 20-foot insulated tack room has three doors for easy access from any of the three aisles.

- Cross-ties are located on both sides of the tack room in the side aisles, and in the central aisle.

- Aisles are 11 feet wide by 11 feet high.

- Electric overhead doors on the front of the barn offer hands free operation and need no room to slide or swing.

- Sliding doors between the arena and aisles minimizes dust in the barn.

- Aisle flooring is rubber brick over a gravel base.

- Tack room and wash rack flooring is rubber tile over concrete.

- The wash rack floor slopes toward a centrally located drain.

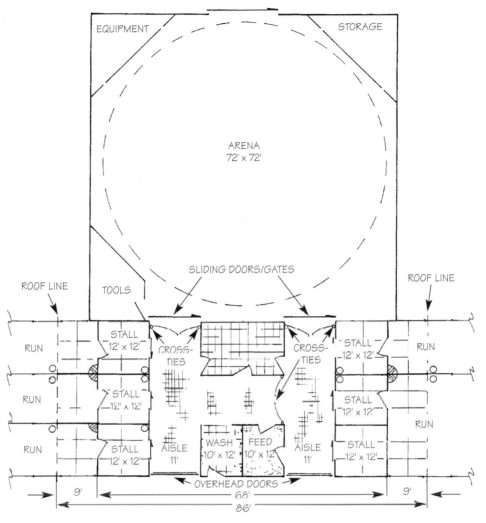

7.24 TRAINING BARN, *plan view.*

- The 10-foot by 12-foot feed room floor is smooth concrete for ease of cleaning.

- The stall floors and the covered portion of the runs are rubber mats over a gravel base.

- The roof extends 9 feet over the runs for shade and to provide a clean, dry feeding area.

- Solid partitions between the covered portions of the runs minimize fighting and food sharing at feeding time and prevent hay from being blown away when windy.

- The runs for the hay stall and the next stall are combined for a double-sized run.

- Automatic waterers serve the stalls and the runs.

DISADVANTAGES

- The large roof area means a lot of water will dump into the pens when it rains so grading to promote drainage away from the barn is critical.

OPTIONS

- Install a heavy-duty *eaves trough* system to carry water away from the barn and pens.

- Extend the barn on one or both ends to make a larger arena or to add more stalls.

- Install a moveable stall partition between two stalls to make a 12-foot by 24-foot foaling or recovery stall.

- Use a middle stall for hay if you need a buffer stall between two horses.

- Add a fourth tack room door on the arena wall.

- Add an observation window in the wall between the tack room and the arena.

- Build an observation room above the tack room that overlooks the arena.

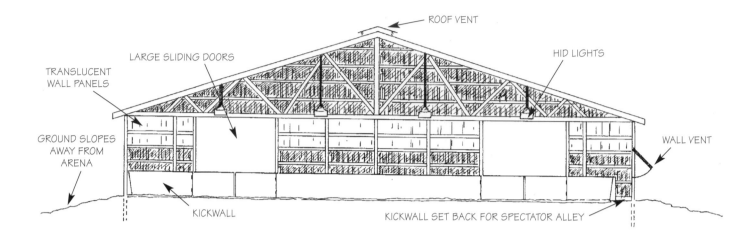

ROOF VENT

LARGE SLIDING DOORS

HID LIGHTS

TRANSLUCENT WALL PANELS

WALL VENT

GROUND SLOPES AWAY FROM ARENA

KICKWALL

KICKWALL SET BACK FOR SPECTATOR ALLEY

7.25 INDOOR ARENA, *section view.*

12. INDOOR ARENA

This indoor arena is designed to be used separate from a full service barn (figs 7.25–7.27). It is larger than the one attached to the preceding Training Barn—it is better to build too large than too small.

- Minimum size of the riding space for some events:

  Reining and cutting: 100 feet by 150 feet

  Dressage: 66 feet by 132 feet or 66 feet by 198 feet

  Pole bending: 80 feet by 126 feet

  Barrel racing: 100 feet by 220 feet

  Jumping course: 132 feet by 264 feet

- The ceiling needs to be at least 15 feet high for safe riding and 20 feet high for safe jumping. Square corners are more useful for training than round corners.

- 10-foot by 12-foot stalls are an efficient size for holding horses between work, but larger stalls would be needed for long-term housing.

DIMENSIONS
- 100 feet by 200 feet
  (100 feet by 170 feet riding area)

- 4/12 roof slope

- 15 feet to top of walls

- 31 feet to peak

FEATURES

- A 4-foot-high angled kickwall of 1-inch plywood around the riding area prevents a rider's legs from hitting the walls, protects the siding from kicks, and separates the riding area from spectators.

- The kickwall is held 4 feet away from the outer wall along one side for a spectator alley.

- Open area between kickwall and lounge can be used for spectator seating, such as for clinics or demonstrations.

- The 12-foot by 30-foot area along the wall opposite the stalls can be used to store equipment such as cones, jumps, and barrels.

- A tractor and drag can be parked between the kick wall and one exterior door. When needed to work the arena, the tractor is driven out the door and into the other access door in front of the stalls.

- Translucent fiberglass panels in the roof and the upper portion of the walls let in natural light to prevent the arena from being gloomy.

- High intensity discharge (HID) lights provide illumination at night and when daylight is not sufficient.

- The 12-foot by 28-foot lounge provides a dust-free, climate-controlled room in which to keep first aid supplies, beverages and snacks, as well as a change of clothes. The 12-foot by 28-foot room shown here is large enough to hold meetings or lessons that don't require riding.

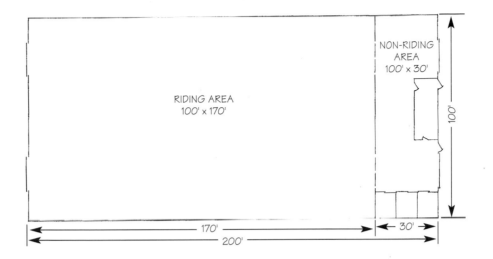

7.26 INDOOR ARENA, *plan view.*

- A continuous roof vent allows rising warm air to escape and draw cooler air into the arena through hinged wall vents that can be latched open.

DISADVANTAGES

- In hot climates, the translucent panels act like a greenhouse and trap heat inside.

OPTIONS

- Extend building to make a full service barn with larger stalls, feed and tack rooms, and wash rack.

- Use a wider roof overhang to block direct light and heat yet admit indirect light through the wall panels.

- Install a toilet and sink in the lounge.

- Install an overhead sprinkler system to dampen footing for dust control.

- Install overhead infrared heaters for winter riding.

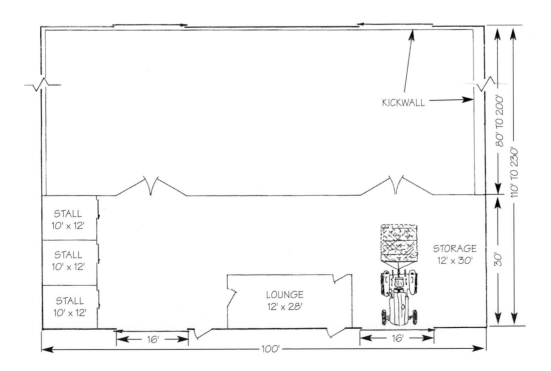

7.27 INDOOR ARENA, *detailed plan view.*

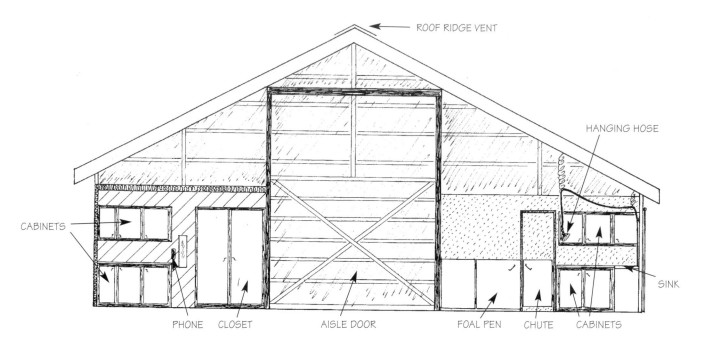

ROOF RIDGE VENT

HANGING HOSE

CABINETS

SINK

PHONE   CLOSET   AISLE DOOR   FOAL PEN   CHUTE   CABINETS

7.28 FOALING BARN, *section A — A view.*

13. FOALING BARN

This barn is designed for horse owners who plan to raise one or more foals every year (figs. 7.28 and 7.29). The waiting room and vet area make it an efficient barn for all aspects of foaling.

DIMENSIONS

- 38 feet by 68 feet

- 6/12 roof slope

- 9 feet to eaves

- 15 feet to peak

FEATURES

- Post and beam combined with open-style truss framing along with a steep roof pitch provide a spacious feeling and plenty of ventilation.

- The floor is textured concrete except for in the stalls, which are rubber mats over compacted gravel.

- The 12-foot by 20-foot vet room has an 8-foot by 8-foot sliding door to the outside, where a veterinarian's truck can back up to the door.

- In the center of the vet room is an AI (artificial insemination) chute, or stocks, for safely containing mares for palpation, ultra-sound, insemination, and other procedures. The chute is located so there is ample room to lead a horse into it.

- At the head of the AI chute is a 6-foot by 8-foot foal pen with 4-foot-high solid walls. This pen provides a safe place for a foal to be contained, and the pen's location allows the mare and foal to be within continual site of one another.

- A gate next to the stocks makes it easy to shuttle the foal into the pen. When vet procedures are completed, the mare can be led through the front of the stocks into the foal pen. Then the mare and foal can be returned to their stall via the gate on the alley side of the foal pen.

- An overhead retractable hose, which is connected to hot and cold faucets on the wall near the sink, hangs by the tail end of the chute.

- The floor slopes to a drain located next to the AI chute.

- To the right of the chute, within easy reach of a vet working at the chute, is a combination stainless steel sink/drain board.

- In the corner of the vet room is a counter with storage cabinets below and cupboards above for towels, medications, and other supplies.

- The insulated waiting room across the aisle from the vet room has a small window into each of the two foaling stalls. The insulated room is large enough to accommodate a foldout couch and

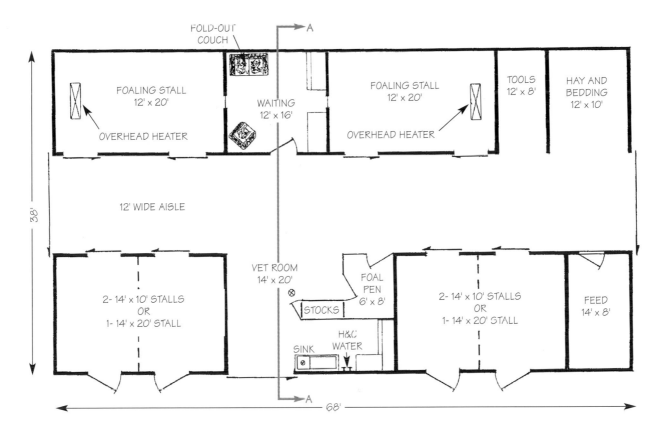

7.29 FOALING BARN, *plan view.*

comfortable chair and can be easily heated by a portable electric heater. Upper and lower cabinets provide storage for snacks and foaling supplies. A small refrigerator can fit beneath a viewing window. There's a closet next to the door for coats, boots, blankets, and other supplies. A telephone provides ready access to the veterinarian.

- The 12-foot by 20-foot foaling stalls, one on either side of the waiting room, are roomy enough for a warmblood mare to foal. Two doors allow the stall to be cleaned with minimal disturbance to the mare and foal.

- An infrared heater is suspended over one end of each stall so the mare and foal can move into or out of the heated area.

- Across the aisle from each foaling stall is a pair of 10-foot by 14-foot stalls that can be used for pregnant mares waiting their turns in the foaling stalls. Each stall opens into a run attached to the barn for easy turnout.

- A divider between the stalls can be removed to make a 14-foot by 20-foot stall for additional foaling space or for a mare and foal that are ready to leave the

foaling stall when it's time to introduce the foal to limited turnout.

- 12-foot-wide doors on each end of the aisle enable a vehicle to enter for stall cleaning.

- Next to the door on one end of the barn, within easy access of a delivery truck, is a twelve-foot by ten-foot area for storing a limited supply of hay and bedding and a 14-foot by 8-foot rodent-proof feed room.

- Rounding out the barn space is a tool alcove in which to keep stall cleaning tools such as forks, shovels, and carts.

DISADVANTAGES
- Roof runoff might create muddy areas in pens and in front of doors.

OPTIONS
- Add gutters to carry water away from entryways and pens.

- Raise walls and/or change roof slope to accommodate a roof overhang to shelter pens and entryways.

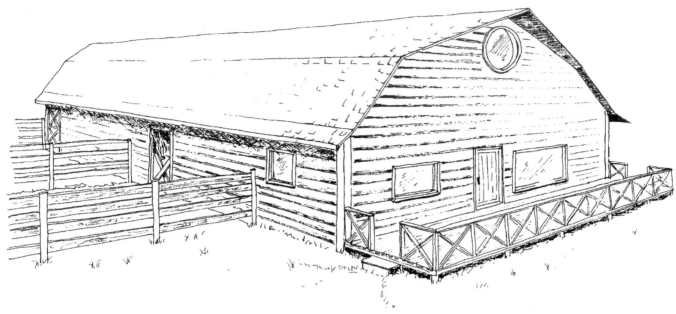

7.30 **LIVE-IN BARN,** *perspective view.*

14. LIVE-IN BARN

This stable/apartment combination offers permanent living quarters for an owner, stable worker, or broodmare manager, or temporary quarters for a barn sitter or visitors wanting a horsey experience (figs. 7.30 and 7.31).

DIMENSIONS

- 36 feet by 48 feet

- 8 feet at eaves

- 20 feet to peak

FEATURES

- Log siding and a fiber cement shake roof give the barn an old-time, traditional look.

- The 12-foot by 36-foot (432 square foot) living space is fully insulated, has a full kitchen, a small bath with shower, and an open area for dining, living, and sleeping.

- A loft over the living space provides an additional 432 square feet of storage space.

- A large round window at one end of the loft provides natural light while a window at the other end provides a view of the barn interior.

- A composting toilet (see the Resource Guide) may eliminate the need for a septic system, and waste water from the kitchen and shower drains into a *dry well* (see Dry Well, p. 112).

- A door provides direct access between the living quarters and the barn aisle, while an adjacent window allows a view of the barn interior.

- The tack room and feed room are located between the apartment and the stalls to buffer noises.

- A porch the full width of the apartment serves as an outdoor "mudroom" for cleaning boots and as a place to relax after a hard day of horse care.

- Gambrel trusses provide more than 12 feet of headroom in stalls and aisle.

- The four 12-foot by 12-foot stalls have rubber mats over a gravel base.

- Water buckets and corner feeders are located so they can be accessed directly from the aisle.

- Each stall has a 4-foot-wide sliding door leading to the barn alley and a 4-foot-wide Dutch door, which can be fastened open along the stall wall, leading to a run.

- A concrete floor in the aisle, feed room, and tack room minimizes dust and is maintenance free.

- The 12-foot by 12-foot feed room has a door to the aisle for feeding and an exterior door for grain deliveries and is a way to enter the barn without passing through the apartment.

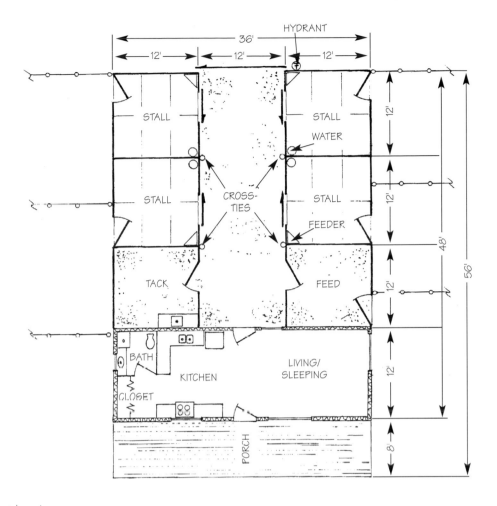

7.31 **LIVE-IN BARN,** *plan view.*

- The 12-foot by 12-foot tack room has a single lockable door for security and a utility sink (that shares the plumbing of the kitchen) for cleaning tack.

- A 12-foot-wide sliding door at the end of the aisle opens to allow a vehicle to back in for cleaning stalls.

- There are two sets of cross-ties in the aisle, one set near the tack room for convenient grooming and tacking and one set halfway down the aisle.

- A freeze-proof hydrant with a hose attached is located just outside the large aisle door for convenient filling of stall water buckets and for bathing a horse outdoors.

DISADVANTAGES

- Wood siding is susceptible to damage from chewing horses unless treated regularly with an anti-chew product.

- Barn interior would be very dark with no natural illumination.

OPTIONS

- Install skylights to provide natural light to stalls and loft.

- Extend the barn as needed to add stalls or increase living space.

- Extend the loft over the feed and tack room for additional living or storage space.

- Exchange the feed room with the stall on the opposite end of the barn and install a moveable wall between the two stalls to make a foaling stall next to the sleeping quarters; install a window between the foaling stall and the apartment to monitor foaling.

7.32 MEETING BARN, *perspective view.*

15. MEETING BARN

This five-stall pole barn has a partial second story that can be used for meetings and other functions (figs. 7.32 – 7.34). Wood panel siding and shingle roof give the barn a rustic appearance and muffle the sound of rain and hail.

DIMENSIONS

- 36 feet by 74 feet
- 4/12 roof slope
- 9 feet to lower eaves
- 15 feet to lower peak
- 20 feet to upper eaves
- 26 feet to upper peak

FEATURES

- A 12-foot-wide by 9-foot-high electric overhead door at the ends of the aisle offer hands-free operation in any weather.

- The 12-foot-wide aisle is wide enough to allow two people leading horses to pass and for a pickup or tractor and cart to be used for cleaning stalls.

- The five 12-foot by 12-foot stalls have automatic waterers and swing-out corner feeders that can be accessed from the aisle.

- The two adjacent stalls have a hinged common wall that opens to make a double stall for foaling or convalescence.

- Two stalls on one end of the barn open into covered pens that can be used to turn out horses in the stalls or to house two additional horses.

- The 12-foot by 16-foot tack room is insulated and rodent-proof.

- A concrete vet/wash area has a sink and hot and cold water for bathing and medical care.

- A pipe rail separates the wash area from the vet area.

- A walk-through door provides access to the vet's truck.

- The 7-foot-wide sliding door can be used to lead horses in and out of the barn and, when left open, can provide cross-ventilation in the barn.

- The rodent proof 8-foot by 12-foot feed room has an aisle door for daily feeding and an exterior door for handy grain delivery or for feeding horses in pens or pastures.

- The hay area is open to the aisle and holds hay for several weeks' feeding.

- An 8-foot sliding door on the outside wall facilitates hay delivery without driving through the barn.

- The centrally located 8-foot by 12-foot tool room keeps stall-cleaning tools and carts out of traffic areas.

- A stairway with landing next to the tack room leads to the second story.

- The 38-foot by 24-foot meeting room gets natural light from three windows on each end and from two glass patio doors.

- The patio doors open onto a balcony, which, if it overlooks an arena, can be used to view demonstrations, lessons, and contests.

- A stairway leading directly from the balcony to the ground provides another access to the meeting room and serves as a fire escape.

- A 16-foot by 12-foot kitchen allows meals to be prepared on-site for meetings and get-togethers.

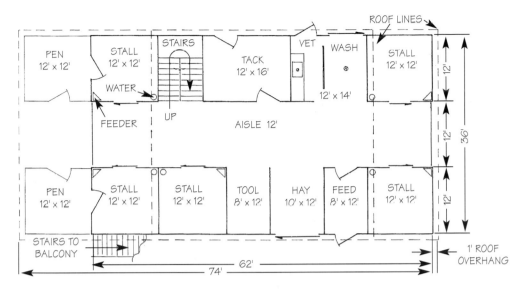

7.33 MEETING BARN, *plan view, level one*

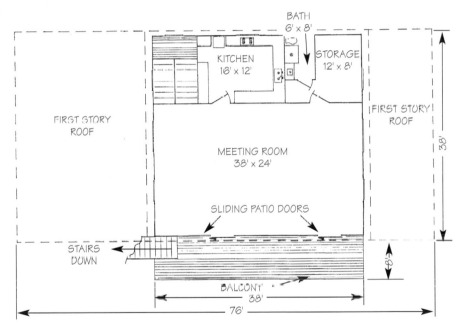

7.34 MEETING BARN, *plan view, level two*

- An adjacent storage room contains a rest room with shower.

- The kitchen and storage room are insulated to keep supplies at a constant temperature, and these rooms are located directly above the wash rack to make installation of plumbing easier and more efficient.

DISADVANTAGES

- Noise and movement of the overhead doors could startle horses that aren't used to it.

- The second story limits the height of the first story ceiling—this reduces air volume and ventilation.

- Absence of stall windows, while increasing safety and decreasing maintenance, means less natural light and ventilation.

- Only two of the stalls open into pens, which means horses in the other three stalls must be led out of the barn for turnout.

OPTIONS

- Convert the meeting room into an apartment.

- Build pens or runs onto stalls that don't have them.

- Build lower level 11 feet high instead of 9 feet for more headroom.

- Add Dutch doors or windows to increase light and ventilation in the stalls.

- Install exhaust fans to ensure adequate ventilation, especially when horses are kept in the barn on a full-time basis.

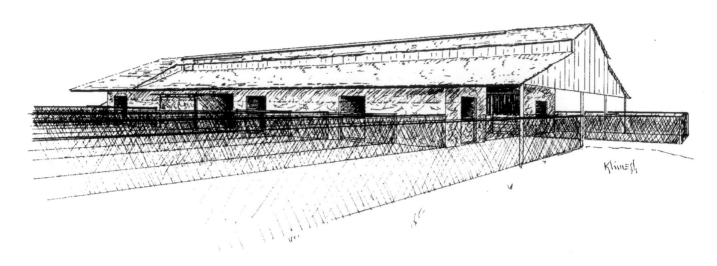

7.35 HOME OFFICE BARN, *perspective view.*

16. HOME OFFICE BARN

More and more people are working at home so they can spend more time with and take better care of their horses. Here's a five-stall barn with a second level heated office from which a person can keep an eye on activities inside and outside the stable (figs. 7.35–7.37).

DIMENSIONS
- 40 feet by 76 feet with 16-foot by 24-foot office
- 4/12 roof slope
- 10 feet to eaves
- 21 feet to peak

ADVANTAGES
- Stucco siding and fiber cement shakes make the barn quiet and fire resistant, which can lower insurance rates in many areas.
- Concrete floor in the aisle and all rooms except stalls minimizes dust and makes cleaning easy.
- Floors in stalls are interlocking rubber mats over a gravel base.
- Clerestory admits natural light through translucent fiberglass panels to the aisle and stalls.
- Gable end wall over the pens is also sided with translucent panels.
- Continuous ridge vent promotes healthy ventilation.

- The roof extends 5 feet on one end to shelter the stairway, 12 feet on the other end to shelter pens, and has a 4-foot overhang along the long pen side to keep snow and rain from dumping directly in front of the doorways.
- It has two phone lines, one that is computer dedicated and one that is fitted with an outside ringer and connected to an extension phone in the tack room.
- The office can be entered from the outside stairway without going through the barn and by an inside stairway that leads from the office to the main aisle.
- The clerestory ends halfway across the office and the roof becomes one uninterrupted slope from the peak to the eaves. This provides headroom for a stairway on one side of the office and a window on the other side that looks directly into the foaling stall below (perfect for all-night vigils).
- A large interior window in the center of the office looks down on the center aisle, stalls, and grooming area. Other windows in the office enable a person to view the outside pens on one side of the barn and approaches on the other side and one end of the barn.
- Security is further enhanced by the absence of windows and doors on the side opposite the pens. This side would be oriented toward the street or road, with the residence located on the other side of the barn in view of the pens.

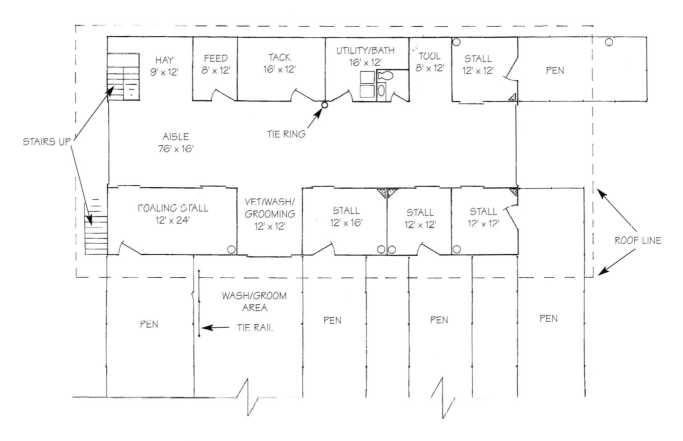

7.36 HOME OFFICE BARN, *plan view, level one.*

- The 16-foot-wide by 10-foot-high electric over-head doors on both ends of the aisle operate at the touch of a button and allow vehicles to drive through the barn for feed delivery, stall cleaning, and vet and shoeing work.

- The vet/wash/grooming stall, which has an 8-foot by 8-foot sliding door, can be accessed by truck from the aisle or from the outside by driving between the pens.

- The tie rail and concrete pad outside the wash stall serve as a sunny grooming/wash area and an additional place for a vet or farrier to work.

- Fencing is V-mesh, one of the safest fences for horses, with a pipe rail on top and bottom, and the bottom pipe buried 4 inches.

- No pens share a common fence—there is an 8-foot buffer zone between pens to prevent play-ing and fighting that could result in injury.

- Dutch doors, which can be opened for ventilation, lead between the stalls and pens, and sliding doors lead from the stalls to the aisle.

- The utility room contains a washer and dryer for horse laundry and has plenty of room for a counter and for shelves and cabinets for storing cleaning products and other supplies.

- The lavatory shares a wall with the utility room, which simplifies plumbing installation.

- The hay storage area holds a few weeks supply of hay.

- The adjoining feed room is rodent proof.

DISADVANTAGES

- The only ways to enter or leave the barn (without going through a stall) are through the large overhead aisle doors or the sliding door in the wash stall.

- A horse could damage its mane and tail rubbing on V-mesh fence.

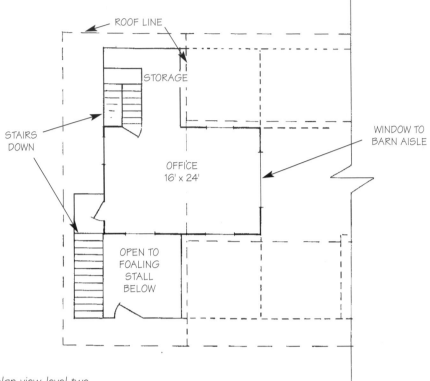

ROOF LINE

STORAGE

STAIRS
DOWN

WINDOW TO
BARN AISLE

OFFICE
16' x 24'

OPEN TO
FOALING
STALL
BELOW

7.7 HOME OFFICE BARN, *plan view, level two.*

OPTIONS

- Make pens off the stalls as long as desired or as space allows.

- Add entrance doors from the outside into the tack room, hay area, utility room, and tool room.

- In cold climates, insulate and heat the tack and utility/bath rooms.

- Replace V-mesh with steel panels, vinyl boards, or other fence.

- Eliminate buffer zones between pens to make wider pens and reduce the amount of fencing required.

- Extend the entire barn on the end opposite the stairway to accommodate more stalls.

- Extend the second floor over the aisle to make a larger office or an apartment.

- Install a skylight in the roof over the foaling stall for more natural light. ∪

CHAPTER EIGHT

CHOOSING MATERIALS

Choosing barn materials is a balancing act involving appearance, cost, safety, durability, and personal preference (fig. 8.1). It's easy to take barn materials for granted. After all, a barn is a barn, right? Wrong. When building a barn for horses you need to consider their size, heft, and habits, which vary considerably from those of sheep and pot-bellied pigs.

Horses are nomadic, and when you thwart their basic urge to move by confining them to stalls or small pens without providing sufficient exercise their frustration will find an outlet. Walls act as barriers to keep horses in or out of specified areas, a task for which your choice of materials is especially critical. Any wall covering (paneling, siding, lining) that horses can contact must be safe and durable. A restless 1,200-pound horse can unleash a lot of energy through chewing, pawing, kicking, and rubbing. These activities can damage facilities and injure the horse if materials are not chosen wisely and installed carefully. Wall covering should be smooth and hard, so there is no place for a horse's teeth to get a purchase and there should be no sharp edges or protrusions that could cut a horse's skin. There is a vast selection of materials for interior and exterior wall covering, but only a few are suitable for use with horses.

Flooring materials warrant special mention because they determine the efficiency, enjoyment, and safety of all barn activities and largely define the character of the barn. An aisle floor should be smooth and level so a horse or handler doesn't trip; yet it should have traction to prevent slipping. The softer and more shock-absorbing a floor is, the less likely a person or horse will be injured if they fall. All floors should be easy to clean, and sturdy enough to withstand traffic, whether from vehicles or hooves. Stall floors present more problems because they must withstand extreme moisture from the gallons of urine a horse produces each day plus constant concentrated impact from hooves.

A roof has a large surface area that is vulnerable to airborne sparks and embers. A barn's number-one defense against wildfire is a fire-resistant roof. The more common, but no less important, duty of a roofing material is to keep the inside of the barn dry. The number-one cause of

8.1 Choose safe, durable barn materials that fit your environment, your horsekeeping style, and your budget.

building deterioration is moisture. Pay attention to roof slope when choosing roofing (see Roof Terms, p. 22). Low slope roofs, less than 4/12, require low-slope roofing, which is generally capable of holding standing water. Inappropriate roofing can allow water to back up under the roofing such as when ice or snow builds up at the eaves. Shingles, for example, are classified as steep-sloped roofing and are not generally recommended for slopes of less than 4/12.

MAKING A CHOICE

Choices of materials dictate not only how your barn will look, but also how it will sound and how safe it will be. Rubber brick or mats in the aisle, for example, will hush the clip clop of hooves, while concrete or wood will make hooves sing. Tile or asphalt roofing will muffle the sound of hail while steel roofing will amplify it like a thousand teenage drummers gone mad.

Don't be afraid to consider materials you are unfamiliar with. Seek advice and feedback from horse owners and builders of horse facilities in your area.

Following are descriptions of materials used in horse barns and reasons why certain materials work better than others for various applications. In many cases, you will be limited by the selection of products available at your local building supply store. But if you know enough about a material to explain what you are looking for, most retailers will be happy to search their catalogs and order products they don't normally stock.

NATURAL FLOORING MATERIALS

Earth and similar materials are often used as flooring because they are inexpensive and available, often being already in place. Dirt, road base, and clay can provide cushion and traction without being overly abrasive. The trouble is these natural floors are readily softened by urine. Holes and depressions can easily form where horses paw or habitually stand and turn. These materials are slow to dry, promote odors, and are difficult to clean. Horses on damp footing are more likely to develop thrush and white line infections than if they were on dry footing.

NATIVE SOIL

Dirt is often used temporarily and ends up being the final floor by default. Depending on where you live, dirt can vary from loose and sandy to hard clay, from thick powder to hard as concrete, from dusty to muddy. Traffic patterns can result in an uneven floor with dips near doors and holes from pawing horses. Maintaining a dirt floor is a never-ending task that includes filling holes, *tamping* or rolling to compact the fill, and leveling.

SAND

Sand varies from clean masonry sand to dirty and dusty fill sand. It is inexpensive (being native soil in some areas), quiet, and perhaps the safest floor to fall on. But sand is constantly shifting underfoot and dust from sand can quickly cover everything in the barn. If sand is your native soil, mix it with dirt or road base and cover it with something solid.

Sand is an especially poor choice for stalls. Its loose surface allows feed, bedding, and manure to become churned into the sand. A horse eating off the stall floor will surely ingest sand, which can lead to sand colic, a potentially life-threatening condition.

ROAD BASE

This mixture of dirt and gravel varies in composition depending on location. Road base can be heavy in clay and can pack very hard or be loose and dusty. It has the same disadvantages as dirt and is unsuitable as a permanent floor but it does make a good base for almost any solid flooring. Road base is classified by size of the gravel it contains, with ¾-inch being best suited for a barn floor base.

GRAVEL

Crushed rock comes in various sizes and purity grades. It drains extremely well and makes a good base for many types of solid flooring. But, like sand, gravel is unstable underfoot and is usually dusty, so is unsuitable as a finished floor.

In stalls, feeding on gravel can cause horses to ingest small particles, which can lead to mineral formation in their intestines called enteroliths. Plus, gravel can work into the bottom of hooves and cause abscesses.

MASONRY/CONCRETE

Masonry includes concrete block, brick, and stone—individual elements that are held together by *mortar*. Concrete, often mistakenly called cement, is comprised of cement, sand, gravel, and water. It is poured into forms, sets hard as rock and is the most durable commonly used building material ever invented. Fiber cement is a mixture of Portland cement, sand, cellulose, silica, and additives, which are molded into siding and roofing products.

FOUNDATIONS

Because concrete can support an incredible amount of weight and is impervious to moisture, fungus, insects, and burrowing animals it is ideal for underground supports (footings and foundation walls), floors, and driveways.

FRAMING

Masonry buildings are popular in hot climates because they tend to stay cool (fig. 8.2, see also fig. 4.13, p. 24). But they can be cold and damp in cooler climates if not properly engineered. Masonry generally costs more than other types of framing, but masonry buildings have minimal

---

THE SECRET LIFE OF ROOFING

According the American Society of Home Inspectors, *asphalt shingles* generally last 15 to 20 years; metal roofing, 15 to 40-plus years; clay/concrete tiles, 20-plus years; slate, 30 to 100 years; wood shingle/shakes, 10 to 40 years.

The fire resistance of most roofing materials is categorized by *UL* Class A, B, or C, with Class A being the most fire resistant. Class A or B roofing materials, such as asphalt shingles, slate, clay tile, or metal, are the best choice for a barn.

upkeep and often qualify for lower insurance rates because of their fire resistance.

Poured concrete, concrete block, and solid rock walls rest directly on footings and require no additional support. Brick and stone can be applied to the outside of these walls or can be attached to a wood framed wall.

One thing to know about masonry: it is very unforgiving—if a horse kicks a masonry wall, serious injury could result to the horse.

SIDING

Fiber cement *planks* are typically 5/16-inch thick and can be smooth or have a wood grain texture. Panels are 4-feet-wide by 8-feet, 9-feet or 10-feet long and come with a smooth, wood grain, or stucco finish. Smooth or textured *soffit* panels are also available. Fiber cement siding comes either primed or unfinished and holds paint well. Although it commonly comes with a 50-year guarantee, it is too brittle to be used on areas of a barn where a horse could kick it.

FLOORING

A properly installed concrete floor is permanent and maintenance free (fig. 8.3). It is waterproof and impervious to insects and rodents. It can be finished with a smooth or textured surface, depending on intended use. A smooth floor would be appropriate in a feed room to make sweeping spilled grain easy but would be too slippery for an aisle, especially for shod horses and especially when wet. In traffic areas, a textured surface is better for traction, even though it is somewhat harder to sweep (see fig. 12.19, p. 158). Since concrete is so hard, it is the flooring most likely to cause injury should a horse or person fall on it.

Concrete is a good choice for any floor in a barn with the exception of stalls. As a stall floor, concrete is too hard for a horse to lie on or stand on for long periods. It must be used with at least 6 inches of bedding or covered with rubber mats. If mats are used, urine can seep between the mats and concrete and cause odor problems.

Brick has been used as a paving material for over 5,000 years. A floor of common unglazed paving brick has fair traction and if installed over a properly compacted base will stay level and last decades (fig. 8.4). Many brick streets laid hundreds of years ago are now carrying auto as well as horse traffic. But if not installed properly, a brick floor can settle unevenly and become wavy. Vehicle traffic can result in two parallel troughs the length of the barn aisle. In high horse traffic areas, depressions can form from the surface of brick wearing away and from individual bricks being compacted into the base. An uneven brick floor can be difficult to sweep clean because of the joints between the bricks.

ROOFING

Concrete and clay roof tiles come in a variety of colors and designs and will outlast the life of most barns. Concrete tiles are less expensive than clay tiles. Quarried slate comes in different colors and grades, depending on its origin. It is virtually indestructible and more expensive than other roofing materials and its application requires skill and experience. Masonry roofing products are heavy and require more support than other types of roofing. If you're considering replacing a different type of roof with concrete tile, it's important to have an engineer inspect the barn's framing to make sure it will support the extra weight.

Fiber cement roofing products simulate the look of shingles, slate, and shakes. Initial products were very long lasting because they contained asbestos fibers. Around 1990, however, the U.S. government crackdown on carcinogens in manufacturing forced roofing manufacturers to switch to less durable cellulose fibers. Since that time, many fiber cement products have experienced early failure.

8.2 *Masonry building. Note non-rusting aluminum grilles.*

8.3 *Concrete floor.*

8.4 *Paving brick lasts for decades and has a distinctive appearance and sound.*

8.5 *Asphalt shingles are the most common roofing material.*

Shingles are commonly 3-feet long and have three tabs or sections. Some shingles contain zinc granules to protect against algae, a common problem in hot, humid areas. Generally, fiberglass-based asphalt shingles have a Class A fire rating, while organic-based shingles have only a Class C rating. Shingles are also rated by *Underwriters Laboratories (UL)* for impact resistance to hail. Ratings are from Class 1 through Class 4, with Class 4 offering the greatest hail protection. Some insurance companies offer discounts for roofs having a Class 3 or Class 4 rating.

Asphalt rolled roofing is similar to shingles but comes in a 3-foot-wide continuous roll. Felt roofing paper *(tar paper)* has no granules and is used only as an *underlayment,* not as exterior roofing.

ASPHALT

Asphalt is a heavy, brown-to-black mineral substance, a mixture of hydrocarbons called bitumens. It is obtained either from natural deposits (native asphalt or brea) or as a by-product of the petroleum industry (petroleum asphalt).

FLOORING

Asphalt paving mixture is a dull black material, made of asphalt, sand, and powdered limestone. Asphalt is applied hot onto a compacted base, leveled, and then smoothed by a heavy roller. This is not a do-it-yourself project. Even though asphalt is cheaper than concrete, it's also not as durable. It is hard and slick when cold, soft and tacky when hot, and can heave and crack during seasonal freeze/thaw cycles. As it cures over six to twelve months, oil rises to the surface and evaporates. The surface can be coated with a *sealer* containing sand to make it less slippery, but only after the *curing* period.

ROOFING

Asphalt is used to impregnate fiberglass mat or organic (cellulose) *felt,* which is then coated with mineral granules to make roofing products. Asphalt roofing is relatively inexpensive, available in a range of colors, and easy to apply (fig. 8.5). Products based on organic felts have been around longer, but fiberglass-reinforced products now dominate the market. Asphalt roofing can last 20 years or more but it is more susceptible to damage by wind, cold, ice build-up, and extreme heat than other types of roofing. And if not properly applied, some types of shingles tend to blow off in high wind.

LUMBER

Lumber is made by sawing trees, commonly Douglas fir, pine, and hemlock, into boards. It is available as rough-sawn (full-dimension) boards, which can vary ¼ inch in dimensions, or as planed boards, which are smoother, thinner, narrower, and more consistent in dimensions. Poles and posts are made by turning tree trunks or large branches on a giant lathe to make them uniform in shape.

FRAMING

Lumber is by far the most popular material for barn framing. It is readily available and easy to work with. It can rot, however, if subjected to moisture. Chewing horses and insects, mainly *termites,* can weaken wood framing and make it unsafe. Wood that has been chewed by horses is not only unsightly but the splinters can injure your horse's mouth and intestines (see fig. 11.6, p. 144). Wood that is exposed to horses will likely need protection by metal "chew guard" edges (see fig. 5.9, p. 37 and fig. 12.7, p. 155) or by periodic application of an anti-chew product.

SHEATHING

Lumber is generally more expensive and takes more time to apply than either plywood or OSB to cover the same area. But it does make good sheathing and is especially applicable if a person has a supply of boards on hand or has access to a cheap source, such as a local sawmill.

SIDING

Lumber siding has considerable visual appeal and nostalgia value. It is the most "barn-like" of all siding materials. It is available everywhere, is easy to work with, and if protected from moisture will last almost indefinitely. But wood siding will rot, crack, and warp if repeatedly subjected to moisture and sunlight, so periodic application of paint or sealer is required. And, like wood framing, board siding is vulnerable to damage from insects and chewing horses. Even if the siding has a relatively flat surface some horse will destroy it (see fig. 11.6, p. 144).

PANELING

Solid wood paneling and siding, such as tongue and groove wainscoting, shiplap, and drop siding, look good on walls and ceilings and since they are generally not exposed to sunlight they require repainting much less frequently than when used outdoors. Another plus is that most solid wood paneling is substantial enough to hold fasteners for shelves and hooks.

STALL WALL LINER

Two-inch-thick rough-sawn lumber and planed tongue and groove lumber work well if applied over adequate framing. Tongue and groove boards join together along their length, making a stronger wall with a smoother, more even surface than a wall made with plain boards. A big plus for lumber is that it is forgiving. If a horse kicks it or runs into it the boards will often absorb the blow and reduce injuries by denting, bending, or breaking (fig. 8.6).

FLOORING

Wood planks make a warm floor with a unique feeling and sound (fig. 8.7). Wood performs best when installed over a base that drains, such as road base, limestone, or gravel, so it is not in constant contact with moisture. Properly installed it will remain stable and level. Even untreated wood, if not contacting the earth, can last for 30 years or more. A wood floor can be taken up and reinstalled relatively easily, for example to repair buried waterlines.

A wooden floor can cause trouble at both ends of the traction scale. It can be very slippery when wet, while a horse shod with traction devices, such as calks or borium, can stick to the floor, creating potential for joint injuries, not to mention scarring, chipping, and splintering the floor surface.

In a stall, wood planks are difficult to clean and sanitize because the surface is porous and usually uneven. Unpleasant odors can result.

For a tack room, planed tongue and groove boards would make a better floor than would rough sawn planks. It would be smoother, so easier to clean, and fit tighter to keep insects out.

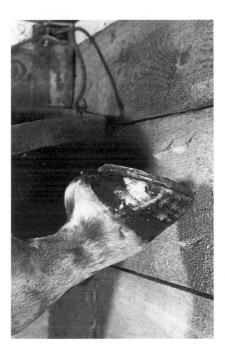

ROOFING

Wood shingles are machine-sawn, while wood shakes are hand-hewn and rougher looking. Their natural look is popular in California, the Northwest, and parts of the Midwest. Wood roofing is subject to rot but if treated and installed properly can last 50 years or more. Shakes and shingles should only be used on roofs with a 4/12 or greater slope so that water drains off and the roofing can dry out quickly. They are very flammable having a UL fire rating of Class B, C, or none at all, unless periodically treated with a fire retardant. Because of this, the use of wood roofing products is limited by some local codes and may adversely affect your insurance rates. Consider their use carefully, especially if your barn is near a wooded area where airborne embers could land on the barn's roof.

8.6 Wood absorbs some of the energy of a kick by denting, reducing the likelihood of injury to the horse's leg.

8.7 A wood plank floor.

PRESSURE-TREATED WOOD

Plain wood will last almost indefinitely if kept dry, but it soon rots when subjected to moisture. Good quality pressure-treated wood, on the other hand, will resist rot for 30 years or more. As its name implies, pressure-treated wood has been treated under pressure to replace its internal moisture with a preservative. The four chemicals commonly used are penta (pentachlorophenol), creosote, CCA (chromated copper arsenate), and borates (from borax).

Because of health concerns, penta, creosote, and CCA have been designated restricted-use pesticides in the United States, available only to certified applicators. Both penta and creosote can have fairly strong odors and are skin irritants. Gloves and protective clothing should be worn when handling freshly treated wood.

CCA and borate treated wood are both considered safe to use around people and horses. CCA forms a chemical bond with the wood and it becomes fixed within the lumber. But it doesn't penetrate to heartwood so end cuts on treated wood need to be treated by hand. CCA treated wood gives off no fumes or vapors and has been found by the EPA to be safe even for playground equipment. Even so, a respirator should be used when cutting CCA treated wood, to prevent irritation by treated wood dust.

CCA treated wood comes rated for its intended use. The higher the rating the more preservative and protection. The most common ratings are:

CCA .25 – for above ground use
CCA .40 – for ground contact
CCA .60 – for below ground structure support

Borates occur naturally in soil, water, plants, and animals. Borate wood treatments are used for protection against termites, beetles, carpenter ants, rot, and fungi. Borate pressure treatment penetrates to heartwood so end cuts on treated wood do not need retreating. Borates are water-soluble, however, and will leach out if used in contact with ground or water, reducing their effectiveness. Borate wood preservatives are odorless, non-irritating to skin and eyes, and considered safe to use around people and horses.

FOUNDATIONS

Pressure-treated posts are used for the foundation of pole barns (fig. 8.8). They

8.8 *Pressure-treated wood used for the bottom portion of the main barn posts and for the splashboard along the lower edge of the siding. OSB used for sheathing on lower portion of wall.*

can be round poles from logs or composite square posts made from lumber, commonly three or more 2 x 6s or 2 x 8s nailed together. In the latter case, pressure-treated lumber and *galvanized* nails are used on the portion of posts that will be underground or within 8 inches of the ground while untreated boards and plain nails can be used for the portion of the post above ground. Pressure-treated plywood or lumber is used for floor or wall framing that comes 8 inches or closer to the ground such as for a splashboard or skirting between the siding and the ground.

PARTICLEBOARD

Particleboard is a composite board made of wood and agricultural byproducts (sawdust, rice and cornhusk, and sugarcane pulp) and a binding agent (usually urea). Some particleboard is manufactured with an overlay of finer particles for smoother faces. Particleboard expands and breaks down if wetted frequently, and it lacks the strength of other panels such as plywood and OSB. Also, driving a nail through it will break a chunk out the backside so it is not used for siding or paneling.

COUNTERTOPS AND CABINETS

The smooth, flat, and hard surface of particleboard makes it ideal as a base for plastic laminates, and it used almost exclusively as the core for countertops.

> ### PRESSURE TREATMENT
>
> **DOES NOT** prevent horses from chewing (except for creosote). Wood treated with penta or creosote should not be used in barns where a horse can chew or lick it. CCA and borate treated wood is harmful mainly because of the splinters, not the chemicals.
>
> **DOES NOT** protect wood from exposure to sun (except for creosote). To minimize cracking and splitting you need to protect exposed wood with paint, stain, or sealer.
>
> **DOES NOT** always protect wood from termites and in some cases not at all. Borate- and creosote-treated wood has the best insect resistance.

Because it is rigid and doesn't warp, it is a good product for cabinets as well.

HARDBOARD

Hardboard refers to tough, dense panels and boards made from wood fibers and binders that are heated and compressed. Hardboard panels are formed smooth or with patterns varying from wood grains and grooves to stucco. It is less expensive than plywood but not nearly as strong.

SIDING

Hardboard siding panels and boards come in a variety of patterns and textures, from wood grain to stucco. This type of siding is relatively inexpensive and easy to install. But it has been known to deteriorate quickly when wet, so it's important that the bottom of siding is eight inches or more above the ground and that the siding is kept protected by paint. Also, hardboard and is one of the easiest siding materials for a horse to kick through (fig. 8.9). If used where horses can contact it, reinforce it with sheathing of ¾-inch plywood or OSB at least to a height of 4 feet.

PANELING

Hardboard siding is also suitable for interior walls except in stalls. It holds paint well and will last indefinitely.

PLYWOOD

Plywood is made by gluing thin layers of wood (veneer) together in a heated press to form a rigid panel. Each layer is placed at a 90° angle to the next so a plywood panel is strong in all directions and doesn't twist or warp like lumber. There are an odd number of layers so that the outer layers, or faces, have the grain running in the same direction.

Plywood is economical because it can cover large areas with less wood fiber than solid wood. It is divided into two general classes: construction plywood and decorative (hardwood) plywood. The latter is used primarily for furniture.

Construction plywood is further classified by exposure durability and grade. Plywood is either suited for interior or exterior use — exterior grade is designated by an X, as in *CDX*. It can be pressure treated for below ground use. Exposure classifications are:

EXTERIOR Waterproof (exterior) glue and composed of C-grade or better veneers throughout.

EXPOSURE 1 Waterproof glue but may include D-grade veneers.

EXPOSURE 2 Water-resistant glue.

INTERIOR Any type of glue and D-grade veneer is allowed on inner and back plies of some grades.

Panel grades either describe the panel's intended use, such as underlayment or concrete form, or letters that identify the grades of the face and back veneers. Grades indicate the size, number, and location of defects, such as knots, splits, and repairs:

N Natural finish that contains only minor surface repairs.

A AND B Solid surface with neatly made repairs and small, tight knots.

C Knotholes up to 1-inch across.

D Knotholes up to 2-inches across.

SHEATHING

C and D grade plywood is used for structural applications like wall and roof sheathing. Many builders prefer plywood to OSB, especially for roof sheathing, because they feel plywood holds fasteners more securely.

SIDING

The most popular plywood siding is T-111 (pronounced "tee one eleven"). It is ⅝-inch thick and has a pattern that resembles vertical boards and presents a smoother, less chewable surface than most board siding. But, as with other wood products, horses will chew exposed edges. And a horse can kick through plywood as thick as 1 inch, so apply it over sheathing if a horse can contact it (fig. 8.9).

PANELING

Thin plywood paneling can be found in nearly any pattern you desire, but if it's less than ½-inch thick it has the same drawback as drywall: the lack of holding power for shelves and hooks. Plywood thicker than ½ inch and plywood siding, such as T-111, make strong serviceable paneling that holds paint and stain well. Better grades of plywood (N, A, and B grades) are used where appearance is important, such as for soffit, interior paneling, doors, and cabinets.

8.9 *A horse can easily kick through hardboard siding, as shown here.*

STALL WALL LINER

Two layers of ¾-inch plywood work well and provide a smooth face that does not invite chewing.

FLOORING

Plywood is suitable as an underlayment, but when used as a finish floor the top veneer will soon wear through and begin splintering.

OSB

Some readers might remember waferboard, or pressed wood, that was popular in the 1970s. It was a less expensive (and poor) substitute for plywood made by gluing randomly placed chips of wood together under pressure to form panels. In 1978, waferboard evolved into *oriented strand board (OSB)*, which is a different animal altogether. One big improvement was to align the layers of wood chips or strands for greatly improved strength—outer layers are aligned in the long panel direction, like plywood, while inner layers are aligned cross-ways or randomly. The layers are glued with waterproof adhesive under heat and pressure.

OSB is less expensive than plywood and has a smoother, tighter surface that's easy to clean. Plywood does have better holding strength for nails or screws. If you penetrate OSB all the way through, the nail will often break portions half the thickness of the panel out the backside, greatly reducing its holding strength. Tongue and groove OSB allows panels to be installed across joists without the need of additional supports *(bridging),* between the joists under the panel seams.

8.10 *OSB (oriented strand board) used for sheathing beneath steel siding to prevent a horse from kicking through the steel.*

SHEATHING

Building codes in the U.S. and Canada allow OSB panels to be used for the same applications as plywood (fig. 8.10).

PANELING

OSB ⅝-inch and thicker works well for interior wall paneling. It is sturdy enough to hold fasteners for hooks and shelves and holds paint well.

STALL WALL LINER

Two layers of ¾-inch OSB work well and provide a smooth face that does not invite chewing. Exposed edges, however, require metal chew-guard edging.

FLOORING

I used one layer of ¾-inch tongue and groove OSB as the finished floor in two tack rooms and treated the floor initially and after four years with a water sealer. It was eight years before the material showed significant wear. It would not last as long where you were tracking mud and snow onto the floor.

DRYWALL

Drywall and wallboard are generic terms for interior surface panels such as asbestos-cement board, gypsum panels, and sheetrock (a U.S. gypsum brand name). Gypsum board, the most common drywall panel, contains a core of gypsum rock, a natural mineral, sandwiched between two layers of paper. Gypsum is naturally fire resistant but shrinks and cracks when exposed to fire. Fire-resistant panels (type X drywall) are made by mixing glass fibers and other materials with the gypsum so they hold together longer under fire. Water-resistant panels *(green board)* have wax added to the core and a green-paper face that is treated with silicone. Drywall panels commonly measure 4 by 8 feet, range from ¼- to ¾-inch thick, with ½ inch being the most common. A 4-foot by 8-foot panel of ½-inch gypsum board weighs approximately 53 pounds.

FINISHED WALLS AND CEILINGS

Drywall (plasterboard) is not well suited for most wall areas of a barn because of its low impact resistance. And it does not hold fasteners well, such as when hanging hooks or brackets. It might be all right in an office or lavatory but even there a more solid material would enable you to attach a hook or shelf anywhere on a wall, whereas with drywall you need to drill for special fasteners or go through into a stud behind the drywall. When installed properly, it makes an attractive ceiling.

FIRE WALLS

Fire walls run from the floor to either the ceiling or the roof and are designed to prevent fire from spreading from one area to another, from your hay storage area to your tack room, for example (see p. 42). They consist of either a masonry or steel framed wall with one or two layers of drywall on each side. The performance of a fire wall can be enhanced by treating the wall surface or framing members with special paints or chemicals. Check your local building code for specifics.

STEEL

Steel is a combination of iron and carbon and often other elements that affect hardness, strength, and other characteristics. It is impervious to chewing damage from horses, rodents, and other animals (fig. 8.11).

FRAMING

Steel framing is often used for large barns and indoor arenas because steel beams can span greater distances than wood beams of a similar size (fig. 8.12). It does, however, usually require large equipment and a specially trained crew to erect. Steel is excellent for posts and grilles because chewing does not damage it. Since steel is so tough and hard, bruising and broken bones are not uncommon when a horse collides with steel framing.

8.11 *Steel is the primary material in a modular barn like this one, from the framing to the grillwork to wall panels.*

MODULAR PANELS

Manufacturers of modular barns use wall panels consisting of a ¾-inch plywood or OSB core with sheet steel laminated to one or both faces (fig. 8.11). These panels serve as siding, finished interior wall, and stall liner. The inner steel is often smooth and galvanized. The outer surface is available in a variety of treatments including textured steel, painted steel, plain plywood, and T-111 siding. These panels can withstand direct horse kicks with only minor dents, and have sufficient cushion to minimize injuries. Most manufactures offer a "kick-through" guarantee.

SIDING, ROOFING

Steel panels used for siding and roofing are economical, go up quickly, come in many colors, and seldom, if ever, need painting. They are typically 26- or 29-gauge thick and ordered precut to any length. As with wood panel siding, a horse can kick through a steel panel, and injury potential is much greater because of the sharp steel edges around the hole. Always install sheathing behind steel siding to prevent kick-through. Another way a horse can be seriously (even fatally) injured with steel siding is when a foot or leg is caught under the sharp

8.12 *Steel framing for large buildings requires large equipment and a specially trained crew. Note the fiberglass blanket insulation enclosed in a plastic vapor barrier.*

8.13 *Steel trim over wood post.*

bottom edge. Attach siding securely to a solid board or other support along the bottom so a horse cannot contact the sharp edge. Likewise, protect all sharp corners and be aware that some horses will chew on exposed edges of steel trim and will rub on protruding nailheads and screws, often ripping out mane and tail hairs.

Steel roofing is fireproof and allows snow, ice, and airborne debris to slide off the easiest of any roofing material (see fig. 11.10, p. 146). Depending on roof slope, a good amount of snow can build up on the roof before breaking free in a sudden, loud avalanche that can startle horses. To prevent avalanches, snow guards, vertical teeth-like barriers, can be attached to the lower portion of a steel roof.

Steel roofing isn't limited to large panels. Individual steel products can provide the appearance of a tile roof, for example, without the weight or can mimic a shake roof without the fire hazard.

Steel trim is sometimes used over square wood posts to improve their appearance and to protect them from chewing horse (fig. 8.13). All steel trim need to be installed carefully and inspected periodically to ensure there are no sharp edges on which a horse could be injured.

ALUMINUM

Aluminum is the third most common element on the planet and the most common metallic element. It is a soft, lightweight, silver-white metal having a strength, lightness, and resistance to corrosion and wear that make it useful for many construction applications. A unique and valuable characteristic of aluminum is that it can be recycled over and over without any degradation or loss of its innate characteristics.

FRAMING AND HARDWARE

Aluminum is used for some framing applications such as doors and windows and for hardware such as grillwork (see fig. 8.2, p. 85).

INSULATION

When polished, aluminum has a very reflective surface making it useful for a *radiant barrier*. Radiant barrier (reflective) insulation is a thin blanket-like product (approximately ⁵⁄₁₆-inch thick) with outer layers of aluminum foil that reflect radiant heat back to the source. A middle layer of polypropylene (bubble wrap-type material) minimizes *conduction* of heat between the two foil outer layers. A radiant barrier reflects a majority of both winter radiant heat loss and summer radiant heat gain. Radiant energy transfer can account for as much as 93 percent of summer heat gain, and up to 75 percent of

8.14 *Translucent fiberglass panels.*

winter heat loss in a barn. Because it also reflects visible light, it will make the inside of a barn brighter as well. Plus, it serves as a wind and moisture barrier.

FIBERGLASS

Fiberglass is just that: fibers of molten glass extruded at a specified diameter. What we commonly call fiberglass is either a rigid composite of plastic resin and glass fibers or a fluffy blanket of spun glass fibers.

SIDING

Translucent fiberglass panels are an efficient and inexpensive way to let natural light into a barn (fig. 8.14, see also figs. 9.5, p.100 and 12.4, p. 154). Some panels have a ribbed profile that matches the profile of common types of steel panel siding. Translucent panels are most effective when used on the gable ends and the upper portion of the side walls. Fiberglass panels can be easily broken by a horse and should not be installed where a horse could contact them.

INSULATION

Fiberglass blankets *(batts)* and rolls are inexpensive, fire and sound resistant, and easy to install. They come in R-values ranging from R-11 to R-38 (see Insulation, p. 28). Birds and rodents like fiberglass for nesting material so it should be carefully covered with a finish material to prevent them from getting to it (fig. 8.15). If fiberglass insulation gets wet (from a leaky roof or condensation caused by a poor vapor barrier) its insulating value will be greatly reduced, besides causing rot and rust by holding moisture against wood framing and wall covering. It will retain its R-value after it dries, but this could take a long time given the limited airflow inside most walls and ceilings.

Blown-in fiberglass is mixed with an adhesive so it adheres to the wall cavity. Nozzles mix water with the fiberglass as it's sprayed, activating the adhesive. Where thickness is not restricted, such as over a level ceiling, fiberglass insulation can be built up to a very high R-value.

FRP AND OTHER PLASTICS

Fiber reinforced plastic (FRP) is a type of fiberglass that is much less brittle than the type used for siding and roofing. It is available in flat panels (sold as bath panel in some home improvement stores) usually less than ⅛-inch thick. Panels have an embossed surface and come in a variety of colors (see figs. 12.18, 12.20, and 12.21, p. 158). FRP is extremely tough and when applied over a sturdy sheathing panel can take the direct kick of a horse without damage.

Polyethylene (poly), the most popular plastic in the world, is found in everything from grocery bags to toys to bullet proof vests. It is available in smooth building panels from 1/16-inch to ½-inch thick. It is also used to make VisQueen® and similar films and *landscape fabrics* (*geotextiles,* weed barriers).

Undoubtedly, a variety of items containing plastic will find a place in your barn, from water buckets to lead ropes.

SIDING

Plastic siding such as vinyl is easily damaged by chewing and kicking, so it is inappropriate where a horse can contact the barn.

PANELING

FRP and poly panels have a shiny, bright "hospital" look that reflects light well and is appropriate in wash racks, vet, and repro areas (fig. 8.16). Both materials provide a durable, washable surface that doesn't encourage mold or bacteria and has a slick hard surface that is easy to clean with a hose and sponge. They are applied to plywood or OSB sheathing using adhesive or special fasteners or both.

FLOORING

Draining flooring made of plastic is available in the form of tiles that lock together or as large mats, which are often one piece the size of the stall. These flooring materials maintain a level floor surface and provide varying degrees of cushion. Less bedding is used because urine drains through the flooring into the ground. But accumulation of urine under the flooring can lead to odor problems.

ROOFING

Like translucent fiberglass panels, there are plastic panels that can be used in portions of a roof to let in natural light. They are either matched to the profile of the steel roofing or applied over a projecting wooden frame.

INSULATION

Spray foam insulation is a two-part liquid containing a polymer (such as polyurethane) and a foaming agent. It is mixed on-site by certified applicators and sprayed as wet foam onto or between wall and ceiling surfaces. It expands while spraying and hardens in minutes into a lightweight plastic insulating material that resembles hard, tan-colored shaving cream. It has the best R-value per inch of any readily available insulation. Spray foam adheres and seals tightly to walls and ceilings and does not shrink, sag, settle, or biodegrade. It reduces air leakage caused by irregularities in surfaces, thereby providing insect resistance and sealing cracks from unwanted odor penetration. The thickness required depends on local codes, personal preference, barn location, and construction type. Most foams do not affect the fire performance of a wall. Spray foam materials cost more than traditional batt insulation but can eliminate the need for *caulking* and a vapor barrier. If your building code does not recognize spray foam as a vapor barrier or as a finished surface, you may be required to cover it with drywall or other paneling.

Rigid insulation board is made of polyisocyanate material (called *ISO, polyiso,* and *foam board*), often with reflective aluminum skin on one or both sides. It has an R-value of approximately 7.2 per inch of thickness. A good choice for barns is thermax finish/insulation board by Celotex, which has embossed white acrylic-coated aluminum on one side and plain aluminum on the other side. It contains glass fibers for added dimensional stabili-

8.15 *Fiberglass is a favored nesting material of birds and they will tear this white plastic vapor barrier to get it. Protect insulation with wire or other covering if birds are allowed inside the barn.*

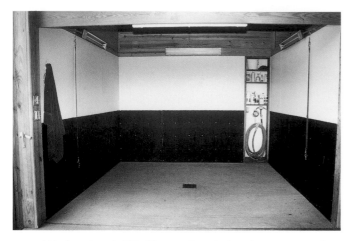

8.16 *Wash rack with FRP (fiber reinforced plastic) on upper wall surface and rubber mats attached to the lower portion.*

ty and chemical additives for fire retardance. It serves as mass insulation, radiant barrier, and vapor barrier. In addition, many codes allow it for exposed insulation/interior finish. It can be installed exposed to the interior on the inside or outside of *purlins* and *girts* and directly to the interior of masonry or concrete. The washable white surface has a light reflectance of 65 percent so brightens up the interior of a barn. Panels come in a range of thickness and lengths up to 30 feet. No added vapor barrier is needed if you tape the joints with Tyvek contractor's tape or aluminum tape. Most foam boards will burn if subjected to a fire of sufficient intensity and, like most common building materials, will release toxic smoke.

There is also a white-faced fiber board, called wallboard or sound board, that can be used under a steel roof to deaden sound of rain and hail and to brighten the inside of the barn. It is less expensive than foam board but is not as rigid, and it can sag over time. Also, it is not washable and is subject to unsightly water stains if there are leaks in the roof. On the plus side, those stains will alert you to the leaks, which you can then repair before they lead to structural damage.

RUBBER

Rubber is a solid natural or synthetic substance that is vulcanized (heated and combined with sulfur) to improve its elasticity and add strength. Rubber is waterproof and resistant to heat, cold, and urine, and lasts for years. It is formed into bricks and tiles of various colors and solid mats (usually black) that commonly measure 4-feet by 6-feet by ¾-inch thick.

PANELING

Rubber mats are sometimes attached to walls over sheathing in stalls and wash racks to provide a smooth, resilient, washable surface that is not damaged by kicking and doesn't invite chewing (fig. 8.16). Black mats soak up light, however, and make a barn interior darker.

FLOORING

Rubber mats over concrete is one of the best flooring combinations for aisles and wash racks (see fig 5.14, p. 39 and figs. 12.12 and 12.13, p. 157). Mats are long lasting and require very little maintenance. Traction on rubber mats is very good when dry and sufficient when wet. A surface pattern on the mats does not significantly improve traction. Mats commonly range from ½-inch to ⅞-inch thick and measure 4 feet by 6 feet. They can be used to cover the entire aisle or just a portion of it. Confining the use of mats to the grooming areas of a concrete aisle could enable you to stay within your budget and still have a great floor.

In a stall, solid mats over properly prepared gravel or road base (see Rubber Mats, p. 134) provide a firm, level surface with cushion for the horse. And, when used with absorbent bedding such as wood shavings, they allow moisture from urine to be removed with each stall cleaning. Rubber mats are heavy to handle when installing, and if not installed properly the mats will buckle at the joints. The resulting uneven surface will make stall cleaning difficult and could cause a person to trip. Interlocking mats have puzzle-piece edges that prevent mat joints from separating (see fig. 12.10, p. 156). If used in a stall over a poorly draining base, such as concrete, odors caused by accumulating urine can be a problem.

CAUTION: do not use old conveyor belting for flooring because it is dangerously slippery when wet for people and horses and can lead to serious injury.

Rubber brick is available in a variety of shapes and colors. It is durable, quiet, and provides a resilient floor with excellent traction whether wet or dry (see fig. 5.14, p. 39). It can be installed over a hard surface like concrete or in a sand base over a draining surface such as gravel. It is considered by many horse owners to be the best (and most expensive) barn aisle floor money can buy.

Rubber tile is also available in a variety of colors. It is 1-inch to 1¼-inch thick, and designed to go over a solid, impermeable surface such as concrete or asphalt. Rubber tile has many of the advantages of rubber brick, but since it is thinner and on a solid base, it doesn't provide as much cushion.

FASTENERS

The fasteners you use can affect the safety of your horses, the longevity of your barn, and how much maintenance you'll need to do down the road.

Nails are commonly measured in units called pennies, designated by the letter "d", spoken as *"penny."* In England during the Middle Ages, nails were either sold by the pound or the count, and *"d"* (from denarius, a Roman coin) was the designation for both the English penny and a pound of weight.

Today "d" refers to nail length. As the penny size increases, so does the length and thickness of the nail. The shortest nail with a penny measurement is a 2d, which is 1-inch long, and the longest is 60d, which is 6-inches long. Nails that are shorter than 2d or longer than 60d are measured in inches.

Nails are usually sold by the pound—the larger the nails the fewer per pound.

NAIL TYPES

COMMON General-purpose nail with a relatively large head and thick shank.

SINKER A common nail with a head that tapers on the bottom to countersink it into the wood with less deformation of the woods surface; often has a checkered pattern on the head to prevent the hammer from slipping off.

BOX Thinner version of the common nail for use with wood that splits easy; reduced diameter means it doesn't hold as well as a common nail.

DUPLEX Also called double-headed or *scaffold nails,* have double heads. One head is driven flush with the wood, the other head remains exposed to allow easy pulling. Use for temporary braces and concrete forms.

JOIST-HANGER These nails provide the same heft as larger 8d common nails but in shorter lengths for *joist hangers* (a common nail 1½-inch long is only a 4d size— way too skinny to provide the shear strength the joist hanger requires.)

BRAD A slender, small nail with almost no head.

FINISH Has a small, dimpled head only slightly larger than the shank; used for trim and cabinet work where a nail set fits in the dimpled head to drive the head below the surface and the hole is filled.

CASING Heavy finish nail but with a flat, not dimpled, head; often galvanized; used for door and window casing and trim.

DRYWALL Thin nail with a ringed shank and a broad, cupped head that is driven slightly below the drywall surface; has been largely replaced by drywall screws.

ROOFING Galvanized nail with a large head for holding down asphalt shingles and felt.

ALUMINUM ROOFING For corrugated metal or plastic roofing; has rubber washer under head for watertight seal.

MASONRY Made of hardened steel for fastening to concrete walls and floors.

NAIL SHANKS

Ring shank and spiral or screw shank nails are used where holding power is very important. They can be almost impossible to remove without causing damage to the lumber.

NAIL COATINGS

BRIGHT Shiny and smooth with no coating. Nails coated this way are easy to pull out and will rust if they get wet; commonly used for framing that is protected from weather.

GALVANIZED Zinc coating that resists rust and weathering. Nails with this coating have even less holding power than bright nails; use for any work exposed to the elements or within 8 inches of the ground and for damp wood, freshly pressure treated wood; streaking occurs on cedar or redwood siding and shingles because of acids in these woods, which react with the zinc. Use aluminum or stainless steel nails with these woods.

CEMENT Increase holding power; difficult to remove. Heads often will break off before the nail comes out.

VINYL Work like cement-coated nails, but use a newer chemistry to make driving easier, provide extra holding power, and keep hands cleaner.

NAIL LENGTH AND SPACING

As a general rule, the nail should be three times as long as the thickness of the top piece of wood through which it is driven, so ⅔ of the nail is driven into the bottom piece.

PULLING NAILS

A straight claw hammer with a fiberglass handle is a handy tool for pulling nails smaller than 16d. Wooden handles tend to break when hammers are used for pulling. A block of wood under the head of the hammer will increase leverage and to prevent marring the surface of the material you are working with. If you have a tough time grabbing the nail head, don't strike the hammer with another hammer, you could chip the hammer faces. Instead try prying sideways with the hammer.

Nails 16d and larger should be pulled with a crowbar. Again, a block under the bar will increase leverage.

A cat's paw is a marvel of simplicity and function. Once you've used one, you'll wonder how you ever got along without it. The rounded head of a cat's paw is driven into the wood near the nail head and it grips the nail shank and scoops the nail out of the wood. It often works even if the nail head comes off. It will leave a gouge mark in the wood, but the nail will almost always come out.

A flat bar (wonder bar, super bar) is good for pulling nails up to 16d. It works particularly well for removing roofing because the flat shape is easy to slide under shingles.

AVOID SPLITTING

To avoid splitting wood when driving nails near the end of a piece of wood follow these tips:

- use a box nail instead of a common nail

- avoid driving two nails in the same grain of the wood

- drill a small pilot hole

- start the nail farther from the end and angle it into the support

- place the nail with the widest axis of the diamond-shaped point across the grain

- blunt the point of the nail with a hammer so it breaks the wood fibers rather than acting as a wedge U

CHAPTER NINE

UTILITIES AND DETAILS

Ahandy person using common sense and a few precautions could install most of the plumbing and wiring in a barn. Contact a licensed plumber or electrician for help with work that is beyond your capabilities. Some professionals will act as coaches and allow you to do most of the chimp work while they complete the critical parts. This can save you money and give you a better understanding of the inner workings of your barn. Then, if problems should arise later, you'll have an idea of how to diagnose the problem and get it fixed. There are many excellent how-to books on plumbing and wiring available at building supply stores and libraries. What I will discuss here are the practical aspects of deciding how extensive the utilities in your barn need to be and how best to design them.

ELECTRICITY

Electricity is the lifeblood of your barn. It provides power for three necessities: light, heat, and pumping water. Poorly installed plumbing might flood the barn floor, but bad wiring can burn the barn down—or kill a person or a horse. Don't mess around. If you aren't confident that you can handle wiring, call a professional.

THE CODE

The NEC (National Electric Code) is a guide for safe wiring, and, although it does not itself have the force of law, many local building authorities adopt it outright or use it as a template to make their own codes. The NEC is revised and published every three years by the National Fire Protection Association, an insurance industry group. See the Resource Guide for where to obtain a copy. To find what regulations apply in your area, check with your local building department and with your local electrical utility, which may have special requirements for electrical installation.

Some states require a licensed electrician to install all wiring. Others let

9.1 *Locate the service panel where it will be easily accessible.*

you do everything but the actual hook up. Ask your local electrical inspector how much of the wiring you are allowed to do. If you decide to tackle the job, take the time to do a neat and precise job. Inspectors tend to look very carefully at wiring installed by homeowners.

Most jurisdictions require a permit and inspections of all wiring. You can be forced to tear out wiring done without a permit and do it again once a permit is in place. Worse, if fire caused by uninspected wiring destroys your barn, the insurance company may refuse to pay. Get the permit.

POWER BASICS

Electricity from the local utility company is typically supplied through three overhead or underground wires called *leads* (pronounced "leedz") or service conductors. An electric *service* or feed consists of two *hot* leads (wires) each carrying 120 volts, and one *neutral* lead. Two hot leads are used together to provide 240 volts when needed. The wires pass through a meter box (usually on a pole) and into the *service panel* of the building where they connect to metal strips called *buss bars* (fig. 9.1). (In some cases, the service splits at the meter to serve the house and the barn.)

A safety *ground* or equipment ground is a wire (often bare copper or having green insulation) that connects from the service panel to a copper rod or galvanized steel rod driven 8 feet into the earth. The neutral wire from the utility is also tied to the equipment ground. Three wires—hot, neutral, and equipment ground—make up the connections to a typical outlet receptacle.

You may wonder why both the equipment ground wire and neutral are needed since both ultimately connect to the same *ground rod*. The equipment ground isn't always needed as evidenced by the large number of electrical appliances that use only two (hot and neutral) prongs. But in electrical equipment, which has an equipment ground connection (a three-pronged plug), the round grounding prong is always connected to any exposed metal parts of the equipment. That way, if an exposed part of the equipment becomes energized by a wiring *fault* inside the equipment, the equipment ground connection causes the hot connection to be directly connected to the service ground, and the *fuse* or circuit breaker would shut down power to the circuit. Equipment with two-prong plugs usually has a non-conducting plastic case so errant electricity should not pass to a person or horse touching the case.

Circuit breakers snap onto the buss bars and transfer electricity from the source to sections of the barn wiring called circuits. Breakers act as safety switches; they trip off to stop the flow of current when a *short circuit* or overload occurs. They can also be operated manually to turn power off to selected circuits.

Electric current doesn't just flow into a lamp or other appliance and stop. Like a drive belt on pulleys, it needs to follow an entire circuit back to the source in order to work. It leaves a breaker through a hot wire (usually black), passes through whatever appliance it is powering, and returns to complete the circuit though a neutral wire (usually white). In addition to the neutral wire, a ground wire (bare copper) offers current another path back to the service panel in the event of an electrical short or overload. As mentioned, the ground wire is connected to a long metal rod that is completely buried in the soil.

Electric cable is comprised of two or more insulated wires grouped together within a covering or sheath. The most common type is nonmetallic-sheathed (NM) cable, which is covered by flexible plastic (often mistakenly referred to by the brand name "Romex"). Underground feeder (UF) is a plastic-sheathed cable suitable for wet areas and for direct bury. Armored cable (AC, historically BX) is covered by a flexible metal casing.

Cable is categorized by sheathing, gauge (thickness), and the number of leads (wires) it contains. For example, NM 12-2G means that the cable has nonmetallic sheathing, 12 gauge, two leads (one neutral, one hot), and a ground wire.

Conduit is plastic or steel tubing through which cable is run to protect it from damage. Cable buried in poured concrete must be in conduit, even UF cable. The transition from buried cable to a building is usually required to be in conduit.

If the electrical requirements of your barn are small, you may be able to run a branch circuit from your house or other building or from an existing meter to power the barn. If the barn is far from existing service you may

need to install a new service and meter. Consult with your local electrical utility.

CIRCUITS

Voltage can be confusing. A circuit called 110 volt, 115 volt, or 120 volt all refer to the same thing. North American utilities are required to supply a 240-volt feed, plus or minus 5 percent, in two 120-volt legs. Because of resistance in building wiring, 240 volt often drops to 220 volt or 120 volt drops to 110 volt by the time it reaches an outlet.

It is better and safer to have more circuits than too few and to limit each circuit to ten or twelve outlets. Keep in mind future updates and a maximum load demand on each circuit when making a wiring diagram.

Using *Ohm's* law you can figure out how many appliances or lights you can plug into a circuit without tripping a breaker. It is watts = amps x volts. A circuit in the U.S. is typically 15 amps and 120 volts, so it could safely handle 1800 watts. A rule of thumb is to never operate a circuit at more than 80 percent of its capacity, so a goal of 1440 watts would be safer. This allows for the burst of current necessary to start some motors or certain types of lighting.

Make a separate circuit for lights, for outlets that power heaters, and for other outlets. That way if the heaters should trip a circuit breaker, you won't be groping in the dark to find the service panel. Locate heater outlets around the room and use a different color outlet for them (outlets commonly come in dark brown and shades of white). Separate circuits are also needed for built-in appliances, such as a washing machine or refrigerator in the tack room. A 20-amp circuit should be placed within 6 feet of a washing machine. An electric dryer requires a separate 240-volt circuit.

OUTLETS

A common outlet, or *duplex receptacle,* can accept two plugs at a time. Grounded outlets, those with round hole for the grounding prong on plugs, are required by code to actually be connected to a ground wire. Whether you install an outlet with the grounding hole up or down makes no difference.

As with circuits, it's better to have too many outlets than not enough. Install some near the floor and some around 4 feet from the floor. That way when trunks and boxes block the lower outlets you'll have access to the higher ones. No point along the floor line of a wall should be more than 6 feet horizontally from a duplex outlet. Do not mount outlets facing up, such as in a floor or counter, unless they are designed with covers for this purpose.

Install one or more weather protected outlets on the outside of the barn where a horse cannot reach them.

They will be handy for plugging in clippers, a weed trimmer, or a trouble light. All outdoor boxes and those used in wet areas, such as near a wash rack, must be specifically listed for outdoor use, and contain the appropriate gaskets and fittings for weather protection (fig. 9.2).

GFCI OUTLETS The NEC requires *GFCI* (ground fault circuit interrupter) outlets outdoor or wherever you're likely to encounter water or dampness, such as in a wash rack, bathrooms, and within 6 feet of a sink (fig. 9.3). A GFCI continuously monitors for equal current flowing in both the hot and the neutral wires. If the slightest amount of current leaks to ground, say through a person's or a horse's body, there will be more current flowing in one wire than the other and the GFCI will shut off all current flow in about 1/40th of a second. It is more sensitive and faster than a fuse or normal circuit breaker and fast enough to prevent current from flowing to ground and causing bodily harm. It can protect you and your horses from shocks, for example, if a tank heater shorts out or if you horse chews through a wire.

There are several types of GFCI units. One replaces a circuit breaker in the service panel and it protects that entire circuit. This type can be a nuisance in older buildings because very slight and harmless electric leakage, typical in many older buildings, will constantly cause it to trip.

Another type of GFCI is the receptacle type, which replaces a conventional receptacle outlet. It has a reset and a test button in the center and protects anything plugged into it. Some can be wired to protect all other outlets on that circuit, which are downstream from it (but not upstream). GFCI outlets are relatively inexpensive ($8.00 to $12.00). They come with stickers reading "ground fault protected" that are used to mark outlets downstream of the GFCI. To find which outlets these are, trip the GFCI with the test button and use a radio or light to see which outlets are dead. A GFCI outlet is bulkier than a regular outlet, so use an oversize box when installing it. In fact, use deep boxes everywhere. Regular boxes always seem crowded.

Note: A surge protector or even some devices that have a surge circuit in them when used with or downstream of a GFCI will constantly trip the GFCI.

Another type of GFCI is the portable type that plugs into an existing three-prong grounded outlet. Some models are incorporated in extension cords for use in damp locations, such as for a water tank heater.

Note: If you are at all unsure of how to properly install a GFCI outlet, you should contact an electrician.

LIGHTS

Lighting determines the atmosphere within a barn and affects the safety and efficiency of everything from feeding to grooming to cleaning stalls to just walking through.

General (ambient) lighting can be supplied by a combination of windows, doors, skylights, translucent panels, and electric lights. It allows you to move around safely without falling over things and to find items easily without groping in the dark. Work (task) lighting focuses on smaller areas where you need to see what you're doing without shadows and glare. In the feed room, for example, *task lighting* helps you see to portion feed, read labels, and measure supplements and medications accurately. In the grooming area, side lights might improve your clip job. Outside the barn, entrance and path lighting can make access safer. Lights that illuminate pens can be invaluable when you need to catch a horse, make emergency pen repairs, or do chores after dark.

NATURAL LIGHTING Skylights (roof windows) and translucent wall panels are an inexpensive means of getting natural light into a barn (fig. 9.4). An added benefit is that the UV light in sunlight contains a powerful and

9.2 Weatherproof outlet and switch. Locate switches and outlets where a horse cannot reach them.

9.3 GFCI (ground fault circuit interrupter) outlet.

9.4 *Translucent fiberglass panels that match the pattern of steel roofing.*

9.6 *The window part of a skylight is often a bubble-shaped section of glass or plastic mounted on a rectangular frame.*

9.5 *Translucent fiberglass panels are typically less expensive than the siding they replace.*

9.7 *Windows protected by steel grilles.*

inexpensive natural killer of bacteria and viruses. Skylights of UV-pervious plastic are superior to glass in this regard because glass usually blocks a large percentage of UV. Generally, a 10 percent skylight area in a roof is suitable for a healthy environment. In hot climates, however, skylights on the south slope of a barn roof can make the inside of the barn uncomfortably warm.

Translucent fiberglass panels are formed with various rib configurations and are typically used with steel roofing that matches the rib pattern. This option is less expensive than manufactured skylights and easier to install. Fiberglass panels can also be used as siding on the gable ends and the upper parts of the walls and doors (fig. 9.5).

Domed skylights with frames work well with shingle roofs and steel roofs where fiberglass panels can't be found to match steel roof panels (fig. 9.6). The window part of a skylight is typically bubble-shaped or flat glass or plastic mounted on a rectangular frame.

Daylight tubes consist of a highly reflective tube 10 to 20 inches in diameter that brings sunlight into a ceiling fixture, such as in a tack room or feed room. The tube extends a few inches above the roof and is protected by a weatherproof dome. Some skylight tubes have built-in vent fans. An 8-inch tube is about equivalent to a 100-watt incandescent lamp; a 12-inch tube is about equivalent to a 250-watt bulb.

Windows are a good source of light, but windows that a horse could contact must be protected by sturdy grill-work or a heavy screen (fig. 9.7). This prevents injury to the horse and damage to the window. It also helps keep the window clean.

Large doors can be a good source of natural light when left open (see fig. 4.15, p. 26). But besides letting in light, open doors also let in wind, flies, birds, dogs, and other creatures that might not be welcome. One way to solve this problem is to install giant sliding screens over barn doorways so that doors can remain open for light and ventilation but birds (and other animals) are blocked out.

ELECTRIC LIGHTS For safety and convenience, have a light controlled by a switch in every room in the barn. The switch can either control the light directly or an outlet that a light is plugged into. Control main aisle lights from several entrances using three-way switches.

Light bulbs, more accurately called lamps, are rated by two criteria: watts, the electricity it takes to run them, and lumens, the amount of light they produce. Both watts and lumens are usually listed on a lamp's packaging. The more lumens a lamp produces per watt, the more energy efficient it is. Generally, it costs less to use one big lamp than to run several small lamps that put out the same amount of light. Once lights are installed in your barn, 80 to 90 percent of the continuing cost will be electricity and 10 to 20 percent for lamp and fixture replacement.

The three main types of electric lights are incandescent, fluorescent, and high intensity discharge (HID). They differ in how they produce light, how efficiently they operate, and the color of light they produce.

INCANDESCENT The incandescent lamp has the classic light bulb shape and an Edison screw-base (fig. 9.8). It works by heating tiny wire filaments made of tungsten. They are not very efficient, converting only 6 percent of electricity to light; the rest goes to heat (which is why you can keep a small cupboard from freezing with a light bulb and also why a bulb covered with dust and cobwebs could catch fire). Incandescent bulbs burn out in 500 to 1,000 hours (20 to 40 days of continuous light), much more quickly than other lamps. They are cheap, however, and easy to replace. Also, the light they produce is one of the truest as far as color rendition. It has very little effect on the perceived color of your horse's coat or mucous membranes. Fixtures that hold incandescent

bulbs and connect them to the barn wiring are rated according to their ability to withstand heat. Plastic fixtures are generally limited to 60-watt bulbs. Higher-rated fixtures are made of ceramic or steel. If you want more light, be careful about simply screwing in a bigger bulb. Using a 95-watt bulb in a fixture rated for 60 watts will likely result in charred and brittle insulation on the wires and increased the risk of fire from heat and/or shorted wires. If you need more light in an area of your barn, add more fixtures or replace fixtures with larger ones or a different type (see following section on quartz lights), but DON'T exceed a fixture's ratings.

The average life expectancy of a bulb is usually printed on the package. If bulbs are burning out much quicker than the manufacturer's rated life it may be they are getting too hot, usually because you're using a bulb with too much wattage for the fixture.

Occasionally, the service coming into a barn will supply more than the standard 120 volts, which can cause bulbs to burn out prematurely. Test your barn circuits with an inexpensive multimeter available at electronic, hardware, and building supply stores. If *voltage* is over 125 volts you need to contact your power company. If the voltage is only slightly more than 120 volts, use 125-volt or 130-volt bulbs, which will last longer. This trick will cut down on how often you replace bulbs with normal circuits as well. For example, a 100-watt, 130-volt bulb will last twice as long as a 100-watt, 120-volt bulb. The tradeoff is that 130-volt bulbs put out about 25 percent less light. Although 130-volt bulbs are not always easy to find, my local Ace Hardware store had them in stock, and at a lower cost than 120-volt bulbs.

Another way to minimize your ladder time changing bulbs is to use bulbs labeled "long-life." They are more expensive than standard bulbs, but they really do last longer, plus they cost less to operate.

Vibration and shock are common causes of premature lamp failure, such as with bulbs located near a door that slams, on the stall of a wall-kicking horse, or on the ceiling beneath a loft floor used for square dances. In these situations, bulbs labeled "rough service" or "shock resistant" stand a better chance.

Flickering is okay for candles, but it will cut the life of an incandescent bulb short. If you have a bulb that flickers, it is likely the result of intermittent electrical contact caused either by a bad light socket or a poor electrical connection somewhere in the wires leading to the light, most likely right at the fixture. Flickering can cause the bad connection to get hot and possibly start a fire. If the connection looks good, there could be a bad neutral connection, a dangerous situation that should be checked by either the power company or an electrician.

9.8 *The 95-watt incandescent bulb on the left puts out less than half the light of one of the 40-watt flourescent bulbs in the fixture on the right.*

9.9 *Quartz halogen light.*

QUARTZ Quartz, *halogen* lamps also produce incandescent light by heating tungsten filaments (fig. 9.9). But instead of a glass vacuum bulb, they use a clear quartz tube filled with halogen gas. Quartz lamps last longer than incandescent bulbs because the tungsten that burns off the filament combines with the halogen gas and is redeposited on the filament, rather than on the inside of the quartz lamp. Not only does this extend the life of the filament, it keeps the lamp at full brightness as it ages. Quartz lamps cost more than incandescent bulbs, but they burn brighter and more consistently, are 10 to 20 percent more efficient, and last up to four times as long—up to 4,000 hours or 5½ months of continuous light. Unlike incandescent bulbs, which protrude from the fixture and throw light in all directions, quartz lamps are enclosed in a fixture having a polished aluminum reflector that focuses the light in one direction. The light from quartz lamps has little effect on the true color of objects.

Standard quartz floodlight fixtures from 150 to 500 watts are commonly stocked in hardware and building supply stores. They are comprised of a sturdy cast aluminum housing and a clear glass plate. The lamp is completely enclosed to protect it from contamination and to contain it in the unlikely event the lamp shatters. Cleanliness isn't critical when handling glass incandescent bulbs, but handling quartz bulbs is another matter. Oil, salts, and other contaminants from your fingers can react with the quartz and create hot spots that cause the bulb to fail more quickly or even explode. A quartz light should never be operated without the glass cover securely in place. Quartz lamps are usually packaged with a small sheet of plastic foam for handling the bulb. Clean gloves, a cloth, or a plastic sandwich bag also work well. If the bulb is touched, clean it with isopropyl alcohol to remove any traces of grease and salt.

Quartz floodlights are a good choice for lighting barn aisles, stalls, or pens. Not only do they put out more light per watt than incandescent lamps, but you can use a higher wattage lamp without fear that the fixture will overheat the barn wiring—the swivel arm on a quartz floodlight holds the lamp housing away from the base. And quartz fixtures are more compact than long fluorescent lights, so they catch less dust and are easier to clean.

FLUORESCENT Fluorescent lights are the coolest, most energy efficient, and most popular commercial light source in North America (fig. 9.8). Unlike incandescent and quartz lights, fluorescent lamps don't heat a filament to produce light. Instead, the inside of a fluorescent lamp is coated with phosphors, chemicals that give off light when hit by UV *radiation.* The lamp is filled with inert gas (argon or argon-krypton) and a small amount of mercury. Electricity arcing between two electrodes in the lamp heats the mercury, which gives off UV radiation.

A 40-watt fluorescent bulb puts out twice the light of a 95-watt incandescent bulb and uses less than half the electricity. It typically costs four times as much but lasts ten times longer. Some fluorescent bulbs are rated as long as 20,000 hours—over two years of continuous light! Longest life is best achieved, however, if the light is left on for long periods without being turned off and on frequently. Fluorescent lamps come in many shapes, with the most common being the 4-feet-long, 1½-diameter tube called T12. Fluorescent fixtures typically hold two or four of these lamps.

The color of fluorescent light varies significantly depending on the type of phosphors used in the lamp. Some light makes red and green look dull and brown. I once visited a vet clinic where the fluorescent lights were being replaced because they gave a whitish cast to a horse's gums—a distinct drawback when trying to assess the health of a horse's mucus membranes!

Fluorescent fixtures contain a part called a ballast, which regulates current. The type of ballast determines how well a fluorescent fixture performs. Bargain fixtures often use cheap ballasts that might only last two to four years.

Preheat ballast fixtures are the most readily available. They are also the slowest to start. They use standard T12 lamps, and work well to 50°F. Below that temperature they can dim appreciably, flicker, and be difficult to start. They have separate starters that preheat or jump start the lamps with an extra boost of electricity. Starters need to be replaced periodically. (It's a good idea to replace them whenever the lamps are replaced.) Preheat lamps have a two-pin cap on each end.

Instant-start (cold-start) fixtures use a higher starting voltage to provide full light output instantly. They some-

---

FLUORESCENT LAMP TERMINOLOGY

Example: F40CW-T12

F = fluorescent
40 = wattage
CW = color:
  CW (cool white), WW (warm white), BL (black light)
T = tubular
12 = diameter in 8ths of an inch
  (8 = 8/8 = 1 inch; 12 = 12/8 = 1½ inchs, etc.)

---

times make a bothersome hum and the higher starting voltage can shorten lamp life. You can spot instant-start fixtures by the single-pin caps at the ends of the lamps; all other types have two pins.

Rapid-start fixtures come on quickly and make less hum than instant start fixtures. They are the most popular fluorescent fixture for commercial use.

Cold temperature, or 0 (zero) ballast, fixtures work well to 0°F and use standard T12 lamps. These fixtures usually need to be special ordered.

Consider using 240-watt instead of 120-watt fixtures. They require less amperage so you can run more fixtures per circuit. Some fixtures can be installed to use either wattage.

COMPACT FLUORESCENT LAMPS Manufactured since the early 1980s, compact fluorescent lamps (CFLs) with an Edison screw-base provide a long-lasting, energy-efficient substitute for standard incandescent bulbs. Ranging from 5 to 40 watts, screw-in CFLs are available in two types: integral units, which combine the lamp and ballast, and modular units in which the lamp can be replaced separately from the ballast. Although CFLs are relatively expensive, $10.00 to $20.00, they can provide energy savings of 60 to 75 percent over a standard incandescent bulb and last ten times longer: 10,000 hours.

CFLs do, however, have significant drawbacks. Even though the base fits, the lamps themselves are generally bigger than incandescent bulbs and they won't fit into some fixtures; like larger fluorescent lamps, CFLs may not start or light well in temperatures under 50°F; they can affect the accuracy of colors; some types may produce an annoying flicker and cause radio interference.

HID (HIGH INTENSITY DISCHARGE) HID lamps were originally developed in the 1930s for outdoor applications such as street lamps (fig. 9.10). HID lamps typically consist of a sealed arc tube inside a glass bulb. The inner arc tube is filled with a mixture of gases (vapor) that emit light when ionized by electric current. The color of emitted light depends on the gases within the lamp, which may include sodium, metal halide, and mercury. Metal halide lamps have the most natural light, mercury lamps produce a blue-green light, and sodium lights produce a golden light. Like fluorescent lamps, HID lamps require ballasts to provide the proper starting voltage and to regulate current during operation.

Available from 35 to 1,500 watts, some types of HID lamps have the longest life (5,000 to 27,000 hours) of any type of lamp. HID lights are the most efficient light sources to run but the most expensive to buy. A 150-watt metal halide fixture and lamp, for example, costs over $100.00 compared with $10.00 to $20.00 for a 150-watt quartz fixture and lamp. HID lamps need two to six minutes to warm-up, and, when they are turned off (or the power is interrupted), they need between five and fifteen minutes to start up again. Because of this, HID lights are not good where they would be turned on and off frequently but would be well worth considering for an arena, yard light, or a barn where lights are on for long periods.

HOW MUCH LIGHT IS ENOUGH? The amount of light you need depends on the space, the task, and the location of the light. Materials used on the inside of the barn will determine how light is distributed. Dark-colored surfaces such as walnut-stained wood or black rubber mats absorb a lot of light. Light surfaces, on the other hand, such as bare concrete and white insulation board (see Chapter 6, Materials), reflect light, so less light is required to illuminate the space.

You can get an idea of how much illumination various lamps provide by visiting barns and other buildings and taking note of the type, wattage, and placement of lights. A single 100-watt incandescent bulb might be adequate in

9.10 *HID (high intensity discharge) light.*

one feed room, while another feed room might require several 100-watt bulbs. For a 10-foot by 12-foot stall, a single 150-watt quartz fixture or a fluorescent fixture with two 40-watt lamps mounted 11 feet high is usually sufficient. In a 12-foot by 12-foot tack room, plan on at least three 100-watt incandescent or 80-watt fluorescent lamps. Outdoors, a 300-watt halogen or HID fixture mounted 12 feet high will light an area 50 feet away well enough to be able to clean a pen after dark, and it will light an area 100 feet away to allow most people to walk safely.

MAKING A PLAN Good barn lighting doesn't just happen, it is planned. Write down specific lighting instructions at the beginning of the barn project. Otherwise, the contractor might place light fixtures where they are easiest to install, not where they will do the most good. Planning barn lighting includes determining the type, size, number, and placement of light fixtures. It also includes locating enough outlets for temporary and emergency plug-in task lighting. For example, outlets near each stall and in the grooming area will allow you to plug in portable lights for vet or foal care.

Choose light fixtures that put light where you need it. Lights should provide adequate illumination for the activity and be placed so as to prevent shadows on your work. Fixtures placed at the four corners or along each side of a grooming area or wash rack, for example, will provide more even, useful light than fixtures placed directly overhead. Nondirectional lights like fluorescents that flood an area with light are good for *ambient lighting.* Hooded incandescent or quartz fixtures that focus light directly on a specified area are good for task lighting such as over a sink or desk. Be sure to locate task lighting so it doesn't glare in your eyes as you do your work.

If you are planning to improve lighting in an existing barn, walk around and through the barn at night with the lights on and make notes of areas that need better lighting (fig. 9.11). When planning a new barn, start with a floor plan and imagine everything you'll be doing in the barn and where you'd do it. To locate switches where they'll be most convenient, walk through the floor plan in your mind, imagining yourself turning lights on as you enter an area and turning lights off as you leave. Switches should be located along the main traffic routes of the barn at a convenient level, usually 4 feet from the floor. Determine if some lights, such as the main aisle lights, need to be operated from two or more locations. Indicate lights, switches, and outlets on the plan and label lights L1, L2, L3, etc., switches S1, S2, S3, etc., and outlets O1,

---

AVOID GLARE

The entire barn should be lighted evenly so your eyes don't have to adjust to dramatic changes from very dark to very light areas. Glare, such as from bare bulbs, disrupts vision due to a phenomenon called phototropic impulse, where the eye is instinctively drawn to and adjusts to the brightest light source in the area. Likewise, sunlight streaming through windows can make it difficult to see darker areas adjacent to the windows. If you've photographed or videotaped a horse in an indoor arena with windows along the side, you know what I mean. The higher the windows are on the walls, the less glare they produce at eye level. Translucent fiberglass panels diffuse sunlight, providing a more even, less glaring light than clear glass.

O2, O3 and so on. On another paper describe details of each labeled item on the plan. Figure a cost estimate and make a shopping list. A list might begin like this:

L1 40-watt, 4-foot double fluorescent, grooming area

L2 40-watt, 4-foot double fluorescent, grooming area

S1 Single pole switch, grooming area

L3 95-watt incandescent in "jelly jar," grain room

S2 Single pole switch, grain room

L4 300-watt quartz, aisle

S3 Three-way switch for aisle

O1 North stall

O2, O3 Grooming area

Don't forget to include outdoor lights. On a dark night, a little extra light is quite welcome. A light high on the barn can make walking to and from the barn at night safer. If you need to handle a horse after dark, a light over a pen is better than holding a flashlight in your teeth. Glare is especially important to avoid for outdoor lights because of the extreme contrast between darkness and bright light. Place outdoor lights high so they do not create glare in the line of vision or very low as with path lights. For path lights, a hood can be used to direct the

9.11 *A good way to evaluate the lighting of an existing building is to walk through and around it at night, making notes and sketches of where to add or increase lights.*

light away from the eyes and onto the ground. Be careful where you place path lights so a loose horse can't contact them. When positioning lights under a roof overhang, make sure the roof doesn't shade the light from illuminating what you want to see.

SWITCHES Single pole switches operate lights from one location. Three-way switches control lights from two locations. *Four-way switches* are used in conjunction with three-way switches to operate lights from three or more locations. Waterproof switches should be used outside and in areas that might get wet, such as wash racks (see fig. 9.2, p. 99). Make sure switches next to stalls cannot be reached by horses. For fluorescent lights, avoid switches that say "incandescent only."

Outside lights can be controlled automatically by a light sensor (photocell) to come on at dusk and turn off at dawn. Some outdoor fixtures have a photocell built in; you can add separate photocells to the wiring of existing fixtures. Make sure no lights are aimed at the photocell or the light will go out as soon as it comes on! A yard light that's on all night is good for security but be aware that the light will affect your view of the stars and may annoy your neighbors. Wire all automatically controlled lights to a manual switch as well so they can be turned off when desired.

Motion sensors can turn lights on automatically to warn of intruders, scare away deer, or light up a path as you approach the barn. Infrared switches turn lights on when they detect heat from an approaching person (or dog, deer, or other warm body). The sensors must have a direct line of sight to detect motion in a given area. Ultrasonic sensors use high-frequency sound waves above the range of normal human hearing to detect movement of objects, whether warm or cold. Ultrasonic sensors usually can detect small movements and do not require a direct line of sight to occupants, but wind-blown leaves and other debris can trigger the lights.

An adjustable time-delay feature on motion sensor switches allows you to specify how long the lights stay on after motion is detected. A long time delay reduces the chance of the sensor turning off the lights while you're still in the area but wastes energy if the light is frequently activated by animals or blowing debris.

Have you ever wished you could control the barn lights from your house? Remote control units using X10 technology make that possible. They send FM signals through your existing wiring to operate lights connected to X10 switches at distant locations. A controller plugged in the house, for example, can operate lights at the barn and along the path to the barn, just as long as the lights are powered by the same electrical service. Note: some equipment using similar technology, such as plug-in intercoms, might interfere with X10 controllers.

9.12 *Jelly jar and grille.*

9.13 *Plastic conduit and incandescent bulb inside a jelly jar.*

SAFETY

Faulty wiring and light fixtures are common causes of barn fires. Use only fixtures having a UL label. All lamps in a barn should be protected from dust and impact (figs. 9.12 and 9.13). Dust and cobwebs on a bulb not only reduce light output but can be a real fire hazard because the heat from the bulb could ignite them. Light bulbs break easily upon impact and can result in injury from shards of glass and fire from the hot filament. One way to protect incandescent and HID lamps is by using a sturdy glass cover, sometimes called a "jelly jar," along with a metal grille. This will reduce light output, however, especially when the glass cover gets coated with dust. Fluorescent lamps should be protected by a plastic cover and by a moisture-proof cover in a wash rack or other wet area.

The best protection is to keep fixtures out of reach. Don't underestimate the reach of a rearing horse. Light fixtures in a stall should be at least 11 feet from the

9.14 *Automatic waterer.*
Photo courtesy of Nelson Waterers.

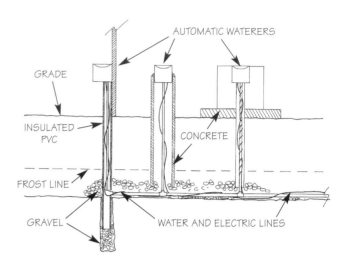

9.15 *Automatic waterers: left, on a wall (utilizing ground heat to prevent freezing); middle, on a pipe; right, on a pad.*

SOURCE

If your barn will be connected to the city water system, the most important thing you need to know is where the main shutoff *valve* is located so in case a pipe breaks or you need to work on the barn plumbing you can turn the water off.

If you have a domestic well, you may be able to tap into your existing house water lines and utilize the pressure tank in the house. Most likely, you will want a separate pressure tank in the barn. Consult a plumber for advice on the best size and where to locate it.

Choose a watering system that will fit your horse-keeping style and that will ensure your horses always have access to fresh water.

AUTOMATIC WATERING

Installing an automatic waterer properly involves considerable planning, labor, and expense, but once it's in place it can provide your horse with a constant, labor-free supply of fresh drinking water (fig. 9.14). But, if not installed properly and monitored regularly, an automatic waterer can give you a false sense of security. Unless the waterer is equipped with a water consumption indicator (see Nelson Mfg. Co. in the Resource Guide) or you actually see a horse drinking, you don't know if he is getting water, and even then you can't determine how much he is drinking. You might assume your horse is drinking sufficient water when, in fact, he is not. Or you might go to the barn one day and find your horse's stall has become a pond or skating rink because the shut-off valve malfunctioned, a water pipe froze and burst, or Mr. Ed found a new toy.

An automatic waterer is comprised of a water bowl, a valve, and a housing or base, which contains plumbing and electrical components. Some mount on a wall, some on a vertical concrete or PVC pipe set in the ground, and others bolt to a concrete pad (fig. 9.15). One waterer can serve two stalls when installed in the wall between the stalls. The wall is cut out, or built around the waterer so a horse on either side can drink. The space between the waterer and the wall should be minimal to prevent a horse from getting a foot caught and to discourage playing and fighting between horses.

Electric lines are needed to keep the units from freezing and water lines must be buried below frost line. Underground water and electric supply lines are brought to the waterer in a trench and connected within or beneath the waterer's housing. The occurrence and depth of rock at the site will influence the practicality of installing automatic waters. Decide before excavators leave the site if you want automatic waterers. They are more difficult and costly to install once the barn is underway.

There are three types of valves used to regulate water in the bowl.

1. A float valve buoyed up by the water. The float connects to a lever arm that opens the valve when the water level goes down and closes the valve when the bowl fills.
2. A paddle valve activated by a horse pressing a paddle close to the water surface. Water flows in when the horse presses the paddle and stops when the horse stops pressing.
3. A balance valve kept closed by the weight of the water in the water bowl. As the bowl empties, the valve opens to refill the bowl and then closes as the bowl gets heavy with water.

Manufacturers provide detailed installation instructions for their specific models. It helps to know ahead of time what materials and labor are involved in properly installing any type of automatic waterer outdoors or inside a building.

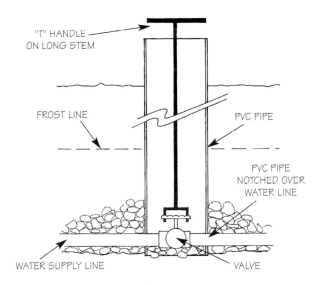

FROST LINE

Frost line varies from 0 in the southern-most states, to around 3 feet in the middle states to over 5 feet in the northern United States and Canada. Ask your building department or excavation contractors who have operated in the area for several years what the local frost line is. Even inside an enclosed building, pipes should extend below frost line. In warm regions, bury water lines deep to protect them from freak freezes, which are increasingly common. Water expands with incredible force when it freezes, and if frost reaches your buried water pipes they can burst. Locating and repairing broken water pipes can be a time-consuming, costly job even in warm weather. In the dead of winter it's near impossible. You may be forced to turn off the water supply to the broken line and wait until spring to start digging. For sound winter sleep, bury deep.

9.16 *Shutoff valve.*

PREPARING FOR INSTALLATION Determine where you will tap into water and electric lines and plan the trench route. You'll need a trench at least 4-inches wide and deeper than the frost line. Water and electric lines are laid in the bottom of the trench and brought vertically to the surface at the waterer location.

Be sure to install an accessible water shutoff valve somewhere between the main water line and the waterer. If anything goes wrong with the waterer, you want to be able to quickly turn off the water. One way to do this is to install a valve in the supply pipe that lies in the trench (fig. 9.16). Notch a 6-inch diameter PVC pipe and set it over the valve and the water line. This access pipe extends above the ground and is fitted with a removable cap. To open and close the valve, use a long steel rod with a handle on the top end and prongs that engage the valve handle on the other end.

MOUNTING ON A PIPE Round waterers designed to mount on the end of a pipe set in the ground are especially safe for horses. Some models mount in 12-inch or 15-inch diameter concrete pipe and others in 15-inch diameter PVC pipe.

Concrete pipe with slight defects such as chips on the ends are often sold at a discount and can be suitable for a base, especially if the damaged end is set in the ground. The pipe needs to be long enough to extend down to the service trench below frost line and above ground level at least 2 feet. If there is no frost in your locale, the pipe should be least 2 feet deep for stability. Twelve-inch diameter concrete pipe weighs around 100 pounds per foot, so you'll need several strong people or equipment such as a tractor with a loader to set the pipe upright in

the hole. If you hire a *backhoe* to dig the trench, have the operator set the pipe before leaving. Have four or five pails of gravel on hand to cover the bottom of the hole at least 12-inches deep for drainage.

Seal between the edge of the waterer and the top of the concrete pipe with caulking or *grout*.

MOUNTING ON A PAD Some automatic waterers mount on a concrete pad. Sharp edges and corners of the pad should be rounded before the concrete sets to prevent injury to the horse. The unit is usually anchored by means of galvanized bolts set at least 2½ inches into the concrete when it is poured. If mounting bolts are not included, use ⅜-inch by 4-inch galvanized *carriage bolts* or a 4-inch-long piece of ⅜-inch diameter threaded galvanized rod that is bent at the bottom end to secure it in the concrete. A template is included with the waterer for positioning the mounting bolts in the concrete. As the concrete sets, check the bolts for spacing and alignment.

If you are mounting the waterer on existing concrete, drill holes in the concrete with a masonry bit and secure the automatic waterer using ⅜-inch *anchor bolts*. If the unit does not set level, use zinc-plated washers to shim between the housing and the concrete.

MOUNTING ON A WALL Wall-mount waterers are commonly used in stalls. The wall, whether wood, metal, or concrete, must be thick enough and dense enough to hold the fasteners.

With a wood wall, ⅜-inch by 2-inch *lag screws* are commonly used. A wall of metal-covered wood less than 1-inch thick, popular in prefabricated stalls, is not thick enough to hold a lag screw securely. Instead, use carriage bolts, which go completely through the wall. If the bolts project into another stall, cut them off flush with the nut and file them smooth or use rounded acorn nuts, which cover the ends of the bolts.

With a poured concrete or concrete block wall, ⅜-inch diameter *expansion bolts* are used. These bolts have a sleeve the length of the thread that expands to grip the side of the hole as the bolt is tightened. You will need to drill holes in the wall for the bolts using a masonry bit. If the unit does not meet the wall flat, use galvanized washers to shim between the wall and the waterer.

Water and electrical lines for a wall-mounted units can be installed inside the wall or enclosed in a steel or thick-walled plastic pipe. The pipe should be set tight against the wall to prevent trapping a horse's foot.

WATERLINE FREEZE PROTECTION You can prevent an automatic waterer from freezing by using ground heat, electric heat, or both. Natural ground heat can be utilized by extending a hole beneath the waterer from 1 foot to 4 feet below frost line, depending on the manufacturer's recommendation (fig. 9.15). This could mean digging a hole up to 10-feet deep, in which case a backhoe would be essential. The hole is lined with 8-inch to 12-inch diameter drain tile, PVC pipe, or specially designed insulated liner pipe. The water supply pipe and electric line enter a hole in the liner at the level of the supply trench and rise in the center of the liner to the waterer. The water supply pipe should not contact the mounting base or the liner pipe or it will be likely to freeze at that point. Do not fill the space between the water pipe and the liner with insulation. Air from below the frost line, which is a relatively warm 50°F, must be free to rise through the liner and warm the water pipe and the water bowl.

Depending on the installation, ground heat can prevent water pipes from freezing even in sub-zero temperatures.

9.17 *Water bucket.*

But ground heat alone usually won't prevent water in the bowl from freezing when the temperature inside the barn drops below 20°F for more than a day. Most automatic waterers offer optional heaters that automatically turn on when the temperature drops to 40°F or so.

One way to ensure the water supply pipe doesn't freeze is to wrap it with electric heat cable (see Insulating and Heating Pipes, p. 111). Heat cable is available in hardware and building supply stores or supplied by the automatic waterer manufacturer. The cable comes in various lengths and has a sensor that turns on the cable at around 40°F. As with the ground heat method, the water supply riser pipe is inside of a 6-inch to 8-inch diameter liner pipe, which protects the heat cable from damage and helps insulate the water pipe from the frozen earth. Heating cables are one of the main causes of barn fires. If you use them they must be installed properly and inspected at least once a year.

MANUAL WATERING

Filling a bucket, tub, or tank manually enables you to monitor if and how much your horse is drinking (fig. 9.17). A bucket secured by a wall bracket is the most common manual watering method for stalls, with an emphasis on manual. In order for a horse to have fresh water, buckets must be filled three to five times daily and scrubbed regularly. A bucket or tub that sets on the floor is not appropriate for a stall. A bucket can be knocked over and a tub is difficult to clean without getting the stall floor wet.

Mount the bucket on the stall's aisle wall, if possible, so it can be filled with a hose without entering the stall. To keep water clean, mount the bucket as far as is convenient from hay and grain feeders.

Plan to have a faucet or hydrant within 50 feet of every stall to allow filling buckets with a hose of manageable length.

To prevent water buckets in stalls from freezing you can use a freeze-proof bucket, a heated bucket holder, or an insulated bucket holder. Any electric watering device must be installed in a way that makes the cord inaccessible to the horse.

A freeze-proof bucket has thermostat-controlled electric coils embedded in the walls of the bucket. It must be mounted so the cord can be unplugged each time the bucket is removed for cleaning.

A heated bucket holder attaches to a stall wall and holds a standard water bucket. You can change the bucket without having to unplug the bucket heater.

An insulated bucket holder uses no electricity and holds a standard 5-gallon bucket. Insulation in the walls and bottom of the holder, plus a plastic or Styrofoam disc that floats on top of the water, conserve heat from the water to delay freezing. The colder the air, the more frequently the water in the bucket needs to be changed to keep it from freezing. Unless the temperature in the barn is below 20°F, an insulated bucket holder will keep water ice free for at least several hours.

PIPE

The type of pipe you use for waterlines is often personal preference—what you or the plumber are accustomed to working with. But check local codes because some will not allow anything but copper pipe with nonlead *solder* joints. Use ¾-inch diameter or larger supply lines for a barn because you often need a generous flow of water such as when washing a horse or filling a waterer. When working with plastic pipe, be sure to purchase glue that is suitable for the specific plastic you're using.

COPPER   Copper tubing is still the traditional choice for water lines. It is sold in straight sections and in rolls and in a variety of diameters and weights. Type K, type L, and type M, from heaviest to lightest, are typically used for water-supply lines. Although copper is resistant to corrosion, it doesn't work well with some well water or soft, acidic water. Even so, copper will last a long time unless you have really corrosive water.

Copper lines are joined with lead-free, solid-core solder in a process called *sweating*. The biggest danger for a typical do-it-yourself person is setting something on fire when sweating joints that are near combustibles. Plastic pipe is less expensive and easier for most people to install. It is also more resistant to corrosion. There are many types of plastic pipes and some are better suited for specific uses than others are.

POLYETHYLENE (PE)   Black polyethylene pipe is flexible, durable, lightweight, resistant to chemicals and oxidation, and tolerates repeated hard freezing. The pipe fits over ribbed plastic or metal fittings and is fastened with external clamps around the outside of the pipe. Use only all-stainless steel hose clamps from a plumbing supplier; screws on automotive clamps can rust. Softening the pipe by immersing the end into hot water makes is easier to slip over fittings.

PVC   PVC, polyvinyl chloride, is usually white or cream colored. It is typically used for vents, drains, and cold water lines. It distorts at around 170°F so is not often used for hot water lines and should not be used close to a water heater. Connections are made by roughening the joint surfaces with sandpaper (don't use steel wool as it only polishes the surface), cleaning the surfaces with a solvent (use a natural fiber cloth; the solvent will dissolve some synthetic fibers), applying special glue to both surfaces, and sliding the pieces together.

ABS   ABS, acrylonitrile butadiene styrene, pipe is primarily used for vents and drains. It is tough, has high impact strength, and is resistant to chemicals. Connections are made using a fast setting ABS glue that does not require primer.

CPVC   CPVC, chlorinated polyvinyl chloride, is a rigid plastic used for hot and cold water lines. It is less expensive than copper and it connects with glue the same as PVC. It is lightweight, easy to work with, and doesn't corrode.

PEX   PEX, cross-linked polyethylene, has many advantages over other types of pipe. It tolerates temperature extremes and is well-suited for use with both hot and cold water. It is flexible and freeze resistant, so it will not break as easily as other materials when frozen. It comes in white, red, and blue, which enables you to keep better track of water lines. And, unlike other plastic pipes that use messy glue, PEX connects mechanically, using a compression nut, ferrule, and ring.

INSULATING AND HEATING PIPES   Water pipes that are most at risk of freezing and bursting are those in unheated buildings, in uninsulated outside walls and crawl spaces of heated buildings, and inside automatic waterers. You can protect water pipes that are at risk by applying pipe insulation and/or heating cable. When installing plumbing in an insulated building, always install pipes on the warm side of insulation in walls, floors, and ceilings.

Insulation applied to pipes conserves heat from the water running through the pipes to keep them from freezing. Fiberglass insulation up to ½-inch thick and 3-inches wide comes in rolls and is wrapped around the pipe in a spiral. It either has a plastic or foil backing or comes with a separate moisture barrier that is applied over the fiberglass. A similar insulation is comprised of an aluminum sheet bonded to a ⅛-inch thick adhesive-backed foam. Closed cell polyethylene insulation comes in the form of a black tube 3-feet to 6-feet long that's split lengthwise to slip over a pipe. It is easier to apply than insulation that wraps around a pipe. All joints and fittings should be covered as well as the pipe. Pipe insulation is of limited value, but it might offer enough protection if temperatures do not drop below 20°F and if water runs through the pipes periodically. Sometimes, leaving a faucet trickling during a cold snap will keep a pipe from freezing solid.

Installing heat cable under pipe insulation is a more positive way to ensure that pipes won't freeze and burst. Heat cable plugs into an outlet and has a built-in thermostat that turns on at around 35°F and off at around 45°F. This is one case where more is not better—using *too much* insulation (e.g., more than a ½ inch of fiberglass) may cause the cable to overheat, causing fire. Plug the cable into a *GFCI* to prevent fire in case of a short circuit, unplug it when the outside temperature is above 50°F, and check it periodically for rodent damage.

Heat cable is secured to the pipe with electrician's tape or special cable application tape that will not come loose when it gets hot. The cable's thermostat is positioned at the coldest end of the pipe and should contact the pipe and be covered with insulation. Some cables are designed to wrap around the pipe while others run straight along the bottom of the pipe. Spiral applications require a much longer cable. Cables come in lengths from 3 feet to 100 feet, and there are usually instructions on the package to help you figure out how much cable you need. Wrapping plastic pipes with aluminum foil first will provide a more even heat distribution.

Study your instructions carefully. Some cables cannot be used closer than 1 foot to combustible materials, which rules out using them in most walls, floors, and ceilings! Never operate a heat cable on a plastic pipe that doesn't contain water and don't use heat cable on a garden hose. Finally, the time to install heat tape is in the cool of autumn, not the dead of winter.

FAUCETS

A *hose bibb (bibcock)* is a faucet to which a hose connects. A *sillcock* is a bibb with a flat back for fastening to a wall. A hydrant is a vertical pipe usually with a lever handle.

Regular faucets are compact and are designed with the shutoff valve at the handle. They can only be used where they are not subjected to freezing temperatures.

Freeze-proof faucets are built onto a pipe stem that projects into the wall of a heated room or building (fig. 9.18). Their shutoff valve is located at the end of the stem where it's warm. The stem slopes slightly downward toward the spout, so when the water is turned off it drains from the stem, preventing the spout from freezing. If the space behind a freeze-proof faucet isn't heated, the valve and waterline will freeze.

Freeze-proof yard hydrants are essential in cold climates and good insurance against freak freezes in areas that normally don't freeze (fig. 9.18). The shutoff valve on a freeze-proof hydrant is located at the bottom of the pipe, below frost line. A small drain hole next to the shutoff valve drains water from the vertical pipe when the hydrant is turned off. The water drains into a pocket of gravel placed below the stem when the hydrant is installed. Freeze-proof hydrants are available in a variety of lengths to accommodate frost depths in different areas. The spout should project high enough above the ground to fit a tall bucket under it. A hydrant installed in an aisle or other traffic area can cause injury to a horse and can be damaged by equipment or horses. Protect it by

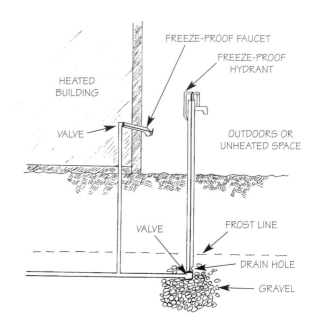

9.18 *Freeze-proof faucet and hydrant.*

installing one or two 6-inch diameter pipes or pressure-treated posts close to the hydrant but so they don't interfere with its operation.

TIP: Use "T" or "L" connections of galvanized steel, not plastic, for connecting supply lines to the bottom of a hydrant. When connecting poly (PE) pipe to metal fittings use double clamps, especially where the fittings will be buried.

WASTEWATER

Wastewater from the washing machine, wash rack, sink, and shower is called greywater, and you may have more than one option for dealing with it. Any water that contains toilet waste is classified as backwater, and it must drain into an approved septic system or city sewage system.

OPEN DRAIN Where open drains are legal, pointing the drain down the nearest hill is a simple, practical method of handling greywater, especially the low volume produced by a small barn. This method requires minimal materials, no electricity, no maintenance, is simple to build, and lasts indefinitely. On flat ground the soil may become over saturated and scum might accumulate on the ground along with odors. Also, surrounding plants may be killed by root suffocation and mosquitoes could use the stagnant water as a breeding ground.

DRY WELL Another alternative for handling greywater, if local regulations allow it, is to run the barn drain into a seepage pit, or *dry well* (fig. 9.19). This is an area where water is collected and allowed to percolate naturally into the surrounding soil. You can purchase ready-made plastic units in some areas or build your own. Specifications are not critical. Dig a pit at least 10 feet from the barn that is

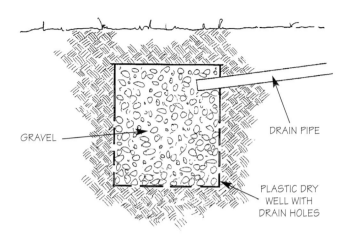

GRAVEL

DRAIN PIPE

PLASTIC DRY WELL WITH DRAIN HOLES

9.19 *Drywell.*

approximately 4 feet by 8 feet and that extends below frost line or at least 4-feet deep. Line the pit with *landscape fabric* (geotextile fabric) to prevent silt from clogging the dry well. Add a layer of clean gravel at least 2-feet deep. The drain should enter the dry well just below the top of the gravel. Cover the gravel with filter fabric and cover the dry well with soil. Again, check local code to see if dry wells are allowed.

SEPTIC TANK A *septic tank* is a buried concrete or steel tank that typically holds between 500 and 1,000 of wastewater. Sewer pipes bring wastewater by gravity into the septic tank at one end and water leaves the tank at the other end. Odiferous gases are produced in the septic tank as bacteria break down organic material. Every barn drain has a loop of pipe called a *trap* directly beneath it that holds water and blocks gases from flowing back into the barn (it also prevents vermin from entering through the drainpipe). The gases instead flow up a vent pipe *(stack)* that extends through the roof.

As new water enters the septic tank, it displaces water already there, which flows out into a drain field. A drain field is a series of perforated pipes (typically 4 inches in diameter) buried in gravel-filled trenches that are 2-feet wide and 4- to 6-feet deep. Gravel fills the bottom 2 to 3 feet of the trench and dirt covers the gravel. The water is slowly absorbed and filtered by the ground. The size of the drain field is determined by the percolation rate of the soil (how quickly it absorbs water). Clay soil requires a larger drain field than sandy soil does.

WATER HEATER
Hot water is essential for washing blankets, cleaning your hands between horses, and bathing horses, especially on a chilly day.

TANK Standard tank-type water heaters keep a certain volume of water hot at all times. A 30-gallon unit is

adequate for most small barns. If you don't use hot water very often or only in small quantities, keeping a large quantity hot all the time is not energy inefficient. One way to save energy is to install a switch on the water heater and turn it on an hour or so before you'll need hot water and turn if off when you are through. Water heaters require a separate circuit so you could use the circuit breaker as an on-off switch, since the water heater is the only thing on that circuit.

ON-DEMAND Tank-less or on-demand hot water systems heat water as needed as the water passes through copper tubes. They are about 1/3 more efficient than standard tank-type heaters and can handle the hot water needs of just about any barn. They are especially practical where hot water is used only occasionally. Some models are subject to lime deposits within the heating tubes, especially with hard water. This decreases efficiency and increases the cost of heating water. Installing a water softener in the waterline before the water heater can help.

No matter what type of water heater you choose, be sure to install an emergency *pressure relief valve* (which is required, but not always pre-installed) to prevent pipes from bursting in the event of a malfunction. Connect a hose or pipe to the valve outlet and run it to a drain or outdoors. I speak from experience when I say that the valve is bound to blow sooner or later, and without a hose connected to direct the torrent of hot water that is released, everything in the vicinity of the tank will be drenched.

SINKS AND LAVATORIES
A sink is a must for washing your hands after grooming a horse and for washing tack and equipment. A lavatory is a bathroom sink.

A pedestal or a wall-mount sink takes up little floor space so is a good choice in a small bathroom. A pedestal sink usually consists of a stand (base) and a sink. The sink mounts to a bracket on the wall and also sets on the stand.

A vanity cabinet with sink takes more floor space but provides storage underneath and counter space on top.

A kitchen sink can be set in any size counter and can be purchased in nearly any size, shape, and depth.

A utility or laundry sink is deeper than other sinks and is good for soaking and scrubbing buckets, tools, and tack.

Stainless steel restaurant-style sinks incorporating a long, one-piece drain board are great for a barn (see fig. 12.20, p. 158). The drain board provides a solid waterproof workplace to scrub and hose down tack and a place to set buckets and other containers to dry.

SHOWER
Few private barns warrant a shower, but you might consider installing one if you spend a lot of time at the barn

or if you have a large family and frequently find yourself vying for shower time. If you plan to board horses, a shower would give boarders a chance to clean up before heading home.

TOILET

Installing a conventional flush toilet takes planning and know-how. This might be the time to hire, or as least consult with a plumber.

An alternative is to use a composting toilet. Sometimes called biological toilets, dry toilets, and waterless toilets, these self-contained units hold and control the composting of waste without the need of a septic system. They are vented to the outdoors to eliminate odors. Some operate dry while others require a small amount of water at regular intervals.

Aerobic bacteria, molds, and fungi break down wastes to 10 to 30 percent of its original volume and produce a soil-like material called humus. In the U.S., state and local regulations often require humus to be either buried or removed by a licensed seepage hauler. In other countries, humus is used as a soil conditioner on edible crops.

Passive composting toilets are simply vented chambers in which waste is collected and allowed to decompose in cool environments. Active systems may feature automatic mixers, agitators, heaters, fans, and other accessories that speed up composting.

EMERGENCY WATER STORAGE

A horse needs approximately 10 gallons of water per day, more during hot weather and for lactating mares. Most barns rely on electricity to pump water. If electric service is disrupted, having an emergency water supply can minimize inconvenience for you and prevent dehydration in your horses. Don't rely on water standing in pastures because it can contain toxins from fertilizer, herbicides, and pesticides.

BACKUP ELECTRICITY FOR PUMPS If your barn is supplied by a municipal water system, the utility likely has emergency generators to run pumps in case of a general power failure. Call your local water department to find out if backup power is in place. If you have a private well, make sure you'll be able to get emergency power to your pump. A pump that plugs into an outlet can be plugged into a generator if necessary. A pump that is hard wired (connected directly to the barn's wiring) can be modified by an electrician to plug into an outlet (see Emergency Power, p. 106).

TUBS AND PONDS If you use tubs to water your horses, make it a practice to keep them filled with fresh water so they are always ready to carry your horses through a short power outage. If your property includes

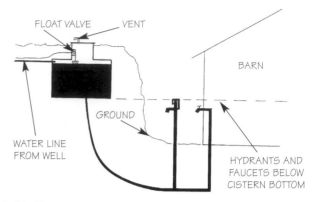

9.20 Cistern.

a natural source of water, such as a pond or creek, have it tested regularly so you know it is safe to use if you have to. Clear a safe approach to the water where you can lead each horse to the water twice a day, or fence in an area with safe access to the water's edge so each horse can be turned out to drink on his own.

CISTERN A concrete or plastic cistern located uphill from the barn can provide water to hydrants by gravity-flow during a power failure and can serve as a source of water for firemen (fig. 9.20). For a gravity system to work, the bottom of the cistern must be higher than the level of the hydrants and faucets at the barn. In cold climates a cistern should be buried so the bottom is below frost line and with 1 to 2 feet of earth over the top to keep the water from freezing. A riser pipe extends a foot or so above ground to provide access for taking water samples and for cistern cleaning and maintenance. In warm areas, the cistern can be above ground. Water stored in a cistern should be tested at least once a year by the county health department to make sure it's safe to drink.

Plastic cisterns are less expensive and easier to handle, but concrete cisterns are better for several reasons. They are less likely to collapse, and they are opaque so they keep out sunlight that promotes the growth of algae inside a cistern. A plastic cistern should have all exposed portions painted black or covered to keep it absolutely dark inside.

The riser and cap of a cistern should be sealed to keep the water inside from being contaminated by rain and snow runoff. It is critical that the cap is vented so air can escape when filling the cistern and enter when drawing water out. Without a vent, pumps will be strained and plastic cisterns are subject to collapse. If the cistern cap doesn't come with a vent, you can make one by drilling through the cap and installing a lawnmower air filter unit or similar apparatus that will let air in but keep dust and insects out.

Install a float valve or a float activated switch that will fill the cistern automatically when the water level drops.

PREVENTING PROBLEMS

You've designed your barn to withstand years of daily use and wear and tear from horses. But it will also be subjected to challenges from natural and unnatural sources that you might not have considered.

SECURITY

A burglar might be more likely to target your tack room than your house, especially if the barn is a considerable distance from the house and near a road.

Install locks on interior and exterior tack room doors and cover windows with grillwork or heavy screen that cannot easily be removed (fig. 9.21). Many modular barns offer window grilles as an option. For custom grilles, check your yellow pages for a local metal fabricator or blacksmith. Your farrier might be willing to make grilles or know someone to recommend.

To deter animal and human prowlers, locate outdoor lights around the barn that are activated by heat or motion.

Consider installing a closed circuit TV system to give you a view from your house of barn entrances, a foaling stall, and any other area you choose (fig. 9.22). It can help you spot intruders, keep an eye out for accidents, and enable you to observe the behavior of boarders and employees.

To make it easier to communicate between the barn and the house or other buildings, install a set of intercoms. One type simply plugs into a common outlet and uses FM signals to send audio signals through existing electrical wiring.

FIRE PROTECTION

Think of your fire plan constantly as you design your facility. Should a fire start in the barn, you want to know about it as soon as possible so you can contact firefighters and save your horses. Make sure the fire number is posted at all phones on the property. Design your barn so there are doors of sufficient size and number to get horses out of the barn quickly and safely. Develop an evacuation plan and practice it on a regular basis with everyone who uses your barn.

FIRE DETECTORS   A fire detector can alert you at the start of a barn fire. Smoke detectors used in houses (typically either ionization or photo cell) don't work well in a barn because dust and condensation can set them off or clog them. A better type for a barn is one that detects heat, either by recognizing changes in heat or by incorporating a small piece of special metal that melts at a very low temperature. These units are better at avoiding false alarms, but they may take longer to trip than a smoke detector.

A plug-in detector doesn't require batteries, although many units have batteries for backup when the main power fails. If you have more than one detector, wire

9.21 *Grillwork on tack room.*

9.22 *Closed-circuit TV and fire extinguisher.*

them in a series so that if one goes off they all do. Install a separate circuit for plug-in fire detectors so they would only become disabled by the main-panel breaker tripping. In the event of a fire caused by an electrical fault a main-panel breaker is unlikely to trip until the fire is well under way. If a fire should occur when the power is off, such as during a storm, plug-in detectors won't work unless they have a built-in battery backup.

Battery-powered units are reliable only if you keep fresh batteries in them—and that can be a big if. Make changing the battery a scheduled event, for example on your birthday, New Year's Day, or when daylight/standard time changes ("change your clocks, change your batteries").

The best solution is to use plug-in units that have battery backup built in or to install both plug-in and battery units. Contact your local fire department for recommendations.

Any type of fire detectors can fail if not properly maintained. The National Fire Protection Association (NFPA)

SECTION III

BUILDING

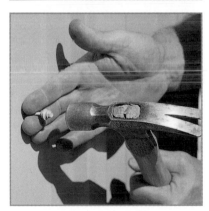

CHAPTER TEN

CONSTRUCTION

The better you understand the construction process, the more likely you will end up with the barn you want. Here I will describe the steps of barn construction and provide building tips along the way that can save you time and make building easier. Since horse barns are most commonly pole barns, I will give that type of construction the most emphasis. Check the Recommended Reading section in the back of this book for books that cover every aspect of pole building in detail.

KEEPING TRACK

If you catch yourself thinking, "I'll remember that," chances are you won't. Carry a notebook at all times to remind yourself of items you need to buy, issues you want to discuss with your builder, tasks that need to be done later. Throughout the building process, document various stages with sketches, notes, photos, and videos. This is especially important for those aspects that will be hidden from view such as trenches for buried utilities and electrical and plumbing in floors and walls (fig. 10.1). When the time comes to find a buried waterline, for example, a video showing the location of the trench and surrounding landmarks will be invaluable and save you the time and expense of trial and error digging. Likewise, keep all receipts, instructions, and warranties that come with materials, fixtures, and appliances, or make sure your subcontractors save them for you. Designate one box or drawer for barn records and be religious about collecting them.

If you are getting a loan for the barn, be certain to discuss with the lender when building can begin. Some lenders do not want any work to take place, not even a survey, until the loan is in place.

The number of inspections required as construction proceeds will likely be stated on your building permit. They depend on local requirements and the complexity of your barn (see Inspections, p. 5).

LAYOUT

Flags on wires or stakes are used to mark off the barn site and surrounding pens to give the excavator an idea of what to do. You may need a survey, especially if you are close to a property line where you have to consider *setbacks* and *easements*.

SITE PREPARATION

GRADING

Site grading involves removing trees and brush and then making a flat area where the barn will stand. Use flagging tape (brightly colored plastic ribbon available at building supply stores) to mark trees and bushes you want to save around the barn site and make sure you point them out to your excavator and other workers.

10.1 *A print or video can later help you locate buried components that require repair or replacement.*

10.2 *Building site higher than surrounding ground.*

FRENCH DRAIN

A *French drain* directly below the eaves can carry roof runoff away so it doesn't wash through pens (fig. 10.3). This is a gravel-filled trench approximately 30-inches deep by 24-inches wide with a drainpipe in the bottom. Slope the trench slope a minimum of ⅛-inch per foot toward a drainage area. Line the trench with landscape fabric (geotextile fabric, sold at garden supply stores for weed barrier) to prevent the tile and gravel from being plugged by dirt. Extend the fabric up past the sides of the trench far enough to cover the top of the gravel once it is installed. Lay a 4-inch diameter perforated PVC or equivalent drainpipe (tile) at the bottom of the trench with the holes facing the bottom. Fill the trench with ¾-inch drain field gravel to within 8 inches of the top. Cover the gravel by bringing together and overlapping the fabric from both sides. If the drain is in a horse pen, install a layer of rigid permeable material, such as draining stall flooring (Equustall or Groundmaster are two examples) over the fabric to prevent a horse from pawing through the gravel and ripping the fabric. Finish with a 4-inch-thick layer of 2-inch rock followed by a 4-inch layer of road base or gravel to ground level.

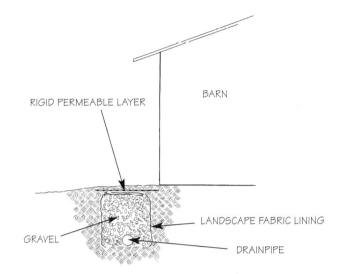

10.3 *French drain.*

10.4 *A building site being cut into a hillside.*

Rain from the area covered by the barn dumps on a line below the eaves. To keep this water from running into the barn, the floor of the barn should be at least 6 to 12 inches higher than surrounding ground (fig. 10.2). Also, the ground should slope away from the barn ¼-inch to ½-inch per foot in all directions so water drains quietly away from the building. A steeper slope can cause erosion from rushing water. Now is the time to taking steps to control mud around the barn. It is harder to do once the barn and pens are in place.

The stall portion of the site must be prepared so that the soil percolates well in order to disperse urine, especially if you plan to use draining flooring. This could involve excavating to a depth of 8 feet and filling the hole with layers of rock, large rock on the bottom and increasingly smaller rocks toward the top. Your builder or county agent can help you determine the percolation rate of your soil.

On a hillside you'll need to cut into the hill and use the dirt to extend a level pad on the downhill side (fig. 10.4). You can either compact the filled area to requirements specified in local building code or let the site stand for a full year to settle. The floor of a barn built on a freshly filled site that is not properly compacted could settle as much as 10 inches the first year.

Cut a diversion ditch around the uphill side of the barn to direct runoff from the hill around the barn.

UTILITY SERVICE

Temporary power is needed at the outset so workers can run their tools. Often this is a weatherproof cable run on the ground from the service meter to the job site. Temporary power is installed by the electrical subcontractor and usually need to be inspected before it can be turned on.

Trenches for utilities are dug after initial grading of the site to ensure optimum final depth (fig. 10.5). Water is brought to the barn by pipes buried below frost line or to the minimum depth specified by local codes. Electric and phone lines are buried to code depth or strung overhead on poles (if code allows). Water and electric lines are trenched into the barn and brought out of the ground at the location of automatic waterers (see

Automatic Watering, p. 108). Building codes commonly allow multiple utility lines be in the same trench with a specified amount of separation between layers.

There are three ways to dig a trench for the service lines: by hand with a shovel, using a trencher to make a narrow trench, or using a backhoe to make a wide trench.

The practicality of digging a trench by hand will be determined by the required distance and depth of the trench and the availability and enthusiasm of manpower.

An easier way to slot the earth is with a self-propelled, walk-behind, or ride-along trencher. You can either hire an excavation professional with a trencher or you can rent a trencher and operate it yourself. If you rent a trencher you will also likely have to rent a trailer to haul it, unless you have a pickup or a trailer into which you can load and haul this heavy piece of equipment.

A backhoe is considerably larger than a trencher. It consists of a large articulating arm, usually mounted on the back of a tractor, to which different sizes of shovels can be attached. Again, you can either hire a professional or rent a backhoe and do it yourself. One advantage of a backhoe is that it can be used to widen the trench where you tap into the existing utility line so there is room for a person to get down and do the work.

Trenches often must be *backfilled* with sand, so plan ahead and have it delivered beforehand. Backfill the trenches as soon as you can after they are inspected to avoid accidents or cave-ins. Use fence or portable panels to keep people, horses, and other animals away from open trenches.

One thing you definitely want to avoid is accidentally digging up an existing utility line. Most states have a nonprofit utility notification center, such as One Call, that is funded by member facility owners and operators. These centers act as a messaging service between excavators and utility companies and are designed to locate buried utilities of all types before excavation takes place. Here's how they work:

- the property owner or excavator phones One Call

- One Call notifies companies with utilities near the excavation area

- each utility company sends out a person (usually at no charge) to locate and mark the service on the ground with spray paint or flags or both

These services are far from foolproof, however, because not all utilities participate and not all utilities are correctly located and marked. Nevertheless, taking advantage of a service such as One Call might save you from injury and the expense of repairing damaged utilities and also avoid inconvenience to the public from disrupted service.

If you damage an underground utility, immediately call the specific company involved and your local One Call office using the emergency or repair number listed in the phone book. One Call will contact all member utility companies in the area in case they need to do extra locating to allow repair work to continue. Keep all people and animals away from the damaged utility until it is repaired. In addition, take the following precautions:

ELECTRICAL LINE Do not touch equipment that is touching the electric line. Turn off power to the line if you have access to the switch.

GAS LINE Evacuate the area immediately. Shut off all equipment in the vicinity and curtail all activities that might cause a spark.

FIBER-OPTIC LINE Do not to look into the cut ends of the cable because severe eye damage can result.

WATER OR SEWER LINE Shut off water to the line if you can. Sewer lines may contain deadly pathogens. Seek medical attention for persons coming in contact with a broken sewer line.

10.5 *Trenches for water and electric lines.*

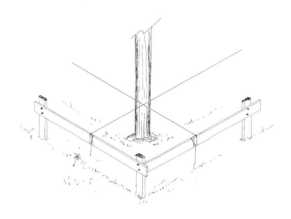

10.6 *Batter boards.*

FOOTINGS

Footings are part of the foundation and the lowermost concrete supports for the barn. For a pole barn they usually consist of a 4-inch to 6-inch thick pad of concrete at the bottom of the pole holes. You may be required to widen the bottom of the pole holes into a bell shape in order to get a pad large enough to satisfy the 16-inch or so diameter required by local code. Belling out the bottom of an 8-inch hole can be slow, arduous work, especially since all loose dirt should be removed from the holes before concrete is added. It's often easier to use a larger posthole auger to begin with.

For a masonry barn, a continuous footing around the perimeter of the barn is usually required. Footings are commonly 16 inches wide by 6 inches deep. A backhoe is essential to dig a trench wide enough for workers to assemble and disassemble concrete forms.

The person laying the footing will need to know where the corners of the building should be. If you had the site surveyed, the surveyor likely drove metal offset stakes just beyond the digging area where they would not be disturbed by excavating. If so, make sure you and the excavator know where the stakes are—it will cost you to have them reset if they are disturbed by equipment. If you lay out the building yourself, *batter boards* can assure footings get installed where they should.

Before concrete is poured, the building inspector will want to make sure the footings are the proper depth and dimensions and that they will be on solid ground, with no roots or loose dirt in the bottom of the holes or trenches.

BATTER BOARDS

After the site is graded, set batter boards to guide the placement of the foundation (fig. 10.6). A batter board consists of two horizontal boards nailed to stakes driven parallel to each wall. Use a long tape measure to lay out the approximate location of the corners of your barn. Place a temporary stake or rock at each corner. Measure diagonally across the corner markers to get the barn approximately square. Measurements should be equal. Drive 2 x 4 stakes for batter boards 6 feet outside the perimeter of the building. The stakes should be securely in the ground and far enough away from the building site to remain undisturbed during placement of the foundation. Attach boards to the stakes approximately 16 inches from the ground. (TIP: When nailing to a stake, hold a heavy hammer or a flat rock against the back of the stake to keep it steady.) Stretch builder's cord between the batter boards (see String Line, p. 139) so the strings cross directly over the corners of the barn. Adjust the strings on the batter boards so the diagonal measurements from where the strings intersect are equal. Make a pencil line on each board where the string lays. Move the strings an inch or so and make a shallow cut with a hand saw on the line. Slide the strings into the saw cuts and recheck your measurements. The saw cut enables you to remove the string lines to allow movement of workers and equipment and put them back in the correct position when it's time to set poles, blocks, or concrete forms. The strings will line up exactly where the barn should be as long as the batter boards are not disturbed. To find the layout below ground level, drop a plumb bob from the point where the strings intersect.

FOUNDATION

Make an effort to keep all barn elements from footings to the roof plumb, level, and square. This will make installation of all subsequent parts—sheathing, siding, and roofing—easier.

CONCRETE

Timber framed and other wood framed barns (except pole barns) usually require a foundation *stem wall* of poured concrete (commonly 8-inches thick) or of concrete block. The stem wall sets on and attaches to the footings and extends above the ground (usually at least 8 inches) to protect the framing and siding from moisture (fig. 10.7). Dimensions and depth of concrete foundations are regulated by local code. Modular barns can usually be set on concrete piers *(caissons),* stem walls, or slabs, and modular barn companies provide instructions and specifications to people who prefer to do their own foundation work.

10.7 *Concrete foundation for a modular barn.*

POLE

With a pole barn, the poles form the foundation and the initial wall framing. The diameter and spacing of poles will depend on the design of the barn. Some poles might be bent, and they should be set so the bend lies parallel with the wall rather than bending in or out.

When setting poles, set the four corner poles, check

10.8 *Temporary pole bracing.*

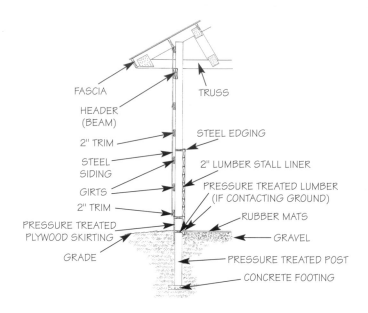

FASCIA

HEADER (BEAM)

2" TRIM

STEEL SIDING

GIRTS

2" TRIM

PRESSURE TREATED PLYWOOD SKIRTING

GRADE

TRUSS

STEEL EDGING

2" LUMBER STALL LINER

PRESSURE TREATED LUMBER (IF CONTACTING GROUND)

RUBBER MATS

GRAVEL

PRESSURE TREATED POST

CONCRETE FOOTING

10.9 *Pole barn section.*

the diagonal measurements at the tops of the poles to make sure they are equal, and brace each pole to two stakes. Framing members are stabilized by each other and by final *bracing* when the barn is finished, but while it is being built, temporary braces are often needed to hold members in place (fig. 10.8). *Duplex nails*, which have double heads, are used for braces because the second head allows them to be easily removed. Stretch a string line around the tops of the four corner poles to use with the batter board string line to set the remaining poles.

SPLASHBOARD AND SKIRTING

A *splashboard* or skirtboard of pressure-treated wood, usually 2 x 8 or 2 x 10, is attached to the outside of the poles, extending 4 inches or more below ground and 4 inches or more above ground (see fig. 8.8, p. 88). It serves to keep small animals and weather out of the barn and to raise the bottom edge of siding off the ground. It also provides a place to firmly attach the bottom of siding to prevent injury to a horse.

I prefer a wider skirting design that consists of ½-inch pressure-treated plywood attached to treated 2 x 4s nailed between the posts (fig. 10.9). A 2-foot wide plywood skirt extends one foot below and one foot above the ground, which provides added protection against burrowing rodents and elevates the siding higher from the ground than a typical 2 x 10 skirtboard does. The exposed portion of skirting should be treated with stain or paint to protect it from the sun.

FRAMING

Framing is the skeleton of the barn to which everything from here on attaches. This is the stage when you begin to get a better feel for the layout and room sizes. Design changes are not uncommon during framing.

Framing is strictly regulated because, if it is done incorrectly or if the wrong materials are used, the barn

can be dangerously weakened. To ensure safe construction, an inspector can order work that is not up to code be ripped out and done correctly.

Barn framing is only as strong as the framing members and connectors. Some lumber suppliers have the impression that horse barns are inferior projects. Don't be afraid to pick through your lumber deliveries to cull out warped, twisted, split, and checked lumber. Talk to your supplier ahead of time and make it clear that this is an important project that requires the best lumber so they'll know what to ship and what to expect to get back. When building, set aside boards that are warped or twisted for return or for use as *blocking* or shorter pieces.

WALLS

Barns with concrete walls need no additional wall framing for support but do require roof framing. Likewise, modular barns often have walls made of panels that fasten together and do not require additional wall framing.

Platform framing is how most houses are built. Walls are framed individually, usually with them lying flat on the ground or floor, and then raised into position. The floor (platform) usually sets on a concrete foundation. This framing is seldom used for barns but may be encountered when remodeling another structure for use as a stable.

Pole framing is the simplest and most common type of barn framing so will be the focus of this section. Once the poles are in place, rows of horizontal boards (girts), commonly 2 x 6s, are nailed to the outside of the poles, spaced at 24 inches to hold the siding (fig. 10.9). A girder (beam, header) is attached to the tops of the poles to support the roof framing.

A girder made of two or more boards will be stronger if the boards are nailed together at regular intervals, rather than placed one on each side of the posts. Do not rely on nails alone to secure girders supporting a roof. At least one of the boards comprising the girder should be notched into the posts. One way to do this is to make a 1½-inch deep notch in one side of every post. Set one board into the notch and tack it in place with nails not to be in the way of the carriage bolts that will be used later to bolt the beams to each post. Nail a temporary wooden block to each post for a temporary support for the second board that will be attached to the first on the same side of each post. Splice beam members at a post and stagger splices so two don't occur at one post. Nail the boards together with three or four 12d or 16d nails at 16-inch intervals. Use two carriage bolts to attach the header to each post.

Depending on the depth of the posts and the height of the barn, permanent diagonal bracing might be required between the posts to prevent wind sway.

Rough openings for windows and doors are cut into the girts and framed. With a pole barn, the poles bear the entire load, and headers over openings generally are not required to carry weight. Horizontal boards between posts at the top and bottom of the opening and vertical boards between those at the sides of the opening will suffice (fig. 10.10).

In the stall area of a pole barn, additional vertical supports might be required between poles more than 4 feet apart to provide sufficient strength for stall lining (fig. 10.10). Use boards the same width as the poles, usually 2 x 6 or 2 x 8, and cut them to fit between the poles at the top and bottom of the stall lining. Use a pressure-treated board at ground level and a regular board at the top.

Interior walls that could be contacted by horses, such as walls along the aisle or adjoining a stall or wash rack, should have 2 x 6 framing. Other walls can be 2 x 4.

CEILINGS

Ceiling framing is sometimes provided by trusses or second-floor joists. And, conversely, ceiling framing often serves as joists for a loft floor. To frame a ceiling in a pole barn, frame walls to support the joists at one end and nail girders to the posts at the height of the ceiling to support the other ends.

ROOFS

Rafter and beam framing is commonly used for small barns and those with complex roofs. This method can require posts on the interior of the barn. One or two persons can build a rafter roof without the need of a crane.
TIPS:

- Lay out and mark one rafter and use it as a template to mark the rest.

- Sight down each rafter and make sure the *crown* (high point in the bend along the edge) of each board is up. That way the weight of the roof will tend to straighten the rafter.

Trusses are preassembled units that enable a much wider free span, often eliminating posts inside the barn. They take less material than a beam and rafter roof and are quicker to erect. You give the truss supplier your barn dimensions—roof slope, post spacing, overhang—and a computer program designs the trusses. It commonly takes two to three weeks from ordering to delivery. Make sure the walls are built using the same specifications you give to the truss supplier. And keep the walls plumb, level, and square or the trusses might not fit.

STALL FRAMING
ADDED BETWEEN
POSTS

WINDOW FRAMING

10.10 *Pole barn window framing and stall supports.*

10.11 *Front-end loader extension used to set trusses in place.*

125

Trusses are heavy and unwieldy and must be installed and braced according to the manufacturer's instructions to ensure that the roof system performs to its designed capacity. Trusses for a small barn can be installed by manpower alone, given patience and careful planning. A crane, although expensive to rent, is the easiest and safest way to get trusses into place. You can improvise by making and extension for a tractor front-end loader from long pieces of pipe to lift one truss at a time into place (fig. 10.11).

To prevent confusion and injury, study the plans and discuss with your helpers beforehand exactly how the truss raising is going to proceed. Erect scaffolding or build a catwalk to stand on while raising trusses. To make a catwalk, nail *cleats* (short boards) about 4 feet from the top of the wall to support the ends of a 2 x 6 or wider plank. Attach 2 x 4 legs for support along the middle of the plank.

PREPARE TO RAISE TRUSSES Mark truss locations on the top of the supporting beam or *cap plate* beforehand, while there is more room to move. Start on one end marking the first truss flush with the outside edge of the cap plate. Mark for subsequent trusses at 24-inch intervals (or whatever the spacing). Mark the other beam starting from the same end.

Prepare temporary bracing to connect trusses to one another. Use 8-foot to 12-foot-long 1 x 4s, which are lighter and easier to handle than 2 x 4s. Mark them with the same truss spacing as on the cap plates. Distribute the pieces and lean them against the inside of wall around the barn where workers can reach them.

Nail temporary 2 x 6 braces vertically near the center of the end walls or on either side of a center doorway. The 2 x 6s need to reach the top *chord* of the truss after it is raised. These braces will steady the end trusses and hold them close to plumb until they can be more securely braced.

Before tipping an end truss into place, check that all of the members in the truss are solidly attached. Start 16d *toenails* along the bottom chord at 16-inch intervals. Then, when the truss is raised, you can adjust the chord flush to the edge of the wall with your foot and lean over and finish driving the toenails.

RAISING TRUSSES Raising trusses is dangerous work. Always follow manufacturer's warnings and bracing guidelines. Amateurs should think twice about attempting to set trusses over 30-feet long.

To raise a truss without a crane, set one end of an end truss on one wall header with the truss upside down. Set the other end on the other wall header. With one or two people on each wall, swing the truss into its upright position. Another person on the ground pushing up on the peak with a 2 x 4 can make this process easier. Nail two

---

GABLE END EXTENSION

There are different ways to extend an overhang at the end of a barn. If the overhang is 3 inches less you can simply extend the roof sheathing past the end trusses or rafters. For wider overhangs, use *lookouts (outriggers)* to support a barge rafter (fig. 10.12). Lookouts are commonly 2 x 4s laid flat and attached flush with the top edge of the second rafter from the end and extended past the end rafter the amount of the overhang. The end truss or rafter is sometimes made lower by 1½ inches so lookouts can set on top of it. If the end truss or rafter is the same height as the others it is notched at intervals along the top edge to accept lookouts.

Cut notches in the end trusses for lookouts before they are raised into position. Measure 1 foot from the top for the first lookout on each side. Locate the others 4 feet on-center down from the top notches (closer for tile roofs to prevent sagging). Precut the lookouts and nail at least the upper ones into place because they can be hard to reach after the truss is in place. Likewise, precut barge rafters, if needed, by measuring off a truss. Tack a dozen or so 16d galvanized nails into the top edge of each rafter to use later to attach the rafter to the outriggers. This saves you from digging in your nail apron while standing on a ladder or climbing on a truss.

---

or three 2 x 4 braces to the end truss and clamp them to stakes in the ground outside the barn. Have one person steady the truss upright while another lines up the ends with the outside edges of the wall. Tack the upper chord to the upright brace and nail the bottom chord to the plate. Loosen the clamp just enough to plumb the truss and nail or screw the braces to the stakes to hold the truss in place.

After the first end truss is raised, plumbed, and braced, the other trusses are braced to it, and to one another, one by one. Lay a brace that you marked earlier on top of the end truss and the second trusses parallel with the wall. Line up the trusses with the marks and nail the braces in place. This will not only set the proper spacing but it will also plumb up the other trusses as you go (assuming the gable end truss is still plumb). The other end truss is the last one to go up, and it should be checked separately to make sure it is plumb.

Purlins can either be cut to fit between trusses or laid across the top of trusses, flat or on edge depending on the roof design. Either way, use 16d ring-shank nails and/or metal hangers or *hurricane clips* to secure purlins to trusses.

SHEATHING

Sheathing, called decking on a roof, attaches directly to the framing to reinforce and, in some cases, to provide attachment for the finish material, such as shingles. Panels of steel, plywood, and hardboard generally don't require sheathing, except on walls where horses can contact the barn. In those areas, sheathing is essential to at least a height of 4 feet to prevent kick-through, minimizing injury to your horse and damage to the siding.

Three-quarter-inch-thick sheathing should be fastened to each framing member using 8d nails spaced 6 inches along the edges and 12 inches in the middle.

STAIRS

A stairway is comprised of *risers,* the vertical parts, and *treads* or steps, the horizontal parts that you step on. Codes regarding stair rise (riser height) and *run* (tread depth) vary and are ever changing. A comfortable rise for stairs is generally considered to be around 7 inches. The best way to find a riser to tread ratio you like is to measure stairs that are comfortable for you to use. One formula carpenters use is to make the sum of the riser and the tread equal 17. Using this method, divide the total rise (measured vertically from the foot of the stairs to the top) by seven (the height of one riser) to get the rough number of steps. If the rise is 96 inches, then 96 ÷ 7 = 13.7 steps. Now divide the total rise by the number of steps (round down to 13 for fewer steps that are higher and round up to 14 for more steps that are lower.) 96 ÷ 13 = 7.38 inches per riser. 96 ÷ 14 = 6.85 inches per riser. Choose which rise you prefer and subtract that number from 17 (carpenter's formula above) to find tread depth. 14 risers at 6.85 inches would use treads 10.15-inches deep; 13 risers at 7.38 would use treads 9.62-inches deep. Exterior steps are generally thought to be better with a 6 inch rise and a longer run.

WIRING AND PLUMBING

After framing is completed, wiring and plumbing are roughed in. The service panel and connections have to be inspected before your power company will hook it up. Switch boxes and outlet boxes are located and attached to the framing, and the wiring is run within and alongside the framing. Wiring for telephones, speakers, security system, vent fans, thermostat, and other devices is done at this time as well, before the walls are paneled. Water and drainpipes are run through the walls, and drains are dug into the floor. A washer/dryer have extra considerations; the washer will need a drain, and the dryer will need an exhaust vent and 220-volt service.

Once the electrical and plumbing rough-ins begin, it becomes harder to change things. For example, if you

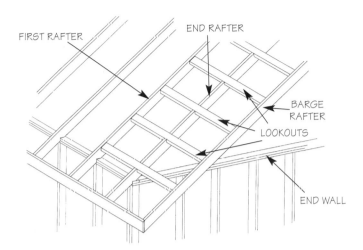

10.12 *Lookouts and barge rafter.*

move a door or a faucet, wires and plumbing might have to be rerouted. This means extra work and more costs.

Switches and outlets are usually installed after insulation and paneling are completed.

SIDING

Siding is the most visible portion of the barn and, along with the roof, the primary defense against weather. On areas where horses can contact the barn, siding with a smooth surface will minimize cuts and abrasions on horses and damage from chewing and rubbing on the siding. It bears repeating that a horse can kick through most any kind of siding that is not reinforced with sheathing.

On the inside of the barn, stalls and other vulnerable areas need to be paneled or protected by boards to prevent the siding from being damaged or pushed off the framing.

WOOD PANELS

Wood panel siding, such as the ubiquitous T-111, is easy to install. Galvanized screw-shank nails are commonly used. Check the first panel you install with a level to ensure it is plumb. Then check every third or fourth panel as you go. A quick way to mark window and door opening is to hold or tack the panel in position over the opening and have a helper trace the opening on the back. Alternatively, you can install siding right over openings and cut them out later using a router with a straight trim bit that is guided by the window or doorframe or by using a *reciprocating saw.*

STEEL PANELS

Steel panels come cut to length and are one of the easiest sidings to install and maintain. You will likely have to cut

10.13 *An abrasive cut-off wheel in a circular saw used for cutting steel panel.*

10.14 *Screws being started with a hammer.*

some panels to fit around windows or to come out even at the end of a wall. Some rental stores and building supply stores have metal shears, a long bar with a hinged blade, that are configured for different panel profiles and that will cut a panel to length with one drop of the blade. Tin snips work best for trimming small, flat areas but are difficult to use on large areas and across uneven ribs. The best way I've found to cut steel panels, whether lengthwise or across the ribs, is using a *circular saw* fitted with an abrasive cut-off blade (fig. 10.13). Slip a board under the panel parallel to, and just off, the cut line. Assume a steady stance and keep both hands on the saw to prevent kickback. Wear eye protection, earmuffs, and a filter mask. This method also works well for cutting fiberglass panels.

Screws with rubber washers are commonly used to secure steel siding to framing, but ring-shank nails with washers can also be used. Nails have a lower profile; so don't encourage horses to rub as much as screws do. But they can work loose, and, ironically, they can also be difficult to pull out if you need to remove or replace siding. Screws hold more securely and are easy to remove for replacing panels. Apply screws to the flat parts of the panel, not to the ribs, so a horse will be less likely to rub his mane and tail on them.

Use an electric drill with a special driver to install screws having a rubber or plastic washer that seals against the face of the panels. Place screws on the flat portion of the panels and also on the ridge where the panels overlap. You can eyeball the screws to line them up on the girts, but this usually results in uneven lines of screws. Straight screw lines look much better and are not difficult to achieve. Since molding will later cover the corner, hold the first panel back from the corner a couple inches and use two screws to hold it in place. Lay a straight edge, such as a 4-foot builder's level, over the panel and mark a light pencil across the panel at the

center of each girt. Install screws on this line. Each succeeding panel is marked from the last screw of the previous panel to the center of the exposed girt.

TIP: It's sometimes difficult to get self-tapping screws started, especially if you're in a position where you can't apply sufficient force on the drill. Use an awl or a 16d nail to punch a small starter hole in the steel or start the screws by driving the tip through the steel and into the wood (fig. 10.14). Don't over tighten screws. Tighten them just enough to snug the panel against the wood and to seat the rubber washer. Over tightening will cut the washer or squish it out from under the screw head and be a potential leak.

ROOFING

Roofing is dangerous and falls are the leading cause of construction worker fatalities in the U.S. If you feel uncomfortable or unsure about roof work, hire someone to do the work for you. Consider wearing a safety harness (available at construction supply and boating stores) that attaches to a solid spot on the roof (see OSHA guidlelines on fall protection: http://www.osha-slc.gov/doc/outreachtraining/htmlfiles/subpartm.html). Wear soft, rubber-soled shoes—hard lugs or spikes can damage roofing.

Never apply roofing during rain or snow or to wet or damp surfaces. For one thing, the roof will be dangerously slippery. And trapped moisture may cause severe damage to the roofing, insulation, and *deck* (roof sheathing).

SHINGLE ROOF

A shingle roof has four basic components: framing (rafters or trusses), deck (sheathing), underlayment, and shingles. A layer of shingles by itself is insufficient for a roof. Underlayment is needed to prevent water from penetrating to the sheathing.

Asphalt roofing products become soft when hot and are sticky to cut and may be damaged by walking on them. Below 40°F, on the other hand, they become more brittle and may tear, crack, or break, especially fiberglass-reinforced shingles. Avoid roofing during the mid-day hours on hot days, and store roofing in a warm place on cool days until you are ready to install it.

Use fasteners that penetrate at least ¾-inch into the roof deck. If the deck is less than ¾-inch the fasteners should extend at least ⅛-inch through the deck.

DRIP EDGE

Drip edge is a metal strip that's nailed along the bottom edge of the roof to direct water cleanly off the edge without it seeping under the roofing or dripping down the *fascia* or siding. It also supports the part of the shingle that extends past the edge of the roof. Nail drip edge under the underlayment and over the fascia. Cover the nailheads with roofing cement then stick the felt down. At the *rake* (gable end overhang), install the drip edge over the felt and fascia. This will prevent wind and blowing rain from getting under the felt. When using more than one piece of drip edge, lap upper pieces over lower pieces.

UNDERLAYMENT   For underlayment, builders' felt (tar paper), which comes in rolls, is the most popular material. It is made in a wide variety of thicknesses and is gauged in pounds. Typically, a roll of No. 15 felt will cover about 400 square feet and a roll of No. 30 would cover half that area because although the roll is roughly the same size and weight, the felt is twice as thick.

Special eave protection *(double eaves course)* must be used in Snowbelt regions (National Building Code, Section 9.26.5) to avoid water backup from ice dams at the eaves. Mineral-surfaced or smooth-surfaced rolled roofing can be used in warm weather, but when it's cold these products must be warmed to allow them to relax and stretch. If applied cold, they might later wrinkle and buckle raising gaps along the edge of finished roofing material. Self-adhering eave protector membranes made of polymer-modified

---

HOW MANY SHINGLES DO YOU NEED?

The surface area of a roof is measured in squares, one square being 100 square feet. Shingles are sold in bundles, with three bundles usually covering one square. Figure the total square footage of the roof (length x width) and divide by 100 to get the number of squares needed. Multiply by 3 for total bundles of shingles.

ROOF JACKS

Roof jacks are steel brackets that hold planks in a level position on a slope. They are helpful for support on roofs steeper than 4/12 and good along the eaves on any slope in case you slip or something slides down the roof. To install roof jacks, drive a nail almost home through the decking and rafter underneath a completed row of shingles. Hook the jack on the nail and hammer the nail down. Nail the jack on the lower hook slot. Attach the companion jack in a like manner and set a sturdy plank (2 x 8 or larger) on the jacks.

---

asphalt are more flexible in cold weather. Laying felt is much easier and faster with two people; one rolling and one stapling or nailing. Position the felt roll slightly overhanging the gable end (it is easiest to trim it flush later) and the bottom edge of the roof. Working toward the far end, unroll about 5 feet of felt, square it with the roof edges, press out any wrinkles, and fasten it in place as you go. Proceed at 5-foot intervals to the far end. Overlap the second row of felt on the first row by 2 inches. Work up the roof this way to the ridge. Leave the ridge gap exposed if you will be installing a continuous ridge vent and continue underlayment on the other side. If there will not be a continuous ridge vent, fold the felt over both sides of the ridge (overlapping at least 2 inches) and fasten it. Once the roof has underlayment, it can withstand exposure for a few days. However, if it gets wet, the felt may wrinkle up a bit, which increases its chances of tearing by wind. If necessary, tack a row of wood lath over the seams to keep underlayment in place.

The best way to lay shingles in straight lines is to snap *chalk lines.* Snap the first one to guide the top of the first course (row) of shingles. After the first course of shingles is laid, snap a vertical line from eaves to ridge, parallel to the rake, to indicate the inside edge of the first shingle. This mark will be a guideline for the first shingle in the odd number rows. After the second course is laid, snap a parallel line for the inside edge of first shingle in the second and following, even number rows. (This is for a 6-inch offset; offset may also be 4 or 5 inches.)

Lay a starter course of "tabless" shingles made by cutting the tabs from regular shingles. Shingles are best trimmed using a razor knife—with a hook blade cut from the front surface, with a straight blade cut from the back. To keep water off the fascia, let the shingles overhang from ¼ inch to ¾ inch on the ends of the roof (rake) and at the eaves. More overhang than this will cause shingles to sag.

To minimize water penetration, stagger the joints of the first course over the starter course. Measure the length of a shingle (usually 36 inches) and divide it into the length of the roof in inches (including how far you want the shingles to extend past the rake) to determine how the shingles will lay out. This lets you cut the first shingle, if necessary, to avoid ending up with a 1-inch-wide strip at the far end. Nail each shingle in the first course at each end and middle tabs about ½ inch to ⅝ inch above the tabs. Stagger the first shingle of the second course 6 inches short of the first course shingle, so their tabs do not set directly above the first row tabs.

For nails not covered by shingles, put a spot of roofing cement under the head of the nail before driving it home and add another spot over the nail. Air-powered staplers are fast but are prohibited by codes in some areas because they can drive staples clear through shingles, so the shingles are not held in place. Pneumatic nailers, however, are acceptable because nailheads have a larger bearing surface than staple heads and are less likely to be driven through the shingle.

Racking is a fast method of shingling where you lay down as many shingles as you can reach without moving. You nail down the first row about three to six shingles across, then do the second row, and the third row. The end tabs of the rows are left unfastened so when you move, the next shingles can slide into position under the loose ends. The trouble is, applicators often leave out nails when sliding shingles in during racking, and if the shingles are brittle they are often damaged. Also, because you are working in a small area, color shading problems are exacerbated by racking. The Asphalt Roofing Manufacturers Association and National Roofing Contractors Association both discourage racking.

An application method that generally produces more even color mix and more consistent fastening is aptly named the "typewriter" method. You lay down one complete row the length of the roof before returning to start the next row.

On a roof that changes slopes (see fig. 8.5, p. 86 and fig. 11.11, p. 147), like a gambrel or a gable with a shed extension, install a metal *flashing* where the roof breaks, extending at least 4 inches over the lower shingles and 6 inches or more up the slope or wall. Start the upper slope like you did the eave, with an extra layer of felt and a set of starter shingles.

The upper-most courses and the rake edges are especially susceptible to wind lift. Most asphalt shingles have patches of *sealant* on the underside that bonds the shingles together when heated by the sun. When shingling in cold weather, use one or two spots of trowel grade mastic to glue every tab down. For sealing the long edges of rolled roofing, apply roofing cement from a 5-gallon can using a regular 9-inch painting roller on an extension. Keep mineral spirits nearby in case you need to clean the adhesive off something.

STEEL PANELS

Perhaps the hardest part of installing a steel roof is ordering materials correctly. The factory precuts each piece according to your order, so you must first figure out exactly how many pieces you will need and how long each piece must be. If you can wait to order after framing is completed, you can measure panel lengths directly on the roof. Measure from the top edge of the sheathing (where the roofing will end at the peak) to the bottom edge, adding an inch for overhang at the eaves. If plans call for a continuous ridge vent, determine the dimensions and how the steel will join with the vent and adjust panel lengths accordingly.

If you want to order steel before the roof is built, study the working plan closely to calculate panel lengths. If you've ordered trusses, the truss company can provide the exact length of the top chord of the truss to help you determine steel lengths.

Installing screws in straight lines is even more important on a roof than with siding because you are usually screwing into the relatively narrow 1½-inch-wide edge of the purlins. Every missed screw is a potential leak (see method for straight screw lines on p. 128). Carry a small tube of silicone caulking (available at hardware stores) for filling holes from missed screws. Using an electric drill or driver with an adjustable clutch can help prevent over tightening screws, especially when installing steel over insulation board.

SKYLIGHTS

Skylights are notorious for leaking. But leaks can be prevented by careful installation. When translucent fiberglass panels are used with steel roofing panels, leaks are usually due to over or under tightening fasteners or missing framing with fasteners. Use screws with rubber or plastic washers and drive them perpendicular to the roof so the heads contact the panels flat. Tighten screws just enough to compress the washer firmly between the screw head and the panel, not so much that the rubber washer is squeezed out around the head. Overlap panel ends at least 12 inches and position every joint over a purlin.

GUTTERS

Gutters and downspouts divert runoff from the roof to minimize mud around the barn (fig. 10.15). Gutters should be sloped toward the downspouts approximately 1/16 inch per foot; otherwise water can overflow the gutter. In snow country, ice and snow can rip gutters off a barn unless some type of shield is applied to allow it to slide over the top of the gutter.

If water empties onto the ground, place a splash block at the mouth of the downspout or extension to prevent erosion. An alternative is to run the downspout extension into a French drain (see fig. 10.3, p. 121) containing a drainpipe that empties to daylight on the discharge end.

10.15 *Gutters and downspouts can divert roof runoff so it doesn't fall off the eaves into pens.*

FLOORS

With concrete, it is not critical that the base be absolutely level. But, with mats, brick, or a wood floor the base should be as level as you can make it and sloped for drainage if required. One way to level a large area for a floor is by using a *transit level* to make *witness marks* on posts and walls around the perimeter of the floor, then measure down from the witness marks to mark the level of the floor. Most rental stores stock transit levels with tripods. Some transit levels have lasers that make marking easier.

HOW TO LEVEL A FLOOR BASE

You'll need a stable platform in or near the floor area you want to level. The platform should be between waist to chest high, such as a barrel. Place a relatively square piece of OSB or plywood on the platform and set a standard builder's level on the board. Use shims and spacers under the board so the level's bubble reads level. Rotate the level 90 degrees and shim as needed so the bubble reads level again. Rotate 45 degrees and check again. Continue until the bubble reads level at all points around the circle.

Sight down the top of the level, like sighting down a rifle, and line up on a post or wall. Have a helper make a witness mark at that point (fig. 10.16). If you are working alone, push a stickpin into the wood, resight, and adjust until the pin is on the mark.

Measure down from each sight mark and make another mark at the desired level of the base.

Drive steel pins (½-inch conduit works well) into the ground near each mark and level with the mark. Pins

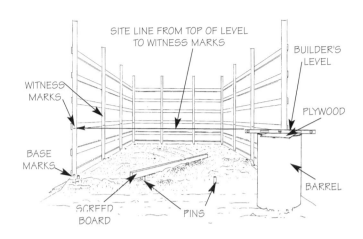

10.16 *Leveling a floor base.*

6 inches to 12 inches long work in most soils, while softer soil requires longer pins for them to be stable.

Add road base or another fill to just above the top of the pins.

Use a straight 2 x 4 on edge for a *screed* to work the gravel level with the pins. The screed should be long enough to span two pins. Hold one end of the screed on a pin and pivot it, dragging the gravel level as you go. Do the same off adjacent pins until the entire area is level. For areas wider than 8 feet, drive additional pins in the interior of the area, using a straight 2 x 4 and level to level them with the perimeter pins.

HOW TO POUR A CONCRETE FLOOR

Pouring a concrete floor is not rocket science, but once it sets, the floor is permanent. If you don't know what you are doing you might want to hire a professional or at least enlist the aid of an experienced friend. It is physically demanding, messy work that has to be completed in a relatively short time. The better prepared you and your helpers are, the easier it will go. Concrete is alkaline and will ruin leather boots and make your skin crack. Wear rubber boots and old clothes and protect your hands with gloves or a barrier hand cream or both.

A barn floor should be at least 4 inches thick over a 4-inch-deep base of compacted road base; 6 inches thick if vehicles will be driven over it. Reinforce the floor with a grid of ½-inch *rebar* (steel reinforcing bars) on 2-foot centers or with 6-inch by 6-inch 10-pound wire *reinforcing mesh*. Bolts set in concrete for securing walls later should be not less than ½ inch diameter and embedded at least 3 inches.

PREPARE THE BASE The first step in preparing the base is to remove all organic matter such as grass and twigs and excavate to a depth of 8 inches.

Next, haul in road base, distribute it evenly in a level 4-inch layer, and compact it with tamping bars, rollers, a rented tamping machine, or stomping feet. A tamping bar can be made by welding a plate or disc of steel that's at least ¼-inch thick and 6 inches across onto the end of a 5-foot length of 1½-inch to 2-inch-diameter pipe. Tamp the base until it no longer shows a footprint when you walk on it.

INSTALL FORMS Existing aisle walls can serve as part of the forms. Use 2 x 4s and stakes to fill in the gaps between walls. Reusable concrete forms are available at rental stores. Where walls are serving as forms, either snap a chalk line on the walls to mark the height of the finished floor or drive nails for markers halfway into the wall at 16-inch intervals at the level of the finished floor. Make the top of the other forms the height of the finished floor. If building forms, drive 2 x 4 stakes flush against the outside of the form boards at 2-foot intervals for support. Concrete weighs around 150 pounds per cubic foot, so don't be afraid of making the forms too strong. Place stakes so the narrow edge is against the form. Nail the form boards to the stakes with scaffold nails, which have double heads, to make removing the forms easier. Hold a heavy hammer, brick, or stone behind the stake when nailing to keep the stake from moving. Paint the inside of the forms with diesel fuel to make them easier to remove once the concrete has set.

If hydrants are located in the aisle, box around them with wood and fill the space with gravel (see fig. 12.17, p. 157). Then, if the hydrant is accidentally turned on without a bucket beneath it or if a hose should pop off, the water will have a place to drain without flooding the floor. Alternatively, install a drain beneath the hydrant.

A floor should have *control (expansion) joints* every 10 feet to control cracking. One way to provide these joints is to score a line in the surface of the concrete before it sets. If the slab cracks, it will crack along the straight line. Another way is to place pressure-treated form boards across the width of the floor at intervals to be left in the floor to serve as expansion joints. Locate embedded form boards exactly under the center lines of walls that will later set on the floor, such as for a feed room or utility room. The bottom wall plates can then be screwed or nailed to these forms, eliminating the need for setting bolts in concrete or drilling concrete to install fasteners later.

Reinforcing wire or rod should end up in the center of the slab's thickness. Wire reinforcing mesh is easier to use than rebar, but, because of the weight of the concrete and movement of workers, it almost always ends up next to the ground where it does absolutely no good. Rebar is more rigid and is wired together and is held off the ground by being wired to steel rods driven into the ground at intervals. It is less likely to end up next to the ground.

ORDER CONCRETE Concrete is sold by the cubic yard. For an area the size of a barn floor you will likely have it delivered or haul it yourself using a rental mixer (fig. 10.17).

You can specify what strength you want—a "5½ sack mix" is suitable for a barn floor. This means there are 5½ sacks of cement per cubic yard of concrete.

To find how much concrete you will need, multiply the length of the aisle by the width to get square feet and multiply that by the thickness in feet (a 4-inch-thick floor is ⅓ foot) to get cubic feet. Divide cubic feet by 27 to get cubic yards. A quick formula is one cubic yard for 70 square feet of slab 4-inches thick. Concrete trucks typically carry between 8 and 10 cubic yards. Figure extra for waste and variance in the depth of concrete. While you don't want to have concrete left over, the most expensive concrete you'll ever buy is that extra half yard you have to order when you come up short.

10.17 *Rented mixer for hauling premixed concrete.*

10.18 *Floating and edging is done after screeding. Note 2 x 4 expansion joints embedded in the concrete.*

To avoid having to dump leftover concrete on the ground, frame up a simple form for a tie area or a walkway ahead of time.

PLACE THE CONCRETE Make sure to clear a path to the barn so that when the concrete truck arrives, it can get as close to the pour site as possible. An experienced concrete hauler can use chutes on the truck to deliver the right amount of concrete just where it is needed.

The wetter the concrete, the better it will flow down the chute and into the forms and the easier it will be to finish. If it's too wet, however, the coarse *aggregate* in the mix will settle to the bottom, resulting in weaker concrete above. Drier concrete generally sets up stronger, but it doesn't flow as well and takes more work to move and to finish. A good rule of thumb is to keep concrete wet enough to flow but dry enough to keep the coarse gravel suspended in the mix.

Moisten the base with a hose before the concrete is placed. Use shovels to take concrete from high spots and move it to low areas. Concrete sometimes expands once it is poured; so don't be surprised if it seems to "grow." Tap the sides of the forms with a hammer and tamp the mass of concrete with a shovel to settle the large aggregate from the surface and to prevent honeycombing (hollow areas). Avoid stepping on the reinforcing rod and forcing it down.

SCREED When the forms are filled, a straight board is used to screed, level, or strike off the concrete. A screed board can simply be a straight 2 x 4 or 2 x 6 that is a foot or more longer than the forms. Concrete should be struck off as soon as possible after it has been poured. Rest the screed on top of the forms and, with a person on each end, work the board back and forth in a sawing motion while slowly moving down the length of the forms. If you use a bowed board with the *bow* down, the floor will have a slightly concave shape, which will encourage water to drain down the center of the floor.

FLOAT Floating can be done immediately after screeding to remove ridges and bring finer aggregate to the surface for a smoother surface (fig. 10.18). A bull *float* on a long handle is used to reach the center of wide slabs. Hand floats can be made from a piece of plywood 3- to 5-inches wide by 12- to 18-inches long and fitted with a handle. Round the corners and edges to help the float ride on the surface without leaving ridges in the concrete. Elevate the leading edge as you move the float so it doesn't dig in. Don't float too much or else you will bring excess water to the surface.

EDGE After floating, use a rounded *edger* to remove sharp corners along the sides of the slab. Wait until the concrete is set enough to hold the shape of the edger and

10.19 *Concrete slab covered with plastic to keep it wet for curing.*

run it back and forth between the forms and the concrete. This will make the floor safer and give it a finished appearance. Edging is a good way for the younger members of your team to get some concrete experience.

TROWEL Finishing with a *trowel* will give the smoothest surface. Wait until surface water has soaked in or evaporated and there is no sheen on the surface, but trowel before the concrete gets too hard to work. Don't trowel wet spots and don't sprinkle concrete powder on them to soak them up; it will only flake off later. Instead, soak up the water with a sponge or rag before troweling.

BROOM Brooming will texturize the floor for traction. Drag a stiff-bristled push broom over the surface in a straight or wavy pattern. Brooming can be done after floating and instead of or after troweling and before the concrete sets.

CURE Be careful to not disturb the concrete once is has started to set because it can easily be damaged beyond repair. Forms can be removed after 24 hours, but you risk chipping the edges and corners of the "green" concrete. Three days is considered the minimum curing time; concrete reaches near full strength in seven days and continues to cure for more than a month. Concrete depends on water to cure, so once you have finished the surface, wet the pad thoroughly and cover it with plastic such as VisQueen® or other material to keep the sun and wind from drying it (fig. 10.19). Concrete that's kept wet for a month of curing will be harder and less porous than concrete allowed to dry out after three days. Be patient and keep the slab wet as it cures.

HOW TO LAY A ROUGH WOOD FLOOR

Boards laid across the aisle will give better traction, while boards laid down the length of the aisle will be easier to sweep clean. Level a 4-inch deep layer of gravel over

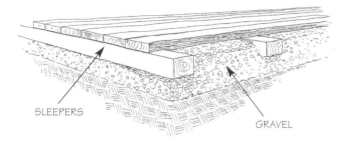

10.20 *Plank floor.*

compacted earth (fig. 10.20). Lay *sleepers* of pressure-treated 4 x 4s or railroad ties on the gravel base perpendicular to the final flooring and at 2-foot intervals. Add gravel between the sleepers level with the tops. Lay 2-inch-thick boards across the sleepers and screw them to the sleepers. Screws won't work out of wood like nails will and are easier to remove to replace damaged flooring. If the floorboards vary in thickness, used cedar shims between boards and sleepers to keep them even and minimize tripping.

LAYING A BRICK FLOOR

In barns, paving brick is commonly laid loose, without mortar, in a bed of sand. A border is needed all around the bricks to hold the floor together. Walls will form most or all of the border and where there are no walls, use pressure-treated 2 x 8s dug into the base, level with the finished floor. Secure them to stakes, if necessary, which don't stick up past the top edge of the boards. Prepare a level compacted 6-inch-deep base of ⅜-inch sharp gravel (sharp gravel packs better and does not shift like round gravel does.) Add 2 inches of sand and roll or tamp it smooth. Lay the brick in the desired pattern. Use string lines to keep rows straight and level. Sweep sand over the finished floor to fill the joints.

LAYING RUBBER BRICK FLOOR

Rubber brick can be installed the same way as clay brick over a draining base or over concrete. If applied over concrete, the floor should slope for drainage so urine and water don't puddle on the surface or collect in pools between the floors. Rubber brick can be cut with a knife or band saw, which makes it easier to fit along the edges of the aisle than clay brick. Matching rubber curbing is available to keep the system together and to provide a finished edge.

RUBBER MATS

The single most important factor that determines the successful performance of stall mats is floor preparation. Stall mats should be installed over a firm level base. Manufacturers recommend using a 3-inch to 6-inch layer of stonedust or ⅜-inch to ¼-inch gravel. Never use sand because it's too shifty to keep mats level. You'll need a tape measure, a piece of chalk (a builder's chalk line would also work), a steel straight edge, and a standard *utility knife* (the type with replaceable blades) for the installation.

PREPARING THE BASE Level the base using an 8-foot-long 2 x 4 (see How to Level a Floor Base, p. 131). Compact the gravel with a tamping bar or mechanical tamper and level it again. Wetting the gravel slightly will help it settle and will also keep down dust.

FIT Place the first mat in the corner of the stall tight against the walls. To provide handles for dragging a mat, clamp locking pliers to its edge. Since the factory edges will likely be straighter and fit more tightly together than the edges that are cut at the time of installation, install the mats with factory edges against one another toward the center of the stall and the cut edges against the wall (this doesn't apply to interlocking mats). The corners of the mats are the weakest part of the floor and the first place that bulges up as bedding works into the joints. Try to lay out the mats so four corners do not come together.

CUTTING Rubber mats are relatively easy to cut with a sharp utility knife; but don't try to cut through in one pass. Instead, apply only moderate pressure to the knife and plan on taking several strokes to cut through. With the mat on fairly level ground, place a 2 x 4 under the mat beneath the line you're cutting so the mat naturally bends down on either side. This opens the cut as you go and prevents the mats from pinching the knife blade. Keep a sharp blade in the knife.

An alternative is to use a reciprocating saw or a jigsaw with a special blade for cutting rubber.

Using a circular saw is not a good idea. Friction melts the rubber, which grabs the blade and strains the saw motor. Also, it produces large quantities of harmful smoke and rubber dust.

INSULATION

Insulating is the last task before closing a wall, floor, or ceiling area. You can install fiberglass batts, rigid foam board, and radiant barrier yourself. Spray foam insulation requires special equipment and is applied by certified applicators.

AIR SPACE

Especially in humid climates, steel panels and other exterior materials will generally last longer if insulation is not applied directly against the backside. Leave a space for airflow so that moisture can escape. The backside of steel panels is typically protected from rust by only a thin coating of primer, and trapped moisture can lead to damage. When insulation is applied on the outside of framing, use *skip sheathing*, 1 x 4s spaced 16 to 24 inches on center, to provide a space between the insulation and steel panels. When using spray foam insulation, install a barrier such as sheathing or chicken wire covered with plastic or paper on the inside of the girts or purlins to maintain an air space next to the steel.

FIBERGLASS

Glass fibers can produce skin irritation, intense itching, and even contact dermatitis. Avoid unnecessary handling of scrap fiberglass materials by keeping waste containers close to the work area. A loose fitting long-sleeved shirt, coveralls, neck scarf, cap, gloves, and other clothing will help prevent irritation by keeping fibers from rubbing against your skin. Eye protection is recommended during overhead application. Do not rub or scratch your skin. Shower at the end of the day with warm water and mild soap to rinse off stray fibers. Wash clothing exposed to fiberglass separately to prevent glass fibers from being transferred to other clothes. If there are a lot of glass fibers on clothes, it is best to presoak and rinse the clothes before washing them. Run your washing machine through an empty cycle before using it again.

Large fiberglass blankets wrapped in plastic are often applied on the outside of the purlins and girts and then roofing and siding applied over it (see fig. 8.12, p. 91). Another method is to install fiberglass between or over the inside of the framing after the siding and roofing are on. One thing is sure—you don't want horses to be able to chew on insulation or tear it out of the walls or ceiling.

Professional installers use a knife with a 6-inch blade to cut fiberglass batts. You can do a good job with a mat knife or razor knife with a short blade. Lay the batt with the paper or plastic face down on a scrap piece of OSB or plywood. Place a metal straight edge such as a builder's level at the cut line and compress the batt to the floor. Make one or two cuts along the straight edge to cut through the batt.

Batts with a paper vapor barrier come in widths that fit between framing that's 16 or 24 inches on center. The paper face goes to the inside of the room and the edges of the paper are unfolded and stapled over the exposed edge of the studs or joists. In most cases, $5/16$-inch-long staples work well for insulation and vapor barrier. All

they need to do is to hold it up until the next layer is applied. If the framing wood is fir or hard southern yellow pine, shorter staples might go in better without bending. Take care to fit the edges and ends of the batts snugly against the sides of the framing, with no gaps for air infiltration. Again, don't push the batts tight against the backside of the siding or roof; rather leave a space for airflow to remove moisture.

If you are using the fiberglass insulation faced with kraft-paper, you don't need another vapor barrier over it. Plain batts require a vapor barrier of 6-*mil* poly or VisQueen® plastic.

FOAM BOARD

Panels of rigid foam board can be cut with a sharp knife and attached with roofing nails and glue to the outside of framing under roofing or siding or on the inside of framing under paneling or other wall covering. If the panels have a reflective face, that face should go toward the inside in cool climates and toward the outside in hot climates. If the panels will be covered, you only need enough nails to hold them in place until they are covered. If they will be exposed, nail them securely onto walls and nail and glue them onto the under side of a roof. Joints between panels should be taped or sealed according to instructions to maintain the integrity of the vapor barrier.

RADIANT BARRIER

Radiant barrier products come in rolls (see Aluminum, Insulation, p. 92). The material cuts with a standard pair of scissors and is secured on the inside of walls and ceilings using a staple gun and sometimes an adhesive. If you have significant air gaps that could allow convection heat loss through air infiltration, you may want to use batts or spray foam along with a radiant barrier.

PANELING

Paneling here refers to interior wall covering that protects framing and components contained therein, such as wiring, plumbing, and insulation.

Paneling used where horses could contact it, such as in aisles, needs to be strong enough to not break should a horse collide with it. This means it should be made of plywood, OSB, or solid wood that is $5/8$ inch or thicker. Thinner paneling material can be used if it is applied over a sheathing that's $5/8$ inch or thicker.

Paneling in other areas of the barn is most useful if it is thick enough to hold fasteners for hooks, shelves, and brackets anywhere along the wall, without having the fasteners go into a framing member. (For a detailed description of paneling options, see materials, pp. 87 to 94.)

STALL LINER

Stall liner is a heavy paneling that protects siding from being damaged or pushed off the framing by a horse from the inside. It also covers the framing and prevents a horse from getting a leg caught between the siding and the poles or other framing members. It must be strong enough to withstand a direct kick from a horse.

Lumber installed horizontally, typically 2 x 8 or 2 x 10 rough sawn or tongue and groove, is a popular choice for stall liner because it is strong and looks good. It should be supported at least every 4 feet by a vertical framing member. With a pole barn, this means adding additional framing between poles (see fig. 10.10 p. 125). All lumber within 8 inches of the ground should be pressure treated to prevent rot. Use screws or ring shank or screw shank nails to attach boards securely to the framing. Fasteners should be flush with the surface or recessed so as not to catch mane and tail hairs. Rounding or *chamfering* the edges of the boards will reduce the chance of splinters and give the wall a more finished appearance.

All wood edges that a horse can reach need to be covered by metal chew guard edging.

SAFETY

A large part of safety around a construction site is common sense: watch what you're doing and where you are going; pay attention to what others are doing; and wear shoes and clothing that are appropriate for the job. Another part of safety is knowing the limits of the tools and equipment you are using, as well as knowing your own limits. Do not exceed those limits.

GENERAL SAFETY

- Fence horses out of the construction area until the barn is completely finished and ready for use.

- Keep the construction area organized and tidy at all times—don't let scrap material or debris pile up on the floor or other areas.

- Wear sneakers or soft-soled shoes with grip when working on roofs.

- Wear goggles when sawing overhead and when cutting steel with a saw or snips.

- Wear a filter mask when cutting treated wood and OSB, and avoid breathing any type of construction dust.

- Wear gloves when handling freshly pressure-treated wood, rough-sawn wood, and steel panels.

- Wear hearing protection during loud operations such as cutting steel siding.

- Do not carry nails or sharp or pointed hand tools such as screwdrivers, chisels, or files in your pocket —buy a carpenter's apron and use it.

- When removing boards, immediately remove protruding nails or bend them down against the lumber.

- Do not strike nails or other objects with the side of a hammer.

- Do not strike one hammer against another hammer.

- Do not use a wooden-handled hammer for pulling nails larger than 8d.

- Use only sharp saw blades in a circular saw.

- Do not carry plugged-in equipment or tools with your finger on the switch.

- Do not handle or operate electrical tools when your hands are wet, when wearing wet gloves, or when you are standing on wet footing.

- Do not use a power hand tool to cut wet or water soaked building materials.

- Do not carry tools by the cord.

- Keep electric cords in good repair.

- Know where power cords are: keep them away from the path of saws and drills.

- Do not drive over, drag, step on, or place objects on a cord.

- Do not remove the ground prong from electrical cord plugs and do not use power cords that have had the ground prong removed.

- Do not use an adapter plug that eliminates the ground to plug into an ungrounded outlet.

LADDER SAFETY

No matter what type of ladder you are using—step, extension, straight, or trestle—understand that they are a leading cause of work injuries (fig. 10.21). Each year in the U.S., accidents involving ladders cause an estimated 300 deaths and 130,000 injuries requiring emergency medical attention. Most ladder accidents can be prevented.

Ladders are divided into three general classes:

- Type I Industrial: heavy-duty with a maximum load of 250 pounds

- Type II Commercial: medium-duty with a maximum load of 225 pounds

- Type III Household: light-duty with maximum load of 200 pounds

Inspection Checklist

- Check for loose or damaged rungs, steps, rails, or braces.

- Remove splinters or sharp edges.

- Check for cracked or broken welds.

- Make sure bolts are tight.

- On stepladders, make sure the spreader (the hinged arms that hold the ladder open) can be locked.

- On extension ladders, replace frayed rope.

- Keep rungs free from grease or oil (you may want to apply an anti-slip coating to the steps of a metal ladder to provide better footing).

- Do not paint or use a painted wooden ladder as paint can hide structural defects.

- Make sure safeties are in place.

Setup Checklist

- If you set a ladder in a traffic area use a barricade to prevent collisions.

- Lock or block any nearby door that opens toward the ladder.

- Set the ladder on a solid, level surface.

- Place the ladder parallel to the surface it rests against.

- Never lean a ladder against an unstable surface.

- Keep the area around the base of the ladder uncluttered.

- Place a straight ladder at a safe angle—the distance from the bottom of the ladder to the wall should be one-fourth of the ladder's height.

10.21 *Pay attention while on a ladder.*

- Make sure both locks of an extension ladder are engaged to prevent overloading a rail.

- Open a stepladder all the way and lock the spreaders.

- When climbing onto a roof or platform, extend the ladder at least 3 feet above the edge.

- If possible, tie off a straight ladder as close to the point of support as possible to prevent shifting.

- Replacing the top rung of a straight ladder with a rope or chain will reduce rocking when leaning against poles

Using a Ladder

- Never allow more than one person on a ladder at a time; ladders are designed to support just one person.

- Pick a ladder that is tall enough to work from comfortably.

- Avoid excessive stretching or leaning. Move the ladder instead.

- Don't use an aluminum ladder, a ladder with metal reinforcing, or a wet wood ladder if there's a chance of contacting an electrical source.

- Use only a trestle ladder to support a plank upon which a person has to work.

- Use both hands to climb and descend. If you need tools, wear a tool belt or raise and lower them with a rope.

- Never turn around on a ladder when climbing, descending, or working. Always face forward.

- Don't overextend an extension ladder.

- Never climb higher than the second step from the top on a stepladder or the third from the top on a straight ladder.

- Carry a ladder with the front high enough to clear a man's head, especially when going around corners.

- Don't leave wood ladders out in the weather.

- Do not use a ladder horizontally in place of scaffolding.

SCAFFOLDING SAFETY

Scaffolding provides a raised platform for working on the upper part of a wall or the lower part of a roof. Scaffolding can be rented or you can make your own using metal gate panels and planks (fig. 10.22). Here are some safety guidelines:

- Make sure scaffold is on solid ground and level and stable before climbing.

- Don't use unstable objects such as concrete blocks, barrels, or boxes to support scaffolds or planks.

- Use wood blocks or plywood supports called mud sills of adequate size under scaffold on soft ground to distribute the load and keep the scaffold from sinking and tipping; mud sills should be level and in full contact with the ground.

- Use solid planks free from saw cuts, splits, and holes.

- Don't span more than 10 feet with 2 x 10 planks.

- Extend planks at least 1 foot beyond supports and nail cleats to the underside to keep the planks from slipping off.

- Don't stand on the extended portion of planks.

- Don't extend scaffold height with boxes or ladders on scaffold platforms.

- No more than one person should stand on an individual plank at one time.

- Do not jump onto, from, or between scaffolding.

- Do not try to carry materials while you climb.

- Wear footwear that has good traction; avoid hard, slick soles.

- Do not overload platforms with materials.

- Keep the scaffold surface uncluttered by scraps, tools, cords, and other obstructions.

- Use containers tied to the scaffolds to keep tools and supplies from falling off.

CLEANUP

You might be surprised by the amount of waste from the construction of your barn (see fig. 2.7, p. 11). Most barn construction waste is recyclable. Designate one area for waste management and pick up and organize the work site at the end of each day. Fence off an enclosure with rolled wire or plastic mesh to keep paper and light debris from blowing away. Stack wood scraps according to size and check there first when you need a short piece for a brace or blocking.

10.22 *Metal panels and planks used for scaffolding.*

Ask your lumber supplier if you can return unused materials for a refund. Many will agree if the material has been kept clean and dry.

Subcontractors tend to use materials more wisely when they have to pay for them rather than when you supply them. Consider a clause in your contract that makes subcontractors responsible for ordering and buying their own materials and for their own waste disposal.

Some materials can be donated to nonprofit groups, such as Habitat for Humanity, then taken as a tax-deductible charitable donation. Brick and concrete waste can be used as fill such as under walkways or driveways.

Approximately half of all barn construction waste is wood. Ground-up wood can be used for mulch, composting, animal bedding, landfill cover, as an industrial fuel source, and in new building products. Untreated wood scraps can be used for firewood or taken to a landfill.

Pressure-treated wood should **not** be burned: period. The American Medical Association advises **against** burning plywood and particleboard as well. Treated wood scraps have myriad uses around a horse place such as wheel chocks, equipment blocks, and gate supports. Brick size pieces and 3-inch-thick slices of posts can be laid in sand for walkways (see Laying a Brick Floor, p. 134). Many landfills accept pressure-treated wood; call before hauling.

Save large leftover pieces of roofing, siding, paneling, and insulation to repair future damage. Haul remaining metal, paper, cardboard, and plastic waste to a recycling center.

Be fastidious about picking up all nails and screws. A magnet on a 24-inch cord or a sweeper magnet on wheels will help find fasteners you can't see.

TOOLS

Following is a list of common tools and what they might be used for during barn construction:

- *100-foot tape measure* – layout of site, footings, and foundation.

- *25-foot* and *16-foot tape measure* – general measuring. (Tapes smaller than 16 feet are too lightweight to be practical.)

- *Builder's cord, dry chalk box (chalk box without chalk)* – string lines for layout and checking straightness of walls and other components.

- *5-pound or heavier hammer* – driving stakes.

- *16-ounce, 20-ounce carpenter's hammer* – driving nails.

- *Crowbar, pry bar* – pulling nails, prying wood apart, and removing braces.

- *Circular saw with carbide-tipped blade* – cutting wood.

- *Hand saw* – cutting where power saw won't reach.

- *Reciprocating saw* – fixing mistakes, cutting through nails, and cutting where a circular saw won't reach.

- *Cordless drill* – installing screws for siding and roofing without having to worry about tangled cords.

- *Saw horses* – elevating boards for marking and cutting, and for low scaffold supports.

- *Framing square* – layout, and marking boards for cutting.

- *Sliding T-bevel (T-bevel, bevel square)* – layout, marking boards for cutting, and marking 90° and 45° angles (12-inch blade makes it handier than a framing square).

- *Carpenter's level* – keeping parts of the barn plumb and level; straight edge.

- *Chalk line* – marking long, straight lines.

- *Plumb bob* – locating foundation locations from intersecting string lines and finding points on floor that are directly below points on ceiling.

- *Step ladder* – for reaching work higher than you can standing on the ground.

- *Straight ladder, extension ladder* – for reaching higher than step ladder and accessing roof and scaffold.

TIPS

EDGES

As you are building, use a hand plane or a router to chamfer the edges on every piece of wood, framing, and wall covering that will be exposed at horse level. This will not only minimize splinters should a horse or person rub against the board; but it will also give the barn a more finished appearance.

STRING LINE

A string line is used to line up walls and other barn components and to check them for straightness (fig. 10.23).

Tie a loop in one end and hook it on a nail. Take the string to the other end of the layout and partially drive a nail where you want the string. Instead of tying the string to the second nail, loop the string around your finger, then rotate your finger six times to twist the loop. Place the loop over the anchor nail. Simultaneously tighten the main string line and pull the free end to take up slack. Lock the string line by pulling the free end away from the direction of the string line. To unlock the line, pull the free end toward the direction of the string line.

To minimize tangles when gathering a string line, make a neat bundle called a tamale. Wrap the string in a figure-eight across the palm of your hand between your thumb and little finger. When you come to the end, tie it around the middle of the tamale. Next time you need a string line, pull on the free end of the tamale to play out the string from the middle of the bundle without untying it. An alternative is to use a dry chalk line for a string line, which allows you to reel in a string line quickly with no tangles.

To prevent sections of a wall or other components you are lining up from touching the string and throwing it out of line, place a small block of wood under the string at each end. String tension will hold the blocks in place. Slip a block of the same thickness between the string and the wall at various points to test the wall for straightness. The string should just touch the block.

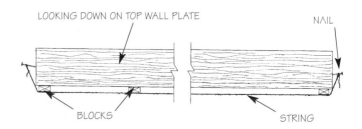

10.23 *String line.*

NOTCHING ROUND POLES

To notch a round pole to accept a board, mark both sides of the notch at the location of the board. Set you circular saw to the depth of the notch, which is usually the thickness of the board. Cut just inside both marks and make several parallel cuts between the marks. Use the straight claw of a carpenter's hammer to chip out most of the wood from the notch and then clean up the notch with a sharp, wide chisel.

CLINCHING

When a nail point protrudes through the back of an exposed board, *clinch* it (bend it over) to avoid injury to your horse and to people. Clinching in the direction of the wood grain makes it easier to bury the nail point but if the nail is close to the end of the board it could cause the board to split. In that case, bend the nail at right angles to the grain of the wood.

MOUSE PROOFING

To prevent spoiled feed and ruined tack, fit doors to feed and tack rooms so there are no gaps for mice. An efficient way to seal the bottom edge is to use a well-fitted threshold. Another is to fasten a strip of heavy rubber belting along the bottom edge on either the inside or outside of the door so the strip just touches the floor.

PAINTING

See the Resource Guide for resources that can help you find the right product for the materials and conditions of your barn.

- The best way to make wood siding last and to prevent peeling paint is to prime all six surfaces of each board before nailing it in place.

- Most wood door manufacturers state that for their warranty to be valid both faces and all four edges of the door must be sealed by paint, primer, or other treatment.

- Prime before you caulk around doors and windows. Caulking will stick to primer better than it will to wood.

- Pressure wash steel siding before painting and let it dry thoroughly. A bonding elastomer (available at professional paint supply stores) applied either as a first coat or added directly to the topcoat will help paint adhere.

- Most paint failures on T-111 siding result from applying paint too thinly.

- A roller presses the paint into the wood fibers and is faster than using a brush. If you use a brush, use a stiff one that will work the product into the wood.

- Use premium paints; they cover better and go on smoother than bargain brands.

If you want a clear finish, use a good quality wood sealer with UV protection. Don't use spar varnish; it will peel. Look for a product with a two- to four-year warranty. On horizontal surfaces, two years is about the most you can expect from a sealer.

Expect to renew exterior stain every three years or so compared with seven to ten years for exterior paint.

LANDSCAPING

Landscaping blends your barn with the land. Detailed techniques are beyond the scope of this book, but there are many excellent landscaping books available. Here are a few suggestions that can affect the safety of your horses and your barn.

Before you or a dirt crew starts grooming the yard area for planting, clean up as much construction debris as possible. Buried wood scraps can promote termite infestation, and buried metal can end up in your horse's foot.

Properly placed trees can help keep your barn cooler in the summer and protect it from cold winds in the winter. But, when planting trees, take into account the size they will be when mature and keep them far enough from the barn so branches cannot rub roofing or fall on the barn. If your area is at risk of wild fires, consider carefully before planting trees close to the barn.

Grass should be kept mowed within 30 feet of the barn to reduce fire danger. Make sure to grade the ground around the barn smooth and level enough to accommodate a mower. To keep horses from pushing on panels and fences in an attempt to reach foliage, keep grass and shrubs at least 8 feet from the edges of pens. Use gravel and rocks in this buffer zone to prevent erosion. ∪

CHAPTER ELEVEN

REMODELING

Remodeling includes transforming a non-barn building into a stable, rearranging space in an existing barn, and expanding a stable. Maybe you need to use a building to house horses temporarily while you are building a new barn. Or you might want to preserve an old building for historic or sentimental reasons and make it safe and useful for horses in the process (fig. 11.1). Although some buildings can be successfully remodeled into a horse barn, others aren't worth the effort. You may end up with an unsafe or unhealthy environment for the horse and at a higher cost than if you had built a new barn.

One of the easiest buildings to renovate for horses is a clear span pole barn that is 10 feet or higher on the inside, the type commonly used for machine sheds. More challenging are masonry buildings with ceilings lower than 9 feet, few windows and doors, and concrete floors (fig. 11.2). A better option is to use such buildings for a more suitable purpose, such as hay and bedding storage or a run-in shed.

There are certain common problems that horse owners encounter when remodeling buildings. I'll provide guidelines to help you evaluate existing structures to see if they are worth the time, effort, and money needed to turn them into a stable. You'll need to answer specific questions as you determine if renovations will satisfy safe horse facility requirements in the following areas:

- Space
- Foundation
- Structural strength
- Roofing
- Flooring
- Water
- Wiring
- Ventilation
- Doors and windows

SPACE

If you keep miniature horses or ponies, you'll have fewer space limitations when it comes to remodeling a building into a barn. Indeed, a single-car garage could be remodeled into a stable suitable for a mini. Full-size horses, however, require much more room (see Stalls, p. 34).

STALLS AND AISLE

Is there enough room to make suitable stalls and aisles wide enough to safely lead horse through the building? Are there posts or walls that will need to be moved or taken out altogether? Can they safely be removed?

Posts and *bearing walls* are there for a reason: to hold up the roof or second story. This is no place for guess work—arrange for an engineer or experienced builder to help you assess the situation before you begin jerking out posts. To safely remove posts and bearing walls, you must first transfer the load they carry to a beam, such as steel I beam or an engineered laminated wood beam supported by other posts. Never remove a post or bearing wall until alternate supports are in place. Take into account how placement of the new posts will affect the space and realize that the new beam will necessarily lower headroom beneath it.

11.1 Well-planned remodeling can preserve and expand a historic building like this dairy barn and make it safe and useful for horses.

11.2 *This concrete block dairy barn is structurally sound but has few doors, and windows of glass block admit only token sunlight and no ventilation. The solid ceiling created by the loft is too low for horse comfort and contributes to the stuffy atmosphere. Remodeling this barn for horses would not be hopeless, but it would be very expensive.*

11.3 *The floor of this remodeled dairy barn was excavated 3 feet to attain a ceiling height of 9 feet and a new concrete floor was poured in the aisle.*

HEADROOM

Will your horse be able to stand normally, head erect, without hitting his head? If he throws his head up or rears, will he crash into trusses, joists, or light fixtures?

A full-size horse needs at least 8 feet of headroom just to stand with his head in a comfortable position. When startled, a horse will quickly raise his head as high as he can, 9 feet or more, in order to see what has startled him. Horses playing or fighting between stalls can rear and reach over 10 feet with their heads. 11 feet or more of clearance to overhead obstructions is the minimum recommended for safety. Lights especially should be at least 11 feet high or located where they are protected by from contact, such as above or between joists or truss members.

As with posts and bearing walls, never cut or remove an overhead joist or truss without being absolutely certain of its function and taking steps to replace it with another structural members.

RAISING THE CEILING One way to gain headroom is to jack up the entire building and build a higher foundation to set it on. This is a big project, but if the building is otherwise sound or of historical value, it is an alternative worth considering. House moving services (check your yellow pages) have the equipment and experience to raise buildings.

LOWERING THE FLOOR An alternative to elevating the building is to dig out the area inside the barn to gain headroom (fig. 11.3). This is particularly applicable for barns where a deep accumulation of ancient animal dung has created a false floor. If the finished floor level is below the surrounding ground, however, there is a danger that water will tend to drain into the barn.

Excavation could be a viable option if the building is on a hillside or in a dry climate and if drainage arrangements can be made to divert water away from the building.

ADDING WALLS

If you inherit an empty machine shed or pole barn, you will likely want to add at least one enclosed room for tack. Start by adding a floor if necessary (see Chapter 9). If the bottom cords of trusses are at least 9 feet high, you should have no trouble building walls on the floor and then standing them up in place as is done in new house construction.

If headroom is limited and you will be attaching to trusses or joists or incorporating them into the ceiling, there may not be enough room to raise a completed wall into position. Then you will have to build the walls in place, piece by piece.

Mark the floor for the bottom plate. Hold a plumb bob on the ceiling so it is over the corner of the bottom plate and mark the location of the *top plate*. Mark the opposite corner of the top plate in similar manner and snap a chalk line between the two marks. Alternatively, use clamps to hold a board that's longer than the top plate is to the trusses or joists overhead. Loosen the clamps and use the plumb bob to position the board as necessary to line it up with the bottom plate then mark the length and the location of the board on the joists or trusses.

Cut the top and bottom plates to length and mark wall stud spacing on 16-inch centers on both plates. Nail the bottom plate to the floor. Hold or clamp the top

11.4 *Shelves suspended from ceiling joists by chains.*

plate in position and mark where nails are required to secure it overhead, then lay it on the floor and start all of the nails. Now hold it in position and drive the nails home.

A wall added over concrete needs to be fastened to the floor to prevent it from moving should a horse lean on the wall or collide with it. One way to do this is with construction adhesive and a cartridge-powered nail gun that shoots hardened nails through the bottom plate and into concrete. These guns commonly use special .22 caliber cartridges. Those activated by striking the end with a hammer cost less than trigger models.

In some cases, a nail-gun will break out a chunk of concrete instead of fastening properly. A more consistent method is to drill holes in the concrete and attach the bottom plate using special screws or any of a dozen or so concrete fasteners or anchors. Masonry bits for regular drills are sufficient for drilling holes in some brick and cinder blocks and in the mortar between them, but many are not up to drilling concrete, which contains rock and rebar. You might be better off renting whatever size bit you need and a rotary hammer, which works by turning and hammering at the same time. Consider where studs will be attached later when positioning anchor bolts.

Once the top and bottom plates are in place, measure between them to find the wall stud lengths. Measure at both ends of the plates and at several points in between because the floor or ceiling may not be perfectly parallel. Cut studs to fit snugly between the plates. Line them up on the marks and check them with a level for plumb. Toenail studs to the bottom plate with 16d box nails from each side and nail through the top plate using 16d common nails.

ADDING SHELVES

Shelves provide a place to store supplies and equipment without using valuable floor or counter space. One way to add a plywood or OSB shelf is to nail a 1 x 2 *ledger strip* or *cleat* to the wall to support the back edge of the shelf. Nail a 2 x 2 to the front edge of the shelf and attach it to the ceiling joists using sections of chain (fig. 11.4).

FOUNDATION

Is the barn setting directly on the ground? Are stones propping it up? Could a rambunctious horse push the bottom of the wall out? Is the concrete foundation cracked or crumbling? Are posts rotting at ground level?

If the foundation is going, the rest of the building will soon follow. Ground moisture will rot the bottom of the walls, causing the building to sag, crack, and come apart at the seams. As mentioned previously, a building can be jacked up while a new foundation is built beneath it, providing more headroom in the bargain. The foundation could be a continuous footing with *pony wall* as high as needed or a series of piers supporting a pressure-treated sill beam around the perimeter of the building. It will be much easier to dig a trench or holes and to pour concrete for a new foundation if the building is moved from the site and then moved back after the foundation is completed.

With a pole barn, you might be able to leave the raised building where it is. Cut off the lower bad portions of the poles and then dig them out of the ground by hand. Pour a concrete pad in the bottom of each hole and install new lower post sections comprised of four or more pressure treated 2 x 6s or 2 x 8s nailed together (fig. 11.5). The old posts set on the center section of the new posts. The outer boards of the new lower section extend alongside and are nailed to the old top sections.

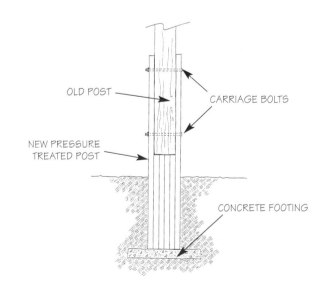

OLD POST

CARRIAGE BOLTS

NEW PRESSURE TREATED POST

CONCRETE FOOTING

11.5 *New post foundation.*

STRENGTH

Are the walls strong enough to contain a horse? If a horse kicks the wall will his foot go clear through, possible cutting his leg? Could the siding be chewed or ripped loose by a horse?

REINFORCING A WALL

Walls framed with 2 x 4s, typical of garages, are generally not strong enough to safely contain full-size horses (see Walls, p. 124). A 1,100-pound horse crashing into or kicking such a wall could knock it loose from the foundation or break the studs, causing the roof to crash down. A building with 2 x 6 framing would be a more suitable candidate for remodeling.

All walls contacted by horses need to be kick-proof up to at least 4 feet from the ground. To withstand a horse's kick, paneling and siding should be solid, full 2-inch-thick boards supported by studs at least every 4 feet; wood-core, steel-faced sandwich panels like those used with modular barns supported every 2 feet; or siding or paneling applied over ¾-inch plywood or OSB supported every 2 feet.

SIDING

Most types of siding can be easily damaged by horses chewing, kicking, or rubbing (fig. 11.6). One way to protect siding is to keep horses away from it by placing turnout pens 6 feet away from the building and making an alley of steel panels from the pen to the stall door. A gate at the pen end of the alley will keep horses away from barn siding.

Inside the barn, all wood edges exposed to horses need to be protected from chewing by regular application of an anti-chew product or by installing chew guard strips (see fig. 5.9, p. 37). Besides being unsightly and potentially dangerous because of ingested slivers, a horse could be poisoned by chewing old painted wood. Paint containing lead wasn't banned in the U.S. until 1978, and most buildings painted before that time contain some lead-based paint, especially on exterior surfaces, doors, and windows. The older the building, the higher the risk of lead-based paint.

ROOF

Does the roof leak? Does the roofing show signs of wear or damage? Is roof framing in good enough condition to justify a new roof? Is the framing strong enough to support a roof overlay or heavier type of roofing?

ROOF INSPECTION

See p. 84 for the life expectancy of common roofing materials. You can get a pretty good idea of the condition

11.6 *The siding on many existing buildings is unsuitable for use around horses. Even the relatively flat surface of the drop siding on this remodeled chicken house was soon marred by horses.*

of a roof from the ground with a pair of binoculars. A more thorough inspection can be accomplished by climbing onto the roof or by looking at it from a ladder. Shingles are easily damaged when they are hot and cold, so avoid walking on them any more than is necessary. And thin steel roofing can be bent by walking in between supports. Place your feet where the screws or nails are; this will also help prevent slipping.

Check for:

- shingles that are loose, cupping, buckling, or are bare of granules

- fasteners that have worked loose—their heads will be raised higher than others

- repairs indicated by different colored shingles or patches of tar

- sagging or bulging sections that could indicate weak framing or rotting sheathing

- mold or decay, splitting, or curling on wood shingles

- torn or buckling flashing in valleys and around roof vents

- loose, projecting nails and screws on steel roofs

- rusty or loose gutters and downspouts

From the inside of the building check for water stains on the rafters and purlins. On a bright day, turn out the lights and look for points of sunlight peeking through, which indicate holes or gaps in the roof.

When shingles curl up at the edges, it generally means that the asphalt in the shingles has aged and the shingles are becoming brittle. This is normally caused by long exposure to heat and UV rays from the sun. Weakened shingles are more easily blown off, torn, or lifted by wind gusts. Damaged shingle edges will allow sun and water penetration to the underlayment and possibly to the deck and framing. The end result is structural rot and interior damage. A deteriorated roof only gets worse with time, and it should be replaced as soon as possible.

If you are lucky with a metal roof, the roof might just need some tightening and minor repairs. Replace loose nails on steel roofing with roofing screws that have a hexagonal head and a rubber washer. Screws should be long enough to go at least 1 inch into solid wood.

Roof framing members that have deteriorated to the point where screws will not hold must be replaced. If you find a hole in steel roofing between purlins where you can't apply a screw into solid wood, fill the hole from the top with silicone caulk.

NEW VS. OVERLAY

If you determine that the roof needs to be replaced, you have two ways to go: tear off the old roofing and replace it or apply a new roof over the old one (overlay). Overlay roofing was more common years ago before felt-based shingles were being replaced by thinner fiberglass-based shingles. Irregularities of the old roof can easily show through the thinner shingles making an unsightly roof. Adding over old roofing means adding more weight to what may already be weakened framing. If the roof already has more than one layer of roofing, check with a professional roofing contractor to see if the framing and sheathing can support another overlay. Some professional roofers discourage overlays altogether, thinking overlay roofs don't last as long as new installations.

If the roof has obviously been leaking for a long time, there is likely damage to the framing and almost certainly to the deck, in which case you will be better off stripping the roof and starting over. Once the roofing has been torn off, you will be better able to see and repair structural damage.

FINDING A ROOFING CONTRACTOR

To get an idea of roofing costs, get three or four estimates from reputable contractors in your area. Make sure the bids include full stripping of the old roof, removal, disposal, cleanup, new drip edge, 30-pound building paper, and good quality roofing in a color and style you like. Keep in mind that cost is only one factor and must be balanced against the quality of the materials and workmanship. As with other contractors, get references and follow them up. Look at roofing jobs they've completed.

Roofing is not technically difficult and the outcome depends to a great extent on how well details are handled. Straight lines and a neat appearance are indicators of a good roofing job. Look for a roofer who is certified by one of the major shingle manufactures and is a member of at least one major roofing trade organization. As with the best farriers, the best roofers are certified and belong to their trade organizations. Choose someone who takes the time to study his field and is knowledgeable about the current issues that may affect his performance.

Educate yourself about the roofing process so that you can ask the right questions. Visit websites of major shingle manufacturers to get an idea of available products and recommended roofing procedures.

Don't confuse the guarantee on the roofing material with the guarantee the roofer gives you on his work. A manufacturer might guarantee materials for 25 years or more, whereas a roofer might guarantee against leaks for only 5 years.

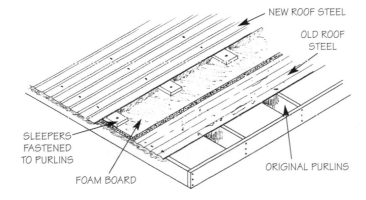

11.7 Sleeper roof.

11.8 A pole barn being extended lengthwise.

11.9 *New truss attached to end of barn.*

11.10 *In order to get snow to dump farther from the barn, this roof was extended by attaching new rafters alongside the tails of the original rafters. Translucent fiberglass was used for roofing instead of steel because it is lighter and allows more light under the overhang.*

BUILDING A SLEEPER ROOF

If the roof framing is in good shape and you don't want to tear off the existing roof, here's how to apply an insulated "sleeper roof" as an overlay (fig. 11.7).

1. Lay 1-inch-thick foam board over the old roof (check the fire rating of the foam board you choose to make sure it is safe for use in a barn).

2. Install 1 x 4 sleeper purlins on the foam board directly over the original purlins or across the rafters.

3. Use 3-inch deck screws to attach the new purlins through the foam board and old roofing, and to the old purlins.

4. Apply new steel roofing over the new purlins.

This type of overlay will reduce or eliminate condensation inside the building because the inside surface of the old roof (the barn ceiling) is kept warm by the insulation above it and air is allowed to circulate beneath the new roof. Although this roof is relatively light, you should have an engineer check the roof framing to make sure it will safely support the added load.

TEARING OFF A SHINGLE ROOF

You may decide to tear off old roofing to replace it yourself or to save money with a contractor. It doesn't require a lot of skill but it can be physically demanding and dangerous. Keep safety uppermost in your mind.

Before you begin, make arrangements to dispose of debris. Rent a large trash container or park a trailer or truck close to the roof so you can toss debris directly into it. A temporary chute will help to funnel debris into the container and help prevent nails from getting lost in the soil around the barn.

You could try and scoop shingles off en masse with a shovel, but it's usually easier and faster to remove them one by one using a flat bar. Pull the nails as you go and collect them in an apron pouch. Once the shingles and tarpaper are removed, check sheathing, fascia, and soffits, for damage. When you are through, comb the ground around the building meticulously with a magnet—every nail you find is one less that could end up in your horse's foot.

ROOF EXTENSIONS AND ADDITIONS

A roof extension is perhaps the most common modification made to horse barns. The roof can extend past the end of a barn for more stalls (fig. 11.8), or it can extend past the side of the barn to add a shed roof for additional horse shelter or hay and equipment storage.

How a new roof ties into an old roof will depend on the existing structure and the planned addition. You can extend the length of a roof at the end of a building by attaching the first new rafters directly to the existing truss or wall on the end of the barn so old and new roof blend together (fig. 11.9). Or you can attach to the wall of the barn below the existing roof in which case the new roof would be separate from and lower than the old roof.

When adding an extension onto the side of a roof, you can sometimes attach new rafters to the sides of the old rafters (fig. 11.10). If the roof meets a wall, you can attach a header to the wall below the existing roof and attach new rafters to the header (fig. 11.11).

11.11 *Adding a roof off the sides of a barn involves attaching a stringer to the barn walls and supporting the ends of the rafters with a beam and posts.*

11.12 *Roof slope changed to maintain headroom.*

When considering a side roof extension, remember that the wider you make the overhang the less headroom there will be at the eaves. Maintain at least 8 feet of clearance wherever horses will pass under the roof. To do this, you may need to change the slope of the new roof so it doesn't drop as fast (fig. 11.12). If you live in snow country, however, snow might pile up where the steeper slope meets the lower slope.

The safe maximum length of an unsupported overhang that is attached to the original rafters is approximately 3 feet. And the new rafters should extend at least 6 feet alongside the old rafters. Overhangs longer than 3 feet need to be supported by posts or brackets. All rafters that butt onto a header require support, usually in the form of a beam and posts.

Wood posts placed within a horse's reach may require periodic application of an anti-chew product to prevent horse chewing damage. Steel posts are impervious to chewing but require special tools for cutting and for welding plates on the top for attaching a beam. Brackets can support a roof extension without the need for posts (fig. 11.13). Check with local blacksmiths or metal fabricators for help with design and construction of roof brackets.

TIPS:

- Use carriage bolts to secure a roof addition to the framing of the building, don't rely on nails.

- To get rafter tails to line up, leave the rafters a bit long and use a chalk line to mark the ends for cutting after they are all in place.

VENTILATION AND INSULATION

Ventilation is directly related to the volume of air inside the building and how much air moves through openings including windows, doors, and vents (see Ventilation, p 26). Windows and doors are relatively easy to add to a pole or timber frame building, but masonry walls present more of a challenge. A continuous ridge vent can be installed on any type of roof and is perhaps the simplest, most effective way to let warm, stale air escape from inside a barn.

11.13 *This 6-foot overhang (also in fig. 11.10) is supported by custom brackets that eliminate the need for additional posts that would clutter the pens and invite chewing.*

CONDENSATION AND INSULATION

A building that has never showed signs of condensation might turn into a rain forest once it becomes a stable. Horses add more humidity and heat to the air than you might think. Proper installation of a vapor barrier and insulation can greatly reduce or prevent condensation. Condensation can camouflage roof leaks, and it's important to find and repair all leaks before applying insulation under a roof. Otherwise a leak might go undetected long enough to rot the framing, leading to expensive repairs or even roof collapse.

When insulating an existing barn, insulation can be applied between the rafters or purlins or attached to the underside of the rafters or purlins (fig. 11.14). Ventilation should be designed into a retrofit when insulation is added below the roof deck so that moist air is not trapped above the insulation.

Fiberglass blanket or batting is inexpensive and readily available, but it is a poor choice for this application. Not only does it absorb moisture, but unless it is well protected, it can provide birds and rodents with an abundance of nest material.

Rigid insulation board with a reflective aluminum or vinyl skin on both surfaces is a better choice. Thermax finish/insulation board by Celotex, for one, has a washable white surface that really brightens up a barn interior.

Spray foam is an attractive alternative because it can be applied quickly and because it so thoroughly seals and insulates even very drafty buildings. However, as mentioned in Chapter 6, some builders feel that foam applied directly to the back of siding and roofing can cause mold and rust problems, especially in humid climates. Check the fire rating of proposed insulation materials to be sure they are safe for use in a barn.

One problem with installing insulation on the underside of an old roof is that it makes it more difficult to spot new leaks. And if a leak should occur, moisture is trapped against the framing, which leads to rot. Plus, many older buildings have relatively low ceilings so no matter what kind of insulation you use, it must be protected from damage and ingestion by curious horses. What's the alternative? Insulate the top of the roof with a sleeper roof (p. 146).

DOORS AND WINDOWS

Are there enough windows for light and ventilation? Are existing doors wide and high enough for horses to pass without banging their heads or scraping their sides? Can you add or modify doors and windows without compromising the strength of the building? Can new doors be made high enough to be safe for a horse?

ADDING A DOOR OR WINDOW

Before making any cuts in an exterior wall, make certain the wall is not load bearing. With a pole barn and timber framed barn, the building load is almost always carried entirely by the vertical posts, and you can usually cut openings anywhere in the wall as long as you don't cut the posts. With other types of framing, the sidewalls are often load bearing; whereas the end or gable walls are generally not load bearing.

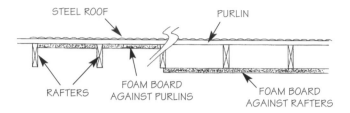

11.14 *Roof insulation retrofit.*

POLE BARN WALL When locating a door or window, make sure there will be room for it to open and close without interference. Mark the *rough opening* of the door or window on the inside wall. The rough opening is larger than the window's actual size. Manufacturers generally recommend a rough opening ½-inch to ¾-inch larger than the door or window. Installation instructions usually include rough opening dimensions.

Before cutting into a wall, be absolutely certain there are no hidden wires or pipes inside the wall. Carefully remove a portion of siding or paneling so you can see inside the wall cavity to locate and identify internal components.

Cut out the opening in the inside wall covering if there is any. Install two horizontal boards between the posts on either side of the opening, one board at the top of the opening and one at the bottom (see fig. 10.10, p. 125). Use lumber having the same width as the poles. Install two vertical boards between the horizontal boards, one at either side of the rough opening.

Drive a nail through the siding from the backside at each corner of the framed opening. On the outside, use a straightedge or chalk lines to mark the opening between the nails. Cut the opening in the siding and fasten the exposed sheathing or girts to the new framing.

Install the door or window in the opening. For a wooden window, center it in the opening and shim as necessary to get it level and plumb. Drill pilot holes and tack the jamb in place. There should always be shims snug between the jamb and the framing wherever you nail.

Aluminum and vinyl-clad windows that come with flanges around the frame are easier to install. You simply center the window in the opening and nail or screw the flange to the sheathing and framing from the outside. You may have to loosen or remove some exterior siding to slip the flange underneath it.

LOAD-BEARING WALL If the wall is load bearing, a header is installed across the top of the window or door opening to transfer the load to the sides of the opening. While the opening is being cut and the header installed, you'll need to temporarily support the load with posts and bracing.

Mark the wall as described for a pole barn wall and check it for wires and plumbing. Install temporary bracing as necessary before removing any studs in the opening. Use these removed studs as *cripple studs* under the sill and over the header.

Install a stud on each side of the opening to obtain the rough opening width for the door or window. Cut *trimmer* studs to support the header and nail them to the wall studs. Build a header and set it in place on the trimmers and nail it to the wall studs. Install cripple studs above the header. For a window, next install the sill piece and cripple studs below it.

Drive a nail through the siding at the corners of the opening and finish as with a pole barn wall.

FLOORING

Is that old wood floor solid enough to support the concentrated weight of a horse? Can you provide enough cushion over a concrete floor to prevent abrasions and joint soreness in your horse? Will accumulating urine and moisture cause mud and odor problems?

It's a rare building that has ideal flooring for horse stalls. Most have either concrete, such as in dairy barns, or dirt. Concrete can be great for aisles and any room except stalls. If the building has a dirt floor, see Chapter 9 for several flooring options.

Dealing with Old Concrete

In stalls, concrete is best suited for short-term use and then only if covered by rubber mats and shavings or other soft bedding. Otherwise, your horse could wear his hooves short to the point of lameness and get sores on his hocks, elbows, hips, and fetlocks from lying down and getting up.

Covering Concrete Long term solutions include either removing the concrete or covering it with a softer, less abrasive material. The simplest option is to install rubber mats directly on top of concrete. This will provide a safe comfortable surface, but urine often gets trapped underneath mats and leads to odors. Your best chance of success is to use interlocking mats—these seal tightly together and minimize the amount of urine seeping through the joints. Also, use absorbent bedding, such as wood shavings, and clean the stalls at least twice a day to remove wet bedding and to keep the stall floor as dry as possible.

Removing Concrete Removing concrete is no picnic. Perhaps the easiest way is to rent equipment or hire a concrete cutting subcontractor to cut the perimeter of the floor area, then use a sledgehammer or jackhammer to break out the middle. The rubble can be hauled away or used to fill in low spots on your property. After the first

two hours, you'll be thinking about hiring the sub to do the entire job.

Repairing and Adding Concrete In aisles and other areas you might want to retain concrete. Broken or otherwise damaged concrete can be repaired or covered by a layer of new concrete or acrylic polymer cement. Gutters in a dairy barn can be filled with concrete or framed in and floored with pressure-treated wood level with the surrounding floor. Realize that with the latter method water or moisture that gets into the gutter will have no way out and may be a source of odors. You may want to make wooden gutter inserts removable so the gutter can be flushed out as necessary.

When pouring a new concrete floor in a barn that already contains stalls, the added height of the concrete can interfere with the operation of doors. It is better in the long run to excavate so the finished floor is at the same level as the old floor. Otherwise you will need to raise the doors, cut off the bottom of the doors, or frame the floor around the doors so they have room to open (fig. 11.15).

WIRING

Is the electric service to the building adequate for extra lights and outlets you might need? Is the wiring capable of handling the extra load required for additional outlets, lights, heaters, or pumps? Is the wiring protected from horses or does it need to be run through conduit? Are there frayed wires that need to be replaced?

Poor or inadequate wiring is the main cause of barn fires. What is especially risky is overloading a wiring system and exposing it to abuse and damage for which it was never intended and from which it is not protected. Anytime you're doing a remodeling job, inspect the wiring and make sure it complies with code. This will involve more work and money for materials like cable, boxes, switches, but you'll sleep better having newer, safer wiring in the barn and will be less likely to be awakened by the smell of smoke and the sound of screaming horses.

Service

To determine if you need to upgrade the service panel, have an electrician look at it and advise you. Also, don't be afraid to call your local electrical inspector for advice. Either or both of these professionals can help you formulate a plan.

Full-Service Panel Unless the building will have an electrical heating system you probably won't need a service larger than 100 amps. A panel with all breaker slots filled doesn't necessarily mean you are using all of the available power. Basic circuits are limited to 15 amps and the number of electrical devices (outlets, lights) that

11.16 *Translucent fiberglass panels used to replace some steel roofing panels.*

11.15 *When adding a new concrete floor in this existing barn, a slot was framed next to each stall to provide space for the sliding doors to operate. This was easier than raising the doors, but the slot fills with bedding and must be constantly cleaned out.*

can be connected to one circuit is usually 12. If your estimated load doesn't justify an increase in amperage service, you can either have a sub-panel *(pony panel)* installed or replace some or all of the 15-amp breakers with twin breakers that fit two circuits into the space of one breaker.

SERVICE UPGRADE If you need to increase the size of your electric service, call your electrical utility to find the size of their service conductors coming into your meter box *(service drop)*. They are commonly 200A. If the service conductors are too small, they will have to be replaced by the power company. If the conductors from the meter to your service panel *(service leads)* are too small, they will have to be replaced by an electrician. If all the conductors are adequate, it is just a matter of turning off the main disconnect switch, if you have one, or having the power company pull the meter to disconnect the power while you or your electrician swap the service panels.

In some areas you are allowed to replace an old fuse panel with a modern breaker panel of the same amperage. But, if you change the size of the service you are usually required to bring all the wiring in the building up to current codes. First contact your local building department and electric utility to find out what you are allowed to do.

If you are allowed to do the work yourself, label wires and make a diagram before unhooking wires so you

know how to reconnect them. Make note of what circuits are 120-volt and which are 240-volt. Once the wires are all removed, install the new panel and hook up the old wires to either one-pole breakers for 120-volt circuits or two-pole breakers for 240-volt circuits.

PROTECTING WIRES

Exposed wiring will need to be replaced with wiring protected by conduit, especially in areas where horses could contact it. Check local code to see what types of conduit you can use. Conduit is not indestructible; it too is subject to damage from the enormous force of a bored horse's teeth. Whenever possible, locate conduit where a horse cannot get at good grip on it, such as in corners or high overhead. And fasten conduit securely to the surface behind it.

ADDING AND REPLACING OUTLETS

An inexpensive outlet tester can tell you instantly if an outlet has dangerous electrical conditions. It is not uncommon for an older building to have two-prong, ungrounded outlets. It is illegal in most areas to install three-prong grounded outlets without a ground wire attached. One way to resolve this is to rewire the building to include a ground wire. The National Electrical Code allows some two-wire systems to be brought up to standard by using a *GFCI* receptacle in the first outlet in each circuit. Although this won't provide a ground, it will give protection against shorts, shocks, and fires.

When replacing an outlet, it must be GFCI-protected if it is located where code requires a GFCI for a new installation.

LIGHTS

Are there enough lights in the building? How many will you need to add? Are existing lights located where horses can't reach them or will they have to be moved.

INSTALLING A SKYLIGHT

One of the quickest and least expensive ways to get daylight into a barn is by adding skylights. With a steel roof, if matching translucent fiberglass panels can be found you don't even need to frame the skylight—simply replace as many steel panels as desired with fiberglass panels (see fig. 9.4, p. 100 and fig. 11.16). A framed skylight is used with shingle roofs, or when you can't find fiberglass panels to match steel panels. The frame extends above the roofing to support a bubble skylight or flat piece of Lexan or other clear plastic. Some skylights set in the frame and attach with brackets; whereas others have a flange that sets over the frame. The latter type seals better.

Here's how to install a skylight frame (fig. 11.17).

It's easiest to mark the skylight rough opening on the underside of the roof where you can see the framing. Drill a hole or punch a hole with a nail through the roofing at each corner of the opening. Up on the roof, use the holes as guides to snap chalk lines outlining the skylight. Using an appropriate saw and blade carefully cut out the opening only through the roofing not the framing. A circular saw with an abrasive blade works well for a

steel roof (see fig. 10.13, p. 128). A carbide blade will work for a shingle roof, but shingles tend to gum up a circular saw blade so you may want to cut the shingles away first with a mat knife. You could use a reciprocating saw instead, but it is more difficult to cut a straight line with a reciprocating saw.

Remove the cutout from the opening and return to the inside of the building. Cut out the portions of rafters in the skylight opening, removing an extra 3 inches to allow for a *double header* on each end. Install headers between the full rafters on either side of the cutout to frame the length of the rough opening. Nail trimmer rafters between the headers as necessary to frame the width of the opening.

Especially if you cut more than one rafter, you may be required to reinforce the rafters on either side of the opening with same-sized lumber that extends the length of the rafters.

The frame must be well sealed where it comes through the roof to prevent leaks. Skylights are notorious for leaking. Carefully remove the shingles surrounding the opening to allow for flashing and tar paper to be installed according to the skylight manufacturer's directions.

REPLACING AND ADDING LIGHT FIXTURES

When adding or replacing light fixtures to an existing electrical system consider:

- Amperage
- Heat safety
- Proper ground
- Physical support

Quartz halogen floodlights are a good choice for replacing standard incandescent fixtures. Not only do they provide more light at lower cost than incandescent bulbs (see Chapter 10), but they also can usually be attached to the existing junction or outlet box.

Fluorescent lights are cooler and typically require less amperage for the same light output. They require more support than just being attached to a junction box. Fluorescent fixtures can weigh more than 25 pounds. A 2 x 4 between rafters or trusses makes a good support. Metal brackets are also available that telescope to fit between framing. The fixtures can also be hung from chains attached to the framing.

AMPERAGE Before adding lights to a circuit or increasing the size of bulbs, determine the load capacity of the circuit by checking the size of the fuse or breaker that controls the circuit in the main service panel. Too many lights on a circuit can constantly cause a breaker to

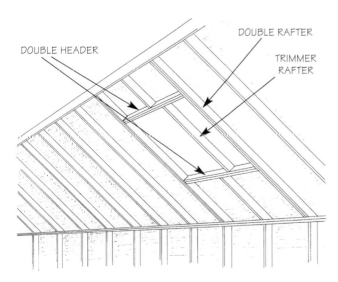

DOUBLE HEADER

DOUBLE RAFTER

TRIMMER RAFTER

11.17 *Skylight framing.*

trip or a fuse to blow. Generally, but not always, the lights are on a separate circuit from outlets and other appliances. To find out which lights and outlets are on a given circuit, turn on all the lights in the building and flip each breaker, or unscrew each fuse, in turn and note which lights go off. Use a plug-in device like a portable lamp or radio to test outlets. Add the wattage of all the lights and other appliances on a circuit to find the total wattage. Divide the wattage by 120 volts (amps = watts ÷ volts) to find the amperage load on that circuit,

For example, if your barn is dark and dismal because it only has five 60-watt incandescent bulbs, you would determine how many lights and of what size you can add this way: the five 60-watt bulbs are using only 2.5 amps (5 x 60 = 300; 300 ÷ 120 = 2.5 amps) on a 15 amp circuit. You could add two 500-watt quartz lamps (2 x 500 = 1000 ÷ 120 = 8.3 amps) and three fluorescent fixtures, each holding two 40-watt bulbs (2 x 40 = 80 x 3 = 240 ÷ 120 = 2 amps) and still draw less than 15 amps (2.5 + 8.3 + 2 = 12.8 amps).

If your calculations show that by adding or replacing light fixtures the amperage requirement would exceed the limit of the circuit, you may be able to install a larger breaker if the existing wires are large enough to carry the load. Fourteen-gauge wires can carry 15 amps; 12-gauge wires are good for 20 amps. Wire size is marked on the cable sheathing (the smaller the gauge, the bigger the wire). If you need to have a new, higher amperage circuit installed, this might be a good time to consult with a qualified electrician.

HEAT Wiring in many older buildings does not have high-temperature insulation. Excess heat generated by some lights, an incandescent bulb in a jelly jar, for example,

can cause this insulation to deteriorate and crack, increasing risk of fire. Some newer fixtures are specifically marked for use with high temperature wire only.

Another heat consideration and potential fire hazard comes with installing recessed or "pot" lamps in insulated ceilings, such as in a tack room or vet room. The National Electric Code requires at least a 3-inch clearance between the fixture and any insulation. Generally a *coffin,* a box covered with plywood, is built around the pot lamp fixture to ensure airflow around it and to prevent it from accidentally getting covered by insulation. Some pot lamp fixtures contain integral thermal cutoff switches that turn the light off if it gets too hot. This type can be covered by insulation but they are usually limited to 75-watt bulbs.

No heat lamp fixture is approved for use in insulation. When installing a heat lamp over a stall or in a bathroom, make sure to allow plenty of airflow around it, using a coffin if necessary. Check local code for coffin dimensions.

GROUND All light fixtures, including fluorescent, require a circuit with a ground. This means an older two-wire circuit will have to be replaced with three-wire cable.

WATER

Are there water lines in the building? Will they have to be moved? If there are no lines, is there a supply line nearby to connect to? If you plan on using automatic waterers, can equipment get into the building to dig a trench or will it have to be dug by hand? If there is a concrete floor in the building, how will you install underground water lines? Will you need to keep water lines from freezing? For help in solving water problems that might come up read Chapter 10 and develop a good working relationship with a professional plumber. U

CHAPTER TWELVE

PUTTING IT ALL TOGETHER

BY CHERRY HILL

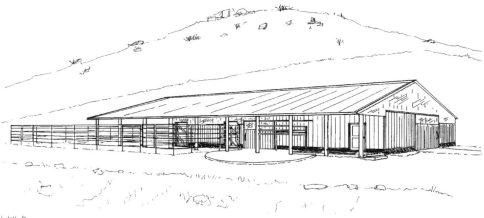

12.1 *The Cherry Hill Barn.*

Now that you have access to a generous amount of information about planning and building horse barns, I'd like to pull it all together by taking you on a tour of my personal barn (fig. 12.1). Richard and I designed the barn to suit the number of horses I usually have, my training program, our style of horsekeeping, and the Rocky Mountain climate. I usually own between six and eight horses, ranging from newborn to senior. We have other horse facilities (pens, paddocks, and pastures) on our property in addition to this barn.

We located the barn downwind from the house set into a treeless hill overlooking the arena, round pen, and

12.2 *Overview of pens and training areas.*

pastures (fig. 12.2). There have been a fair number of forest fires in this area over the last few years, so we chose a safe location away from trees and other buildings. We keep the grass mowed around the barn and we have a separate 1,000-gallon cistern near the barn that is used to water horses and can be used in the case of an emergency.

When I am at the house, I can see the barn, all of the pens, and most of the pastures. When I am at the barn, I can see the house and all of the pens and pastures. The horses that live at the barn can keep an eye on the whole spread—it is a great vantage point and it breeds contentment.

After the site was excavated and the utility trenches were put in (see figs. 10.4 and 10.5, pp. 121–122), we let the site settle for a year, and we built the barn the next year. I say "we" but it was really Richard doing 95 percent of the work while I coached and supplied apple cobbler and oatmeal-nut cookie fuel.

Since most of our winter weather blows in from the north and west, we oriented the front of the barn and the pens to the east-southeast (see fig. 3.6, p. 17). This makes the doors easy to operate in deep snow and wind; there is good shelter under the south and east roof overhangs for the horses; and the morning sun quickly warms the pens on the working side of the barn.

The barn is 52 feet by 33 feet with a 1-foot overhang on the west, a 15-foot overhang on the east, and a

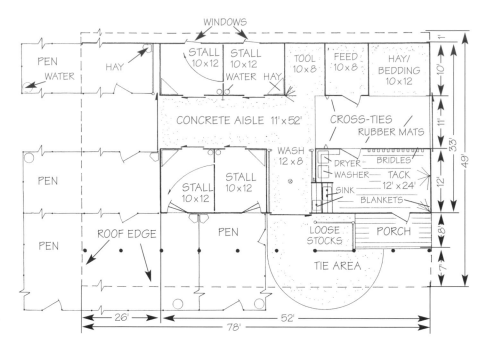

12.3 *The Cherry Hill Barn floor plan.*

26-foot roof extension on the south end (fig. 12.3). (See figs. 11.8, 11.10, and 11.13, pp. 145–147, for details on the roof extensions). The roof has a 4/12 slope with 9-foot-high eaves and a 17-foot peak. There are 11-foot-wide sliding doors at the north and south ends, an 8-foot-wide sliding door at the wash rack entrance, and a person door from the porch into the tack room.

The foundation is 8-inch-diameter pressure-treated posts with a pressure-treated plywood skirting that extends 1 foot above the ground and 1 foot below the ground (fig. 12.4, see also fig. 10.9, p. 124). This deep skirting is the main reason there are no mice in the barn. The siding and roofing are ribbed steel; the walls are not insulated (except for the tack room); the roof is lined with white pressed-fiber soundboard. There are translucent fiberglass panels on the gable ends and on the upper 3 feet of the walls (except for the tack room) (fig. 12.4). The fiberglass panels were a great idea because they let in enough light so I usually don't have to use the electric lights during daylight hours, and the barn has a cheery atmosphere.

STALLS

There are four 10-foot by 12-foot stalls, two on each side of the aisle that I use during very frigid or windy winter weather, during very hot summer weather, and after bathing (fig. 12.5). Heavy-duty solid swinging dividers between each pair of stalls can be opened to create double stalls (fig. 12.6) that I use for foaling or for the rare lay up. The stall walls are 2 x 8 rough-cut pine with grilles of ⁷⁄₈-inch solid rod on the aisle walls. A portion of the grille in each stall opens into the stall for placing

hay or grain into the feeders. All wood edges are covered by the grille frames or by 14-gauge, 2-inch by 2-inch steel angle trim (fig. 12.7). I love the ambiance of wood stall fronts and wanted something sturdy and fitting for Colorado, and the full dimension pine boards fit the bill.

There are sliding stall doors to the aisle (fig. 12.8) and Dutch doors to the turnout pens. When the top of a Dutch door is opened, the stalled horse can see outside (fig. 12.9). When the bottom is opened, the stall can be used as a creep (see fig. 5.5, p. 35).

The two west stalls have windows with solid wood coverings that open out (fig. 12.4). One stall has an infrared heater, which I use to dry a bathed horse in cooler weather (fig. 12.5). We use hanging buckets for water in the summer and have insulated bucket holders for winter. I either feed hay on clean matted stall floors

12.4 *Back of barn.*

12.5 *Single stall with corner feed bin and overhead infrared heater.*

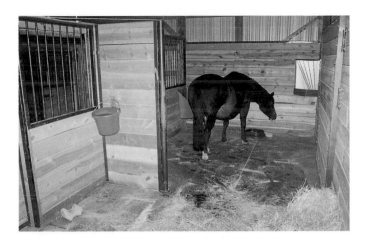

12.6 *Double stall.*

12.7 *Stall edging.*

or in the corner mounted tubs (12.5). The blanket bar on the front of each stall provides a place to store the horse's turn-out blanket and halter; plus, it serves as a handle for the sliding door (fig. 12.8).

We tamped and leveled the native decomposed granite soil in the stalls and pen feeding areas and installed solid, interlocking rubber mats (fig. 12.10). Rubber mats with jigsaw puzzle edges help keep moisture on the surface where it can be absorbed by bedding and also prevent separating and buckling, two common problems with straight edged mats.

TURNOUT PENS

There are four turnout pens with roof extensions off the east and south. The roofed area in each pen is rubber matted. The rest of the pen area is topped with ⅜-inch gravel. Railroad ties divide matted sections from gravel sections to keep the feeding area free of gravel. The majority of the time, we feed hay on ground level, right on the mats. When the footing in the pens is wet (rare in our semi-arid climate), the horses track dirt and gravel onto the eating area, so during that time, I use hay bags, hay nets, or feeders (fig. 12.11).

AISLE WIDTH AND FLOORING

The central aisle is 11 feet wide (fig. 12.12). I can drive my 65-horsepower tractor or my pickup down the aisle to unload hay, bedding, or grain. There is plenty of room for two horses to pass safely, and I find the width ideal for cross-ties.

The concrete aisle floor has a medium texture; the grooming area portion is covered with rubber mats. Looking at the grooming area from the rear, the feed room is on the right and the tack room and recessed grooming tool nooks are on the left (fig. 12.13). The 4-foot-wide tack room door is located on the horse's near side, making it easy for me to carry a saddle out of the tack room and place it on the horse. An overhead vacuum hose connects to the canister vacuum mounted on the tool room wall.

Brushes, curries, cloths, clippers, and other grooming tools and supplies are stored in recessed shelves in the grooming/tacking area (fig. 12.14).

A blanket rod system located at the junction of the stall area and tool room can be swung completely out of the aisle into the tool room or expanded like this for full aeration (fig. 12.15).

LIGHTS

We installed halogen lights in the main barn areas: three 300-watt lights in the aisle, one 150-watt light over each stall, four 150-watt lights in the grooming area (one at each corner), four 150-watt lights in the wash rack (one at each corner), and seven on the outside of the barn (three 300-watt lights and four 150-watt lights) (see fig. 9.11, p. 104). One of the exterior lights is controlled by a remote switch at the house; making the trek to the barn for the night check much safer. We used incandescent fixtures in the feed room and tack room.

12.8 *Stall front.*

12.9 *Dutch door.*

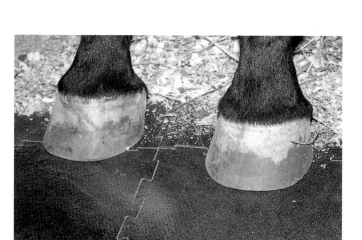

12.10 *Stall mats.*

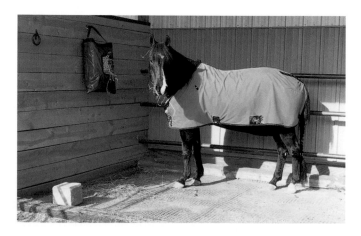

12.11 *Covered pen.*

WATER

The 1,000-gallon cistern located uphill from the barn supplies water to the barn and is automatically refilled from our well. In the event of a power failure, we can still get water to the barn via gravity flow. Between the tack room and the wash rack, in a cabinet under the wash rack sink, there is a water heater and pressure tank that provide hot and cold water to the vet/utility sink, the wash rack, and the tack room (fig. 12.16). We installed one cold-water hydrant inside the barn and one outside to fill buckets and tubs in the stalls and pens.

The freeze-proof hydrant in the barn aisle has a hose hanger and a gravel box around the hydrant, which allows for drainage in the event the hose should pop off the hydrant (fig. 12.17).

WASH RACK

The wash stall (fig. 12.18) is 8 feet by 12 feet with a rough-textured concrete floor that slopes toward a central drain. The drain is covered so it catches hair before it can clog the drainpipe. The rough texture gives good traction, wet or dry, for both the horses and me (fig. 12.19).

The walls are 1/16-inch *FRP* glued to 3/4-inch *OSB*. On the stall side of the wash rack, there are sliding splash panels that are raised and lowered by a rope and pulley system. A 2½-inch diameter pipe rail runs around the wash stall 40 inches from the floor to prevent a horse from contacting faucets, racks, or sliding panels. There are cross-ties at both ends of the wash stall so the horse faces either way. When I am bathing a horse, I generally face the horse away from the aisle with the wash rack door open. When a vet is doing repro work (fig. 12.18), it is handy to face the mare toward the aisle so her hindquarters are near the vet sink where there is easy access to water, a place to plug in an ultrasound machine, and plenty of room to place tools and supplies.

The stainless steel vet/utility sink (formerly from a restaurant) has a sloping 3-foot-long drain board, which makes a great place to scrub and drain grooming tools and buckets (fig. 12.20). The entire sink area can be hosed down. Towel hangers double as cabinet door handles.

There are plastic-coated wire wall racks for shampoos, sponges, and cloths and a hose hanger connected to hot and cold faucets using a Y connector (fig. 12.21). An infrared heater is suspended over the wash rack.

12.12 *Aisle.*

12.15 *Blanket rod aisle.*

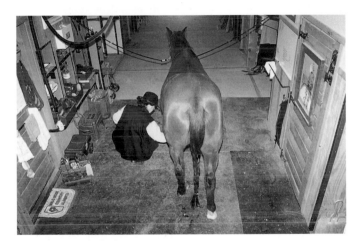

12.13 *Grooming area.*

12.16 *Water heater and pressure tank*

12.14 *Grooming nooks.*

12.17 *Inside hydrant.*

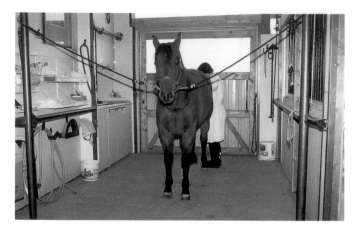

12.18 *Wash rack.*

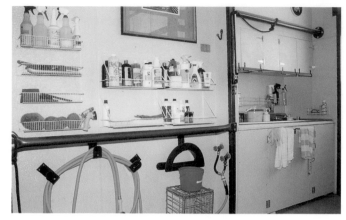

12.21 *Wash rack wall.*

12.19 *Wash rack floor and drain.*

12.22 *Tack room laundry area.*

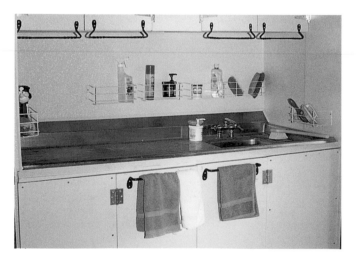

12.20 *Wash rack sink.*

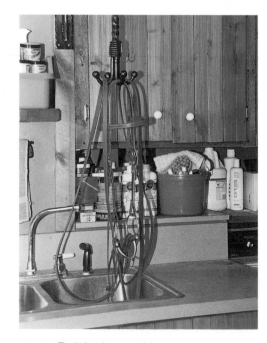

12.23 *Tack hook over sink.*

12.24 *Tack repair counter.*

12.25 *Bridle rack and first aid shelf.*

12.26 *Blanket rod tack room.*

TACK ROOM

The 12-foot by 24-foot tack room is insulated, heated, and vented, has hot and cold water, a washer and dryer, a refrigerator, an 8-foot sink/tack repair counter with double sink (with crane-neck faucet and sprayer), a desk and a file cabinet, storage cabinets and shelves, several large tack trunks, blanket rod systems, a variety of tack hooks, bridle racks, some built-in saddle racks and some standing saddle racks.

There are two doors: one 4-foot-wide door to the tacking/grooming area and one 3-foot wide door to the porch. Above the tack room is an open loft for storage of seasonal or rarely used items, extra buckets, and feeders.

For convenience and to save wear on the home appliances, I wash and dry all horse laundry in the barn (fig. 12.22). The dryer is vented into the wash rack.

There is a tack hook on a swinging arm over the sink, which makes it easy for me to take good care of bits and bridles (fig. 12.23). The 5-foot Formica counter next to the sink provides plenty of room to make most tack repairs (fig. 12.24).

The bridle rack is located next to the door to the grooming area and is topped with a shelf where I keep a first aid kit, helmets, seasonal items, and extra blankets and pads (fig. 12.25).

I use this "Klimesh" swinging-rod blanket system in the corner of the tack room to store saddle blankets, coolers, or sheets (fig. 12.26). There is another blanket rod system next to it that I alternate using for winter blankets or fly sheets.

There is a fan/vent in the ceiling that can be turned on manually or by an automatic timer to remove hot air and draw fresh air through the tack room. During the summer, I set the timer to operate the fan from midnight to 5 am, so warm air is drawn out through the ceiling fan and cool night air is drawn in from a louvered vent near the floor on the north side of the building. A screen behind the louvers keeps insects out. Even in July, when I enter the tack room, it often feels as if I am stepping into an air-conditioned room.

The louvers are closed during the winter. Because the tack room floor, walls, and ceiling are well insulated, a small oil-filled radiator-style heater keeps the tack room very toasty in winter, even during very cold weather. It's a great place to warm up.

FEED ROOM

The feed room (see fig. 5.18, p. 41) is 8 feet by 10 feet with a smooth concrete floor, a feed board, and work counter (fig. 12.27). I rarely need to use the lights because of the translucent panels in the top portion of the west wall. I often feed five different grain products and four supplements to my various horses—foals, lactating mares, horses in various levels of work, idle horses, and seniors. I use plastic garbage cans for feed barrels. They are set on 12-inch-high platforms making it easier to scoop the very last feed out of the bottom of a barrel. Since I buy about a month's supply of each product at a time, I store extra sacks of feed right on the concrete floor. The room is rodent-proof and the door has a horse-proof lock on the outside.

12.27 *Feed room.*

12.28 *Hay and bedding storage.*

12.29 *Tool room.*

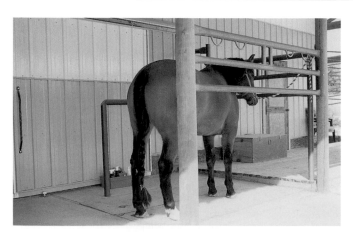

12.30 *Loose stocks.*

HAY STORAGE

We have a separate building for storing twenty tons of hay so we usually only store about 30 bales of hay and 30 bags of shavings in the barn. A 10-foot by 12-foot space at the north end of the barn next to the 11-foot sliding door works ideally for this because of its convenience for unloading (fig. 12.28).

TOOL ROOM

An 8-foot by 10-foot alcove between the stall area and the feed room serves as a tool room where we store a manure cart and forks, hand tools, farrier's tools, and fence repair equipment (fig. 12.29). This keeps the aisles clear and encourages us to practice the adage "a place for everything and everything in its place." Since we both use the tools, this room minimizes the "Hon, where's the _____?" scenarios. The central vacuum is mounted on the tool room/feed room wall and is vented to the outside through the back (west) wall of the tool room. There is a ladder to the loft over the feed room where we store dog transport kennels and more buckets.

TIE AREAS

I like a variety of safe places to tie horses to work on them or to temporarily store them. There are cross-ties in the grooming area near the tack room; two cross-ties in the wash rack; a tie ring in each stall; and a hitch rail and loose stocks on the east side of the barn under the roof overhang.

The hand forged "Klimesh" cross-tie rings are made of very sturdy stock and bolted securely into the wall studs using ⅜-inch by 2½-inch lag screws.

Protected from sun and wind, the loose stocks is a good place to let a young horse stand saddled and learn patience. Often, after a ride, I loosen the cinch and let the horse stand in the shade in the loose stocks while I ride the next horse. It is also a perfect place to let a horse dry after a bath (fig. 12.30).

The hitch rail allows me to tie various horses at the appropriate height and position for that horse. The heavy pipe rails are impervious to chewing so this is another ideal place to teach young horses to stand tied without getting into trouble! The steel loops keep the rope from sliding along the pipe (fig. 12.31).

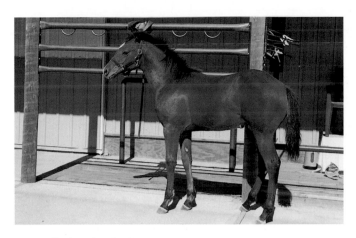

12.31 *Foal tied in hitch area.*

12.32 *Porch and tie area.*

PORCH

The 8-foot by 16-foot porch with slatted redwood floor is on the front (east) of the barn under the roof overhang (fig. 12.32). A blanket rod system is installed under the roof, conveniently located for drying laundry from the tack room or airing saddle blankets. I can leave fancy pads and blankets out all day for a good airing without sun damage.

The porch has a 16-inch-high pipe rail along its front edge. It makes an ideal place to get out of the hot sun in the summer and work on tack or to take a break and put your feet up after writing a book. ∪

HELPFUL BUILDING TERMS

Following is a list of common construction terms and their definitions. Although not all of these terms are discussed in the book, you are likely to encounter many of them while planning and building your barn.

ABS Acrylonitrile butadiene styrene; rigid black plastic pipe used for drain lines.

AC Alternating current; the type of electricity supplied by electric utilities in the United States; also short for armored cable.

Access panel An opening in the wall or ceiling near the fixture that allows access for servicing the plumbing/electrical system.

Adaptor A fitting that enables different types of pipe to be fit together.

Aggregate Minerals such as sand, gravel, and crushed stone with which cement and water are mixed to form concrete; crushed stone is usually designated as coarse aggregate and sand as fine aggregate.

Air changes The amount of fresh air required per hour to replace stale air in a given space.

Ambient lighting General illumination in a room, with no single, visible source of the light.

Amp Ampere; a unit that measures the strength/rate of flow of electrical current through a *conductor;* conductors are rated by the current in amps they can carry.

Anchor bolt A bolt used to anchor a sill to *masonry foundation.*

Armored cable Electrical cable enclosed in a metal *sheathing.*

Asphalt A sticky brown to black bituminous substance, insoluble in water, occurring naturally or obtained as a by-product of refining petroleum and coal tar; used for paving, roofing, and waterproofing.

Asphalt shingles A type of composition shingle made of *fiberglass* or cellulose felt saturated with *asphalt* and surfaced with mineral granules.

AWG *see* Wire size.

Backfill The material used to fill the excavation around a *foundation* to *grade* level.

Backhoe Excavation machine that digs by pulling a boom mounted bucket toward itself; used to dig *footings* and trenches.

Band joist (rim joist) (1) The *joist* that forms the outside perimeter of a floor framing system. (2) A joist that attaches to the ends of the main joists; also called a *header.*

Barge rafter (flying rafter, verge rafter) The last *rafter* at the end of a *gable roof,* often extends past the building and is supported by *lookouts.*

Batt In insulation, a batt is a section of loosely matted fibers that may have one or both surfaces faced with paper or foil; also short for *batten.*

Batten A thin wood strip that covers a joint on vertical board siding.

Batter boards A system of boards attached to stakes set up outside the corners of a building before construction begins and between which strings are stretched to indicate placement of *footings* and other initial building components.

Beam Any large horizontal structural *member* used to support a load over an opening or from post to post.

Bearing wall *see* Load bearing.

Belled pier *see* Caisson.

Berm A small, earthen embankment, usually used for diverting *runoff* water.

Bevel (beveled) To cut or remove an edge of a board at an angle other than a right angle and to the full thickness of the board.

Bibb (bibcock, hose bib) A *faucet* with male threads for a hose connection; the nozzle is often bent downward.

Bibcock *see* Bibb.

Bird blocking Short wooden blocks placed between *rafters* above the *top plate* to keep out birds and small animals.

Blocking Short pieces of lumber installed between *joists* or *studs* to provide a nailing surface for *framing members*, such as when attaching the *top plate* of a new wall parallel to existing ceiling joists.

Board-and-batten siding Wide vertical boards installed close together with the gaps between them covered by narrow boards or strips *(battens)*.

Borate-treated lumber Lumber preserved with borate salts; effective against wood-boring insects, but not against molds and fungi.

Bow A curve or warp perpendicular to the face of a board; often used for *crook*.

Bracing Boards, metal rods, and strips used for strengthening various parts of a building or as temporary supports.

Branch circuits The *circuits* in a building that branch from the *service panel* to boxes and devices.

Breaker *see* Circuit breaker.

Breezeway A center aisle barn with a large door on each end of the aisle.

Brick molding Trim piece that covers the gap between a window or door frame and the exterior finish.

Bridging (cross bridging) Short boards or metal braces attached between *joists* to stabilize the joists and distribute the floor load.

Broom finish The texture created when a stiff broom is pulled across the surface of a *concrete slab* before it has set.

Builder's cord Nylon cord that is stretched tight to lay out a building site, to line up building components, or to check components for straightness.

Builder's level *see* Level.

Building code A set of safety standards that contains the rules necessary for accepted safe building practices.

Building permit An authorized form that allows a person to legally construct or remodel a building.

Building standards Guidelines that detail the minimum design or the performance of a specific material.

Bullfloat (darby) A large flat tool usually of wood, aluminum, or magnesium with a handle used to level the ridges on a *concrete slab* left by *screeding*.

Buss bar (bus bar) One of several metallic strips in the *service panel* onto which *breakers* and wires connect.

BX cable Technically known as *armored cable* or *AC*, it has a flexible aluminum or steel *sheath* over the *conductors;* BX is an old General Electric trademark.

Caisson (belled pier) A pile-like *concrete foundation* made by drilling a hole into the earth, enlarging (belling out) the bottom, and filling with concrete.

Cap Plate Top wall plate.

Carpenter's level *see* Level.

Carriage Bolt A bolt with a domed head and short portion of square *shank* to prevent the bolt from turning in the wood when the nut is tightened.

Casing Trim molding applied around interior and exterior window and door openings to cover the gap between the frame or *jamb* an the wall.

Caulk (caulking) A soft waterproof compound for sealing joints and cracks.

Caulking *see* Caulk.

CDX A grade of plywood; C and D refer to the smoothness of the face (A being the best) and X means "exterior," the glue used to make the plywood resist moisture.

Cement A powdered material composed mainly of limestone and sand that when mixed with water will harden and act as a binder between other materials such as sand and gravel in *concrete;* also used as a synonym for adhesive.

Chalk line A string wound on a reel within a small chalk-filled box; when stretched tight it is snapped to mark straight lines on building components; the mark left by a chalk line.

Chamfer (chamfering) To remove an edge of a board only part way through at an angle other than a right angle.

Chord The main top or bottom component of a *truss.*

Circuit A continuous loop of current.

Circuit breaker (breaker) A switch-like device which automatically trips and opens a *circuit* when the rated current is exceeded as in the case of a *short circuit;* it is not damaged by tripping and can be reset when the problem is fixed.

Circular saw A power saw that uses a circular blade with teeth around the perimeter; Skilsaw is a trade name of a portable circular saw.

Clear span A building with an open area inside that contains no *posts* or *columns.*

Cleat A short length of wood fastened to a *joist,* wall *stud,* or other *framing* member to support horizontal framing pieces, shelves, and other components.

Clerestory An outside wall with windows that is between two different roof levels.

Clinch To bend over the end of a nail that protrudes through the back of a board.

Code Any published regulatory material.

Coffin A wooden box built around recessed ceiling lights to hold *insulation* away from the fixture.

Collar beam (collar tie) A horizontal structural component that connects opposing roof *rafters.*

Column A vertical structural component that supports a *beam.*

Component stall A stall made of preassembled walls that fit between *posts* within the barn and relies on them for support.

Composition roofing A general term for any roofing material having an *asphalt* base.

Concrete A mixture of water, *cement,* sand, and *aggregate;* cement and water are the two chemically active elements in concrete and when combined form a paste or glue that coats and surrounds the particles of aggregate and upon hardening binds the entire mass together.

Concrete block A prefabricated structural component, typically 8 inches by 8 inches by 16 inches, made of concrete that is used for walls.

Condensation The effect of warm, moist air contacting a cooler surface and depositing moisture (condensate) onto the cooler surface.

Conduction The flow of heat from one part of an object to another part.

Conductor A wire used to transmit an electric current; any substance that transfers electricity.

Conduit A plastic or metal tube for protecting electric cable.

Contractor An individual or company offering construction services.

Control joints (expansion joints) Lines cut into a *concrete* surface to ensure that if the *slab* cracks it will do so only along these lines; they are generally ¼ to ⅕ the thickness of the slab and placed every 4 to 10 feet across the slab.

Convection Heat transfer by the natural rising of the heated air and sinking of cooled air.

Coupling A fitting that joins two pieces of pipe.

Course One of the continuous horizontal layers or rows of shingles or of *masonry* brick or block.

CPVC Chlorinated polyvinyl chloride; rigid plastic pipe used in water supply systems, where *code* permits; withstands higher temperatures than *PVC.*

Crawl space A space under a floor that does not have sufficient height for a person to stand erect.

Cripple studs *Studs* shorter than the height of a wall, such as those used over and under a window opening.

Crook A curve or warp perpendicular to the edge of a board.

Cross bridging *see* Bridging.

Crown The high part, or convex part, of a curve, such as along the edge of a board.

Curing The process in which mortar and *concrete* harden; the length of time is dependent upon the type of *cement,* mix proportion, required strength, size and shape of the concrete section, and weather; favorable curing temperatures range from 50 to 70° F; close to maximum strength is achieved in 28 days.

d Refers to a specific nail size; pronounced *penny* and taken from denarius, a Roman coin; originally referred to the cost in pennies of 100 nails.

DC Direct current; the type of electricity generated by batteries.

Darby *see* Bullfloat.

Dead load The weight of structural parts of a building and other fixed loads.

Deck *Sheathing* layer of a roof, typically constructed of plywood or *OSB;* the structural *member* upon which the roofing material (shingles or tiles) is installed.

Double eaves course A double course of roofing installed at the *eaves* of a sloping roof.

Double header A *header* that is double the thickness of the *rafters* or *joists* to which it is attached.

Dovetail Wedge-shaped protrusions on one board fitting into matching notches in an adjoining board.

Downspout The pipe that carries water down from a *gutter.*

Drip cap A horizontal molding used to prevent water from running behind a panel, window, or other component.

Drip edge A continuous strip of material installed along the *eaves* and *rakes* designed to allow water to drip free without backing up under the roofing; usually made of non-staining material such as 26-gauge *galvanized* steel or pre-finished metal.

Dry well A gravel-filled hole in the ground used to dissipate water into the soil.

Drywall Interior wall finish comprised of sheets of *gypsum board* and taped joints; standard width is 48 inches.

Duplex nail (scaffold nail) A nail with two heads used for temporary fastening; the lower head can be driven flush for a tight connection, while the upper head can be grasped for easy removal.

Duplex receptacle A commonly used receptacle (outlet) having two plug-in sockets.

Dutch door A door with two leaves or halves, one above the other.

Easement The legal right afforded a party to cross or to make limited use of land owned by another.

Eaves The bottom edges of a sloping roof; those portions of a roof that project beyond the outside walls of a building.

Eaves course The first course of shingles or tiles at the eaves of a roof.

Eaves fascia *see* Fascia board.

Eaves trough *see* Gutter.

Edger A tool for rounding off the perimeter edges of a *concrete slab.*

Edging Metal strips applied to the edges of boards to prevent horses from chewing the wood.

Elbow (ell) A pipe fitting with two openings that changes the direction of the line.

Electrical box *see* Junction box.

Equipment ground *see* Ground.

Expansion bolt A bolt used to anchor lumber to *concrete* or to *masonry* walls; it has a sleeve that expands to grip a pilot hole when the bolt is tightened.

Expansion joints *see* Control joints.

Face-nailing Nailing perpendicular to the surface.

Fascia board (*eaves* fascia) Horizontal board covering the vertical ends of *rafters;* sometimes serves as attachment for *gutters.*

Faucet A *valve* on the end of a water pipe that controls the flow of water.

Fault The current that can flow in a *circuit* as a result of an undesired *short circuit.*

Felt (tar paper, roofing felt) *Asphalt* saturated *felt,* used as an *underlayment* material in roofing.

Fenestration Refers to the openings (door, windows, *skylights*) in a structure.

Fiberglass Fine filaments of glass made into a fibrous insulating material or molded into a solid material for use as translucent panels and other items.

Finish grade Surface elevation of lawn, driveway, or other improved surfaces after completion of *grading* operations.

Firewall A fire-resistant wall used to restrict or prevent the spread of fire between portions of a building.

Fixture (1) Any permanently connected light or other electrical device that consumes power. (2) In plumbing, a device that provides a supply of water or disposal, such as a sink, tub, and toilet.

Flashing A material, usually metal, used to prevent seepage of wind and water at a roof intersection or projection such as a *vent* pipe or *skylight;* flashing is done before applying final roofing.

Float   A *trowel*-like tool on a handle used for *concrete* finishing.

Floor plan   A drawing, a horizontal section, showing the arrangement of rooms, walls, partitions, doors, and windows and giving dimensions, names, and other information.

Flux   The paste that is used in *soldering* metal joints, such as copper plumbing.

Flying rafter   *see* Barge rafter.

Foam board (ISO, polyiso)   Lightweight, rigid insulation board made of polyisocyanate material and often having a reflective aluminum or plastic skin on one or both sides.

Footings   *Concrete* pads used under *posts* and *foundation* walls to distribute the weight of the structure over a greater area and thus prevent settling; placed below the *frost line* to prevent movement during freezing.

Forced air   A mechanical warm air system that uses a blower to distribute heated air to specific areas.

Forms   Structures usually made of 2 x 4s or 2 x 6s, or other lumber to hold, shape, and support *concrete* as it cures.

Foundation   Comprised of the supporting building components that contact the soil, such as *footing*, *piles*, and *caissons*.

Four-way switch   One of three switches controlling one outlet or fixture; the other two switches are three-way switches.

Framing   The framework of a building, consisting of *beams, columns, joists,* and *rafters,* etc.; the making of such a framework.

Free span   *see* Clear span.

French drain   A gravel-filled trench, sometimes containing a drainpipe at the bottom, used to disperse excess surface water into the ground.

Frost heave   The lifting of the ground or a structure due to the freezing of moisture in the underlying soil.

Frost line   The maximum depth to which the ground freezes in the winter.

FRP   Fiber-reinforced plastic.

Fuse   A protective device containing a thin wire that melts to interrupt the flow of current when the current exceeds a specified *value;* unlike a *circuit breaker,* a fuse cannot be reset and must be replaced after use.

Gable   The end wall of a building having a triangular shape formed by a single *slope* roof on either side of a *ridge.*

Gable roof   A simple triangular shaped roof having two *slopes.*

Galvanized   Coated with zinc to prevent corrosion.

Gambrel roof   A roof having two *slopes* on each side of the *ridge,* with the lower slope steeper than the upper.

General contractor (general)   An individual who does the work of, or oversees the work of, more than two unrelated building trades; often is responsible for a complete building project.

Geotextile   *see* Landscape fabric.

GFCI (GFI)   Ground fault circuit interrupter; a device that senses small imbalances in the *circuit* caused by current leakage to ground and helps safeguard against shocks by shutting off the electricity in a fraction of a second; can be in the form of an outlet or a *breaker.*

Girder   A large *beam* of steel or wood that serves as a horizontal support and typically supports smaller *beams.*

Girt   A horizontal *member* fastened to *posts* or *studs* and to which *siding* is attached.

Glazing   (1) The process of securing a pane of glass into a frame using glazier's points and glazing compound. (2) The glass portion of a window or door.

Grade   Surface level of the ground.

Grade of roofing   Grade A, B, and C are approved fire rating roofs.

Grading   The leveling and shaping of the ground.

Greywater   Waste water not containing toilet or food waste.

Green board   Moisture-resistant *drywall* for use in areas of high moisture, such as bathrooms.

Grille (grillwork)   A steel grating used as a barrier to protect windows and as the top portion of stall walls and doors.

Ground (1) One of the three most common *circuit* wires, along with *hot* and *neutral;* hot brings the current flow in, neutral returns it to the source, and ground is a safety route for returning current; ground and neutral are joined only at the main service panel. (2) **(Ground wire, ground conductor, safety ground, equipment ground)** an electrical *conductor* connected to the earth, usually by means of a *ground rod.*

Ground fault *see* Short circuit.

Ground rod (grounding rod) A rod, usually 8-feet long and copper, driven completely into the earth and used to *ground* an electrical panel.

Ground system In an electrical system, the connection of the *neutral* wire from the main panel to the earth via a *ground rod.*

Grout A thin mortar applied to *masonry* joints; can be purchased as a premix or made from *cement,* sand and, water.

Gusset (gusset plate) A piece of plywood or steel connecting two or more structural *members.*

Gutter (eaves gutter, eaves trough) A long, shallow trough installed under and parallel to the *eaves* to catch and direct water dripping from a roof, generally connected to one or more *downspouts.*

Gypsum A whitish mineral that occurs naturally in sedimentary rocks and which, after processing, hardens when mixed with water.

Gypsum board A panel consisting of a gypsum core, surfaced and edged with covering material, commonly paper, designed for various uses.

Halogen (quartz halogen) A bright, long-lasting light that uses a tungsten filament in a clear quartz tube filled with halogen gas.

Header (1) A beam at the end of a floor or roof opening into which a *joist* or *rafter* is framed. (2) A horizontal *framing member* installed above a door or window to transfer the building's load from above the opening to the supporting wall structure on either side of the opening.

Hose bib *see* Bibb.

Hot One of the three most common *circuit* wires, along with *neutral* and *ground;* hot brings the current flow in, neutral returns it to the source, and ground is a safety route for returning current; ground and neutral are joined only at the main *service panel.*

Hurricane clip A metal connector that joins two boards that cross at right angles.

ID Abbreviation for inside diameter; pipes are sized according to their inside diameter.

Ice dam An accumulation of ice and snow at the *eaves* of a sloping roof.

Insulation (1) Material used to minimize the transfer of heat through the wall, floor and ceiling of a building; classified according to form: loose fill, flexible, rigid, reflective, and foamed-in-place. (2) A non-conducting material, usually plastic or rubber, used to protect electric wires.

ISO *see* Foam board.

J trim Steel trim shaped like the letter "J"; used to cover the edges of steel siding panels.

Jamb The side piece or *post* of an opening such as a door or window.

Joist A horizontal *beam* usually 2-inches thick used to support a floor or ceiling.

Joist hanger A strap-like metal bracket that attaches to a beam to support the end of a *joist* or *rafter.*

Junction box (electrical box) A square, octagonal, or rectangular plastic or metal box open on one face that fastens to framing and houses wires, receptacles, and switches.

Kerf The slot made by a saw cut.

Knee brace A short diagonal brace between a beam and a column to make a rigid connection.

Knockout A removable piece of an *electrical box* or panel that allows cable to enter the box.

Kraft paper A strong, heavy, moisture-resistant brownish paper made from wood pulp treated with a sulfate solution, and used to make bags, wrapping paper, and backing for *fiberglass insulation.*

Lag Screws Large wood screws with a hexagonal bolt head.

Laminated Fabricated in layers that are glued or bonded together.

Landscape fabric (geotextiles, weed barriers) Cloth made of meshed or tightly woven polypropylene used to admit water and yet keep soil or vegetation from passing through.

Latch A general term for a device that holds a door or window closed.

Lead (service conductor) (1) An overhead or underground wire that supplies electricity from a power company. (2) The short length of a *conductor* (wire end) that hangs free in a box or *service panel*.

Ledger (ledger strip) A long horizontal *member* fastened to the face of a wall to support the ends of *joists, rafters,* shelves, or other components.

Level (builder's level, carpenter's level) (1) A hand tool used to check building components to make sure they are perfectly vertical and horizontal. (2) Horizontal.

Lintel A *beam* over an opening.

Live load Weight on a structure consisting of movable objects, animals, and persons.

Load bearing A wall or other similar structural component that supports more than its own weight; cannot be removed without providing an alternate means of support.

Loafing shed *see* Run-in shed.

Lookouts (outriggers) Short *framing members,* usually 2 x 4, that attach to the second *truss,* pass through notches in the end truss, and to which the barge rafters attach; used to extend the roof beyond the exterior wall.

Loose fill *Insulation* manufactured from mineral wool or other fibers that is poured or machine-blown into structural cavities.

Mansard roof A roof having two *slopes* on all four sides of a building, the lower slopes being steeper than the upper slopes.

Mare motel An open shelter usually consisting of steel pipe panels and a roof used for protection from the sun.

Masonry A wall or other structure made of individual *concrete,* clay, or stone units that are usually bonded together with mortar.

Mastic A gummy or paste-like adhesive.

Member An individual component of a structure.

Mesh *see* Reinforcing mesh.

Mil One one-thousandth of an inch; the measurement used to gauge the thickness of plastic sheeting such as used that for *vapor barriers.*

Millwork Generally all building components of finished wood that are made in a woodworking plant or planing mill, including doors, window *sashes,* door frames, stair components, and trim moldings.

Model code A *code* upon which other codes are based.

Modular barn A barn that is constructed from *modules* that are transported to the building site and assembled on a prepared *foundation.*

Module A factory-built complete unit of a building.

Monitor roof A roof with a raised portion over the center aisle to admit light and/or *ventilation.*

Mortise-and-tenon joint A joint in which one piece has a square or rectangular projection (tenon) that fits snugly into a similarly shaped hole (mortise) in the second piece; primary joint used in timber *framing.*

Mullion A vertical or horizontal *member* that divides adjacent window or door units.

Muntin A smaller, secondary *member* that divides the glass or openings in a *sash* or door. The look of a divided light is frequently created with a snap-in muntin grill.

Nailer A piece of wood added between *members* of a framework to provide a nailing surface for all edges of a panel (usually a sheet of *wallboard* or paneling) to be attached.

Neutral One of the three most common *circuit* wires, along with *hot* and *ground*; hot brings the current flow in, neutral returns it to the source, and ground is a safety route for returning current; ground and neutral are joined only at the main *service panel.*

NM Nonmetallic sheathed cable, usually with plastic *sheathing* that contains several *conductors;* the cable is flame-retardant and is limited to use in dry locations.

NMC Solid plastic nonmetallic-sheathed cable for use in wet or corrosive areas but not underground (*see* UF).

Nominal Dimension   A dimension that is greater then the actual dimension of lumber or masonry; in lumber, it is the rough sawn dimension of a board before it has been milled; in masonry, a brick nominal size usually allows for a ½-inch mortar joint to give the full dimension.

OC   On center; *studs, joists,* and other components placed so many inches apart center to center.

OD   Outside diameter.

OEM   Original equipment manufacturer.

Offset gable roof   *Gable* roof with the *ridge* off center of the building, so one side is shorter than the other, and often has a different *slope.*

Ohm   A unit that measures the resistance a *conductor* has to electricity.

Ordinance   A local law enacted by a municipality such as a city or township.

Organic roofing   *Asphalt* roofing using cellulose as a base.

OSB   Oriented strand board.

OSHA   The Occupational Safety and Health Administration, a federal association (part of the Department of Labor) that is responsible for creating and enforcing workplace safety and health regulations.

Outriggers   *see* Lookouts.

Overhang   Commonly refers to the roof portion that extends past the exterior wall; often it is enclosed by a *soffit.*

Overhead door   A door constructed of multiple leaves that is rolled up on tracks to open; commonly used as a garage door.

Overhead service   An electrical service where the *conductors* are brought to a building on poles overhead.

Panel stall   A free-standing stall consisting of completed wall panels that bolt together.

Partition wall   A wall that has no structural function and is installed to divide space.

Pavers   Paving bricks made of clay or *concrete.*

PB   Polybutylene; used for flexible plastic tubing used in water supply systems where allowed by *code.*

PE   Polyethylene plastic material; water pipes will tolerate repeated freezing.

Penny   *see* d.

Permit   *see* Building permit.

PEX   Cross-linked polyethylene plastic material.

Pier   A *concrete foundation* made by drilling a hole and filling it with concrete; the bottom of the hole is sometimes enlarged for more support, making a *belled pier* or *caisson.*

Pigtail   A short, added piece of wire connected by a wire nut; commonly used to extend or connect wires in a *junction box.*

Pile   A shaft-like *foundation* of wood, *concrete* or steel; wood and steel piles are usually driven into the ground, while concrete, piles are cast in holes that have been drilled in the ground *(pier).*

Pitch   The ratio of the vertical *rise* of a roof to the total *span,* expressed as a fraction; for example if the rise of a roof is 4 feet and the span is 24 feet, the roof has a pitch of 1/6 (4/24).

Plank   Generally a large board used as a walking or bearing surface.

Plot plan (site plan)   A drawing showing a complete property, indicating the location of buildings, driveways, *easements,* natural formations, etc.

Plumb   Vertically straight.

Plumb bob   A pointed weight on a string, hung point down over a specific reference point.

Ply   Layer.

Pole barn   A roof structure supported upon wooden *columns* (poles).

Polyiso   *see* Foam board.

Pony panel   *see* Sub panel.

Pony wall   A short wall.

Post (column)   A vertical structural component that is typically utilized to support a *girder* or other *beam.*

Post and beam   Type of wall *framing* that uses *posts* to carry horizontal *beams* on which other framing members are supported.

Power   *Watts,* a measurement of the rate at which electrical energy is used; watts = *volts* x *amps.*

Prehung door A door that is mounted to the *jambs* at the factory and is ready to be installed in a *rough opening.*

Pressure relief valve A *valve* that automatically releases excess pressure in hot water storage tanks to prevent explosion; all equipment used for heating or storage of hot water must have one.

Pressure-treated Wood that has had chemical preservatives forced into it under pressure to protect it from insects and decay.

Punch list A list of items noted during and after construction that have yet to be completed.

Purlin A horizontal *member* between *trusses* to which roofing is attached.

PVC Polyvinyl Chloride; a rigid white or cream-colored plastic material.

Quartz halogen *see* Halogen.

Rabbet A rectangular groove cut along the edge of a board.

Radiant barrier A reflective material, commonly polished aluminum, that blocks the transfer of radiant heat; available in the form of rigid sheets (foil-faced rigid foam or plywood *sheathing*) and rolls of flexible sheeting.

Radiation Transfer of heat by electromagnetic waves; an object in the path of such waves, as from infrared heaters, is heated but the surrounding air is not.

Rafter A sloping roof member that extends from the ridge of the roof to the *eaves* and supports the roof covering.

Rake The edge of a roof on a sloping side; *gable* end *overhang.*

RCA Raised center aisle; a barn with a *monitor roof.*

Ready-mix concrete Fresh concrete that is ready to pour and is transported from a concrete supplier in a cement truck with a revolving drum.

Rebar Reinforcing bars used to increase the tensile strength of *concrete;* comes in standard lengths of 60 feet that are cut to desired length and bent as required.

Reciprocating saw A saw with interchangeable straight blade; blade moves up and down and cuts on the upstroke.

Reducer A fitting that connects pipes of different sizes.

Reinforcing mesh Steel wires woven or welded into a grid of 6- or 10-inch squares used to strengthen *concrete slabs.*

Ridge (peak) The top of a roof where two *slopes* meet; the highest point of a roof that runs the length of the building.

Right-of-way A strip of land, including the surface and overhead or underground space, that is granted by deed or *easement* for the construction and maintenance of such things as utility lines, roadways, and driveways.

Rim joist *see* Band joist.

Rise The vertical distance between the *top plate* line of a barn and the *ridge* of the roof.

Riser In a stairway, the vertical boards placed between *stringers* to support *treads.*

Roll roofing *Asphalt* roofing that comes in rolls 36 inches wide by 36 feet long.

Romex A brand name of nonmetallic-sheathed cable often mistakenly used as a collective term for *NM*-sheathed cable.

Roofing The waterproof covering over a roof.

Roofing felt *see* Felt.

Rough opening The opening formed by *framing members* that is slightly larger than the window, door, or other component that is to be installed.

Rough-in (1) Installing *electrical boxes,* cables, and making in-wall connections before walls are covered. (2) Plumbing installation that includes running the water supply lines and drain, waste and *vent* lines to the proposed location of each *fixture* before walls are covered.

Router An electrical woodworking tool used for cutting grooves, slots, and for rounding edges.

Run The horizontal distance of a roof or stair step.

Run-in shed (shed, loafing shed) A building, usually pole framed, having only three sides and one or more large spaces that horses can enter and leave at will.

Runoff Water traveling across the ground surface.

R-value An indication of a material's thermal resistance; the higher the R-value, the greater resistance to the flow of heat.

Safety ground *see* Ground.

Sash The framework that holds the glass in a window.

Sawhorse A stand, usually used in pairs, used to hold wood while it is being cut.

Scab A short piece of wood nailed on the face of two boards where they join to help position or strengthen them.

Scaffold (scaffolding) A temporary platform-like structure for workmen to stand on.

Scaffold nail *see* Duplex nail.

Screed A straightedge, usually wood, used to strike off or level newly placed *concrete;* screeds can also refer to the form work used to level or establish the level of the concrete.

Screeding The initial leveling, the first stage in the finish of a *concrete slab* after pouring.

Sealant A compound used to fill and seal a joint.

Sealer A liquid applied to a porous surface to seal it and improve the adherence of the finish material.

Section view A drawing showing an imaginary cut through a building or portion thereof.

Septic tank A part of a private sewage disposal system consisting of an underground compartment in which waste is separated, solids biologically digested, and liquids discharged into the soil.

Service The *conductors* and equipment for delivering electricity from the electrical supply system to the main *electrical panel* of a building.

Service conductors *see* Service leads.

Service drop The overhead service connectors from a utility pole to a building.

Service entrance (SE) The location where the incoming electrical line enters a building.

Service leads (service conductors, supply leads) The incoming electrical lines that supply power to the *service panel.*

Service panel (service distribution panel) The wiring and *circuit breaker* box (or *fuse* box) within a building from which utility outlet receptacle wiring originates.

Setback The legal distance a structure or building must be from a property line, centerline of adjacent road, or existing structures.

Settling When a structure sinks and shifts over time as the supporting ground compacts or moves.

Shank The part of a screw or nail that is driven into wood.

Sheathing The first layer of material applied over the framing and under the finish material to add support and attachment for the finish layer, such as on roof and walls.

Shed *see* Run-in shed.

Shed roof (pitched flat roof) A roof having a single sloping surface.

Shed row A type of barn consisting of a single row of stalls with no enclosed aisle.

Sheetrock Trade name of United States Gypsum Company for *drywall* or *wallboard.*

Shell The basic minimum enclosure of a building before installation of interior partitions, plumbing, wiring, etc.

Short Circuit (ground *fault*) Misdirected current caused by a *hot conductor* accidentally contacting a *neutral* or *ground;* a short circuit is an immediate *fault* to ground and should always cause the *GFCI* or the *breaker* to trip or the *fuse* to blow.

Siding Finish material applied to the outside of a building, either on top of *sheathing* or directly to *framing.*

Sill (1) The board laid first on the *foundation* upon which the frame rests. (2) In a window or door, the horizontal *member* laid directly at the bottom of the door or window frame to provide support and closure.

Sillcock An outdoor water *faucet (bibb)* with a wall-attachment flange.

Single pole Type of switch with only two terminals, used to control a fixture from a single location.

Sinker A common nail with a head that tapers on the bottom to countersink it into the wood with less deformation of the woods surface; often has a checkered pattern on the head to prevent the hammer from slipping off.

Skids Timbers placed on the ground that support a building and allow it to be moved by pulling it over the ground.

Skip sheathing Typically 1-inch by 4-inch boards that are attached over solid *sheathing* or at a 90° angle over *rafters* or *studs* to create an air space beneath shakes or wood siding so they can breathe.

Skirting (skirt board, splashboard) Usually a *pressure-treated* 1 x 6, 1 x 8, or 1 x 10 board placed at the bottom of a wall below the siding to protect the siding from ground moisture.

Skylight A framed opening in the roof that admits sunlight into a building; can be covered with either a flat glass or plastic panel or a plastic dome.

Slab A level surface of *concrete,* commonly a floor, usually setting on the ground.

Sleepers Boards placed on the ground to support a floor; boards fastened to the surface of a roof perpendicular to the *rafters* to support a new roof; wood strips fastened to a *concrete* wall or floor for attachment of other materials.

Sliding T bevel (T-bevel, bevel square) A hand tool that consists of a handle and a 6- or 8-inch slotted blade, used for marking 90° and 45° angles.

Slope The incline of a roof as the ratio of vertical *rise* in inches to 12 inches of horizontal *run,* expressed as a fraction or as "X" in 12; a roof that rises at the rate of 4 inches for each foot of run has a 4/12 or 4 in 12 slope.

Soffit The underside of a horizontal surface which projects beyond a wall line, such as an extending roof.

Solder (1) A metal alloy that is melted to join or mend metal surfaces, commonly copper pipe. (2) The act of melting solder into the joint.

Sole plate The bottom horizontal *member* of a frame wall.

Span (1) The horizontal distance between structural supports such as of a *beam* or *truss.* (2) The width of a building.

Spigot *Faucet.*

Spike A larger, thicker version of a common nail, ranging in size from 30d to 60d.

Splashboard *see* Skirting.

Square (1) The amount of roofing required to cover 100 square feet of surface. (2) A 90° angle. (3) A metal tool used to mark right angles.

Stack A general term for any vertical drainage or *vent* pipe.

Starter strip A strip of composition roofing material applied along the *eaves* before the first row of shingles is laid.

Starting course The first course of shingles applied along the *eaves.*

Stem wall (wall stem The *foundation* wall that sets on the *footings;* it is commonly made of *concrete block* or 6-inch to 8-inch-thick poured concrete.

Stile The vertical *members* of window *sash* and panel doors.

Stool Horizontal trim piece attached to the window *sill;* the bottom rail of the lower *sash* in a double hung window rests against the stool.

Stop Small molding strips attached to side and head *jambs* to guide and stop moving *sash* and swinging doors.

Stop valve A *valve* that controls the flow of water to an individual *fixture,* allowing water supply to be stopped to one fixture without affecting the water supply to other fixtures.

String line A nylon line strung tightly between supports to check deviations in straightness or in elevation of building components.

Stringer An inclined *beam* supporting a stairway.

Stucco *Cement* plaster used as exterior wall covering.

Stud One of a series of slender wood or metal vertical structural *members* in walls; wood studs are usually 2 x 4s or 2 x 6s spaced 16 inches or 24 inches on center.

Sub-floor Installed over floor *joists* to provide a surface for the installation of finished flooring tiles and carpet; typically made of plywood or *OSB.*

Sub panel (pony panel) An auxiliary *electrical panel* that receives power from the main *service panel.*

Subcontractor (sub) A trades specialist such as electrician, plumber, or framer who is hired by the *general contractor* for a predetermined amount to perform all or part of a larger contract.

Supply leads *see* Service leads.

Swale A broad, shallow ditch or depression in the ground, either occurring naturally or excavated for the purpose of directing *runoff.*

Sway brace A long piece of wood or metal attached diagonally across the surface of walls and roofs to keep them square.

Sweating Using a torch and *solder* to join copper lines and fittings.

T-111 A plywood siding commonly ⅝-inch thick that is rough to the touch and has vertical grooves simulating boards.

Tamp To pack earth or other material down firmly with a series of blows from a machine or by hand using a flat plate mounted to vertical handle.

Tap A *faucet* or hydrant that draws water from a supply line.

Tar paper *see* Felt.

Task lighting Lighting that concentrates on specific areas for tasks such as grooming, measuring feed, or repairing tack.

Tee A T-shaped fitting with three openings used to create branch lines in a waterline or drain line.

Termites Whitish, ant-like insects that can cause structural damage to buildings by eating wood.

Threshold A strip of metal or wood used to seal the space between the bottom of a door and the floor.

Timber Lumber pieces, larger than a nominal 4 x 4, typically used as *columns* or *beams.*

Timber frame A type of *post and beam* construction that traditionally utilizes joinery rather than nails to connect *members* and make a self-supporting frame.

Toenail To drive a nail at an angle through the edge of a board.

Tongue and groove A type of joint where a tongue or spline along the edge of one board or panel fits into a groove of an adjoining board or panel.

Top plate The top horizontal *member* of a *stud* wall.

Transfer switch A switch used to transfer a load from one power source to another power source.

Transit A surveying instrument mounted on a tripod; commonly used by builders to establish vertical points of elevation, such as for leveling a building site or a floor.

Trap A curved section of drain line designed to hold water, thus preventing sewer gases and vermin from entering the building.

Travelers Wires that carry current between three-way and four-way switches.

Tread The horizontal part of a stair step.

Treated wood *see* Pressure-treated.

Trimmer A *stud, joist,* or *rafter* alongside an opening and into which a *header* is framed.

Trowel A *concrete* finishing tool having a thin, flat, steel blade that is either rectangular or triangular and with an attached handle; used to smooth concrete when it begins to stiffen.

Truss A framework of connected triangles used to support a roof without interior *posts.*

UF Underground feeder cable; electrical cable with wires molded into solid plastic, designed and rated for underground and outdoor use.

U-factor The rate at which heat is lost through a building's exterior walls, roof, windows, doors, and *foundation.*

UL Underwriters Laboratories; a private organization originally founded as a result of the need for insurance companies to help consumers choose safe electrical and safety equipment; UL evaluates equipment voluntarily submitted to it by the manufacturer; equipment that meets certain safety requirements is either UL Listed or UL Recognized; many insurance companies and local electrical *codes* in the U.S. require that installed electrical equipment be UL Listed.

UL Approved A commonly used but technically incorrect term; correct terms are UL Listed or UL Recognized.

UL Listed A form of approval granted by UL to equipment that will be user installed or operated and that is found to meet the safety requirements of the applicable UL standards; UL Listed products are marked with the UL insignia.

UL Recognized A form of formal approval granted by UL to devices that are not used as free standing equipment, but are to be installed into some other system by a manufacturer, electrician, or possibly by an end user; examples include wall switches, wire connectors, wire, *fuses,* and *circuit breakers.*

Underground service Electrical *service conductors* brought to a building underground.

Underlayment (1) A layer of plywood or other panel product installed over a *sub-floor* to provide a smooth, level surface for finish flooring. (2) A membrane material such as *asphalt* impregnated *felt* paper applied under roofing.

Union A three-piece fitting used primarily with steel pipes that joins two sections of pipe and allows them to be disconnected without cutting the pipe.

Utility knife A razor knife with a removable or retractable, disposable blade used for cutting *drywall* and *insulation.*

Valve A device to stop, start, and regulate the flow of liquid or gas through pipes.

Vapor barrier Any waterproof material used to prevent the passage of moisture, such as through walls and ceilings.

Variance An exception to a zoning law, usually granted when extreme hardship would result from adhering to the law.

Veneer In *masonry,* a facing of stone, brick, or other material applied against a structural wall; the thin outer layer of plywood.

Vent An outlet or inlet for air.

Vent stack The upper portion of the soil stack above the topmost fixture through which gases and odors escape.

Ventilation The process of supplying fresh air and removing stale air from a space.

Verge rafter *see* Barge rafter.

Volt A unit that measures the amount of electrical pressure; one volt equals the amount of pressure required to move one ampere through a wire that has a resistance of one *ohm;* volts multiplied by *amps* give the wattage available in *circuit* (V x A = W).

Voltage The driving force behind the flow of electricity, similar to pressure in a water pipe.

Wallboard A general term for manufactured panels used to cover a wall surface.

Watt A unit that measures the amount of electrical power consumed.

Web member One of the smaller components of a *truss* that connect the top and bottom *chords.*

Wire size *Conductors* for building wiring are available in AWG (American Wire Gauge) sizes ranging from 14 to 4/0; the larger the number size, the smaller the diameter; the smallest copper wire for general wiring is 14 gauge.

Witness marks Marks of a constant height made on a wall or *posts* using a *transit;* used to cut posts to the same height, to ensure level application of *girts* or other wall *members,* or to level a floor.

Working drawings A complete set of drawings that provide all information necessary for the construction of a building.

Wye A Y-shaped pipe fitting with three openings used to create branch lines.

Z trim Sheet metal trim shaped like the letter "Z" with right angles; used as a drip cap and to cover the ends of steel panels.

Zoning The division of an area of land into smaller areas the use of which are restricted by law.

RECOMMENDED READING

Engler, Nick. *Renovating Barns, Sheds, and Outbuildings.* Pownal, VT: Storey Publishing, 2001.

Feirer, John L., *Carpentry and Building Construction.* Glencoe McGraw Hill, 3rd edition, 1996.

Fershtman, Julie I., *Equine Law and Horse Sense.* Franklin, MI: Horses and the Law Publishing, 1996.

Fershtman, Julie I., *More Equine Law and Horse Sense.* Franklin, MI: Horses and the Law Publishing, 2000.

Greenwalt, Joni. *Homeowner Associations, A Nightmare or a Dream Come True?* Denver, CO: Cassie Publications, Inc., 1998.

Hageman, Jack M. *Contractor's Guide to the Building Code.* Carsbad, CA: Craftsman Book Company, 4th edition 1996.

Heldmann, Carl. *Be Your Own House Contractor.* Pownal, VT: Storey Publishing, 1995.

Hill, Cherry. *Stablekeeping.* Pownal, VT: Storey Publishing, 2000.

Hill, Cherry. *Horsekeeping on a Small Acreage.* Pownal, VT: Storey Publishing, 1990.

Kahn, Lloyd, Blair Allen, Julie Jones, Peter Aschwanden. *The Septic System Owner's Manual.* Shelter Publications, 1999.

Kardo, Redwood. *Code Check Electrical: A Field Guide to Wiring a Safe House.* Newtown, CT: Taunton Press, 2nd Spiral Edition, 2000.

Kardo, Redwood. *Code Check Plumbing: A Field Guide to the Plumbing Codes.* Newtown, CT: Taunton Press, 2000.

Kardo, Redwood. *Code Check, A Field Guide to Building a Safe House.* Newtown, CT: Taunton Press, 3rd Spiral Edition, 2000.

Leslie, Russell P. *Builders Guide to Home Lighting.* Troy, NY: Lighting Research Center, 1995.

Ludwig, Art. *Builder's Greywater Guide: The Guide to Professional Installation of Greywater Systems.* Santa Barbara, CA: Oasis Design, 1999.

Markell, Jeff. *Residential Wiring to the 1999 NEC.* Carlsbad, CA: Craftsman Book Co., 5th edition, 1999.

McKenzie, Evan. *Privatopia: Homeowner Associations and The Rise of Residential Private Government.* New Haven, CT: Yale University Press, 1994.

Mullin, Ray C. *Electrical Wiring: Residential.* Delmar Press, 13th edition, 1998.

Reader's Digest, New Complete Do-It-Yourself Manual. Reader's Digest Adult, 1991.

Richter, Herbert P. Schwan, W. Creighton, *Wiring Simplified (Based on the 1999 National Electrical Code).* Park Pub., 39th edition, 1999.

Scharff, Robert. *The Roofing Handbook.* New York, New York: McGraw-Hill Professional Publishing, 2nd edition, 2000.

Seddon, Leigh. *Practical Pole Building Construction.* Charlotte, VT: Williamson Publishing, 1985.

Step-by-Step Guide Books, Step-by-Step Guide Books. Salt Lake City, UT, 800-678-1500.

Western Wood Product Association, *Western Woods Use Book.* Portland, OR: Western Wood Product Association, 1996. www.wwpa.org

RESOURCE GUIDE

When you visit listed web sites, you may have to navigate through the site to find the section containing the information you are looking for.

ANTI-CHEW LIQUIDS

Carbolineum Wood Preserving Co.
PO Box 23148
Milwaukee, WI 53223-0248
414-353-5040, fax 414-353-3325

Dyco-Tec Products, Ltd. (aka Dyco Associates, Inc.)
870 Hawthorne Lane, Unit C
West Chicago, IL 60185-1998
630-837-6410, fax 630-837-5904
e-mail: Dyco1@aol.com
www.dycotec.com

Farnam Companies, Inc.
PO Box 34820
Phoenix, AZ 85067-4820
800-234-2269, 602-285-1660, fax 602-285-1803
e-mail. info@mail.farnam.com
www.farnam.com

Nordic National Group
7600 W. 27th St., Ste. 238
St. Louis Park, MN 55426-3163
612-922-9604, fax 612-922-8562

ARCHITECTS AND BARN PLANS

American Institute of Architects
1735 New York Ave., NW
Washington, DC 20006
800-AIA-3837, fax 202-626-7547
www.aia.org

Ashland Barns
990-J Butler Creek Rd.
Ashland, OR 97520
541-488-1541
www.ashlandbarns.com

BarnPlans, Inc.
41-049 Ehukai St.
Waimanalo, HI 96795
877-259-7028
e-mail: dano@barnplans.com
www.barnplans.com

Barns By Gardner
125 Circle Dr.
Fort Collins, CO, 80524
970-224-1560
planitcad@barnsbygardner.com
www.barnsbygardner.com

Gralla Architects
PO Box 538
Lexington, OK 73051
405-527-7000, fax 405-527-6283
e-mail: tcg@grallaarchitects.com
www.grallaarchitects.com

Harrison Banks, Architecture for the Horse Industry
790 Boylston St., Ste. 10-F
Boston, MA 02199
617-236-1876, fax 617-236-1419
e-mail: hbanks@ma.ultranet.com
www.harrisonbanks.com

Homestead Design, Inc.
PO Box 2010
Port Townsend, WA 9836
360-385-9983, fax 360-385-9983
e-mail: craig@homesteaddesign.com
www.homesteaddesign.com

Innovative Equine Systems
3550 Calistoga Rd.
Santa Rosa, CA 95404
800-888-9921, 707-538-4153, fax 707-538-4069
www.equinesystems.com

Thomas L. Croce Architects, Inc.
2962 N. St., Rt. 48
Lebanon, OH 45036
513-934-3957
e-mail: tlcroce@fuse.net
home.fuse.net/tlcroce

Tom Woodruff, Architect
355 Grove Ave.
Winter Park, FL 32792
407-657-0916, fax 407-657-7138
e-mail: TWoodruf@bellsouth.net
www.equiresource.com/commercial/woodruff.htm

Equi-Master, Inc.
Marlborough
PO Box 53039
Calgary, Alberta, Canada T2A-7P1
800-570-3848, 403-291-6860, fax 403-291-6861
e-mail: sales@equi-master.com
www.equi-master.com

ARIAL PHOTOS

Arial Photos of the United States
www.terraserver.microsoft.com

BIRD REPELLENTS

B & W Sales and Marketing, Inc.
1939 Parker Ct., Ste. E
Stone Mountain, GA 30087
770-985-8285
www.net-interprises.com/bandwsales/hotfoot.htm

Do It Yourself Pest Control Inc.
2823 Chamblee-Tucker Rd.
Atlanta, GA 30341
800-476-3368, 770-458-5090
e-mail: postmaster@doyourownpestcontrol.com
www.doyourownpestcontrol.com/4birds.htm

Tanglefoot Co.
314 Straight Avenue, S.W.
Grand Rapids, MI 49504-6485
616-459-4139
e-mail: tnglfoot@aol.com
www.tanglefoot.com

BUILDERS AND CONTRACTORS

A & B Barns
129 Sheep Davis Rd.
Pembroke, NH 03275
800-267-0506, 603-224-7483
e-mail: barns@nh.ultranet.com
www.abbarns.com

American MasterCraft
800-679-1113, fax 800-679-3692
e-mail: info@americanmastercraft.com
www.americanmastercraft.com

Arizona Porta Pens
8123 N.83rd Ave.
Peoria, AZ 85345
800-448-9039, 623-878-9039, fax 623-878-4388
e-mail: azpp1@earthlink.net
www.azportapen.com

B & V Enterprises
885 Flournoy Valley Rd.
Roseburg, OR 97470
Richard Conn, Owner
800-769-2315, fax 541-440-6914
e-mail: bandvent@livestocktrailer.com
www.livestocktrailer.com/barns.htm

Barnmaster
10124 Channel Rd.
Lakeside, CA 92040
or
2501 East I-20
Midland, TX 7970
800-500-BARN (2276)
www.barnmaster.com

Barns By Gardner (*see* Architects and Plans)

BCI Barn Builders
3221 E. Hancock
Muskogee, OK 74401
800-766-5793, 918-687-6432
e-mail: barn@ok.azalea.net
www.bcibarns.com

Cabin Creek Timber Frames
360 North Jones Creek Rd.
Franklin, NC 28734
828-369-5899
e-mail: jbell@dnet.net
www.cctimberframes.com

Cleary Building Corporation
Box 175
Madison, WI 53701-0175
800-373-5550, 608-256-1355, fax: 608-845-707
e-mail: cleary@clearybuilding.com
www.clearybuilding.com

Conestoga Buildings
202 Orlan Rd.
New Holland, PA 17557
877-278-4035
www.conestogabuildings.com

EZ Barns
3761 Government Blvd., Ste. E-4
Mobile, AL 36693
888-666-9752, 334-666-9752, fax 334-666-6704
e-mail: info@ezbarns.com
www.ezbarns.com

FCP Inc.
23100 Baxter Rd.
PO Box 1555
Wildomar, CA 92595
800-807-2276, 909-678-4571, fax 909-678-736
e-mail: info@fcpbuildings.com
www.fcpbuildings.com

Gresham Building Supply, Pole Barns
16091 S.E. Keller Rd.
Clackamas, Oregon 97015
800-291-0330, 503-658-4083
e-mail: brosseau@gbspolebarns.com
www.gbspolebarns.com

Handi-Klasp
1519 West James St.
Webster City, IA 50595
800-332-7990, 515-832-5579, fax 515-832-525
e-mail: info@handi-klasp.com
www.handi-klasp.com

Hardwick Post & Beam
Fleming Rd., Box 225
Hardwick, MA 01037
413-477-6430, fax 413-477-0937
e-mail: ridge@hardwickpostandbeam.com
www.hardwickpostandbeam.com

Harrison Banks (*see* Architects and Plans)

Hearthstone Georgia
120 Carriage Dr.
Macon, GA 31210
877-662-6135, 478-474-9370, fax 478-477-6535
e-mail: hearthstonehomes@mindspring.com
www.hearthstonegeorgia.com

Heritage Building Systems™
PO Box 470
North Little Rock, AR 72114
800-643-5555, fax 800-981-8163
www.heritagebuildings.com/main.html

Innovative Equine Systems
Kentucky Steel Truss Buildings, Inc.
2765 Wades Mill Rd.
Winchester, KY 40391
859-745-0606
e-mail: info@kstbuild.com
www.kstbuild.com

Johnson Barns & Trailers
22307 N. Black Canyon Hwy.
Phoenix, AZ 85027
602-465-9000

King Construction Co.
601 Overly's Grove Rd.
New Holland, PA 17557
717-354-4740, fax 717-355-2469
e-mail: dann@leba.net
www.leba.net/~dann

Lester Building Systems
1111 2nd Ave., South
Lester Prairie, MN 55354
800-826-4439, fax (320) 395-539
e-mail: info@lesterbuildingsystems.com
www.lesterbuildingsystems.com

MD Enterprises, Inc.
1720 East Locust St.
Ontario, CA 91761-9744
800-343-BARN (2276), fax 909-923-1573
e-mail: info@mdent.com
www.mdent.com

Morton Buildings
PO Box 399
Morton, IL 61550
309-263-7474, fax 309-266-5123
e-mail: mmorrison@mortonbldgs.com
www.mortonbuildings.com

National Barn Co.
1739 East Hwy. 62
Fort Gibson, OK 74434
800-582-BARN (2276), 918-478-3538
fax 918-478-3591
www.nationalbarn.com

National Frame Builders Association
4840 W. 15th St., Ste. 1000
Lawrence, KS 66049-3876
800-557-6957, fax 785-843-7555
e-mail: nfba@postframe.org
www.postframe.org

Old Dimensions
RFD #1, Blaney Rd.
Bethlehem, NH 03574
(603) 444-0227
e-mail: info@old-dimensions.com
www.old-dimensions.com

Port-A-Stall
PO Box 4126
Mesa, AZ 85211-4126
800-717-7027, fax 480-649-5290
e-mail: portastall@portastall.com
www.portastall.com

Steinbau Konstruktion Inc.
837 Freemont Rd.
Pleasant Valley, NY 12569
845-635-2265, fax 845-635-4344
www.castlemall.com/steinbau

Thomas L. Croce, Architects (*see* Architects and Plans)

Timber Frame Business Council
217 Main St.
Hamilton, MT 59840
406-375-0713, fax 406-375-6401
e-mail: nancy@timberframe.org
www.timberframe.org

Walter's Buildings
Jack Walters & Sons, Corp.
PO Box 388
Allenton, WI 53040
or
Hwy. 41, 6600
Midland, CT 53002
800-225-2591, 414-629-5521
www.waltersbuildings.com

Wick Buildings
405 Walter Rd.
Mazomanie, WI 53560
800-356-9682, fax 608-795-2534
e-mail: info@wickbuildings.com
www.wickbuildings.com/horse.htm

BUILDING CODE

American Wood Council
1111 19th St., NW, Ste. 800
Washington, DC 20036
202-463-2766, 800-AWC-AFPA (800-292-2372)
fax 202-463-2791
e-mail: AWCINFO@afandpa.org
www.awc.org

Buildingteam.com
www.buildingteam.com/codes/index.asp
*Search building codes, authorities and local utility information,
by city/county or state*

Code Check
www.codecheck.com

International Conference of Building Officials
(OCBO)
5360 Workman Mill Rd.
Whittier, CA 90601-2298
800-284-4406, 310-669-0541, fax 913-764-2272
www.icbo.org

Wood Truss Council of America
One WTCA Center
6300 Enterprise Lane
Madison, WI 53719
608-274-4849, fax 608-274-3329
e-mail: wtca@woodtruss.com
www.woodtruss.com/wtca/wtcaindex.html
Construction laws, general code information and links

BUILDING MATERIALS

CertainTeed Corporation
750 East Swedesford Rd.
PO Box 860
Valley Forge, PA 19482
610-341-7000, fax 610-341-777
www.certainteed.com
*Foundations, siding, roofing, insulation,
windows, ventilation*

DuPont
800-441-7515, 302-774-1000
e-mail: info@dupont.com
www.dupont.com
Tyvek contractor's tape

EchoStar, Inc.
230 Center Dr. #201
Vernon Hills, IL 60061
800-211-7170, fax 888-780-9870
www.ecostarinc.com
Recycled building products

Farm Tek's TekSupply
1395 Rte. 5
South Windsor, CT 06074
800-835-7877
www.TekSupply.com
Poly-Max polyethylene panel

Georgia-Pacific Corporation
PO Box 1763
Norcross, GA 30091
800-BUILD-GP
www.gp.com
Roofing, plywood, OSB, insulation,
gypsum board, lumber, siding

Kemlite Company, Inc.
PO Box 2429
Joliet, IL 60434
800-435-0080
www.kemlite.com
FRP, fiberglass, PVC, polycarbonate panel

National Gypsum Company
2001 Rexford Rd.
Charlotte, NC 28211
800-NATIONAL, 704-365-7300, fax 800-392-6421
e-mail: ng@nationalgypsum.com
www.national-gypsum.com
Drywall

New City Resources Inc.
NCR Industrial Centre
250 Baseline Road, East
Bowmanville, ONT, Canada LIC 1A4
905-697-3888, fax 905-697-0980
e-mail: info@newcityresources.com
www.newcityresources.com
Polyboard, Firex fireproof panel

USG (United States Gypsum Co.)
125 South Franklin
Chicago, IL 60606-4678
800-874-4968, 312-606-4000
e-mail: usg4you@usg.com
www.usg.com
Drywall

Western Wood Products Association
522 SW Fifth Ave., Ste. 500
Portland, OR 97204-2122
503-224-3930, fax 503-224-3934
e-mail: info@wwpa.org
www.wwpa.org
Lumber technical and regulatory information

COMPOSTING TOILETS

Biolet USA, Inc.
150 East State St.
PO Box 548
Newcomerstown, OH 43832
800-5BioLet (US), 800-6BioLet (Canada)
fax 740-498-4073
e-mail: info@biolet.com
www.biolet.com

Bio-Sun Systems Inc.
RR#2, Box 134A
Rte. 549 Jobs Corners
Millerton, PA 16936
800-847-8840, 717-537-2200, fax 717-537-6200
e-mail: bio-sun@ix.netcom.com

Clivus Multrum Inc.
15 Union St.
Lawrence, MA 01840
800-4-CLIVUS, 1-978-725-5591, fax 978-557-9658
e-mail: forinfo@clivusmultrum.com
www.clivusmultrum.com

Sancor Industries Ltd.
6391 Walmore Rd.
Niagara Falls, NY 14304
800-387-5126 (USA), 800-387-5245 (Canada)
fax 416-299-3124
e-mail: info@envirolet.com
www.envirolet.com

Sun-Mar Corp.
600 Main St.
Tonawanda, NY 14150
800-461-2461, 905-332-1314, fax 905-332-1315
e-mail: compost@sun-mar.com
www.sun-mar.com

CONCRETE AND MASONRY

Concrete Fastening Systems
1192 E. 40th St.
Cleveland, OH 44114
888-498-5747
e-mail: info@confast.com
www.confast.com
Carbide drill bits, concrete fasteners

Dynobond Inc.
PO Box 693
Mt. Brydges, Ontario,Canada N0L 1WO
519-438-5869
www3.sympatico.ca/dynobond
Acrylic polymer cement for concrete repair

Interlocking Concrete Pavement Institute
1444 I St. NW, Ste. 700
Washington, DC 20005-2210
202-712-9036. fax 202-408-0285
e-mail: icpi@icpi.org
www.icpi.org
Contractor locator, application and installation guides

Masonry Advisory Council
1480 Renaissance Dr., Ste. 401
Park Ridge, IL 60068
847-297-6704
e-mail: info@maconline.org
www.maconline.org
Articles, cost guide, contractor locator

National Ready Mixed Concrete Association
900 Spring St.
Silver Spring, MD 20910
888-84NRMCA (846-7622), 301-587-1400
fax 301-585-421
www.nrmca.org
Homeowner's guide to concrete

Pave Tech, Inc.
PO Box 576
Prior Lake, MN 55372
800-728-3832, 952-226-6400, fax 952-226-640
e-mail: sales@paveedge.com
www.pavetech.com
Paver brick information, installation and safety guides

Portland Cement Association
5420 Old Orchard Rd.
Skokie, IL 60077
847-966-6200, fax 847-966-8389
e-mail: info@portcement.org
www.portcement.org
Information on all aspects of concrete

Quikrete Companies
1790 Century Cir., NE
Atlanta, GA 30345
800-282-5828, 404-634-9100
www.quikrete.com
Consumer help line, info, glossary, projects, concrete calculator

Roadware Incorporated
2100 Wentworth Ave.
South St. Paul, MN 55075
800-522-7623
e-mail: sales@concretemender.com
www.concretemender.com
Concrete repair materials

CONTRACTOR LOCATORS

Builders Websource
www.builderswebsource.com
Forum, books, and videos that cover all aspects of building

Buildscape
www.buildscape.com
Maintains a searchable database of over one million architects, builders, and tradesman

Contractor.com
240 South Broadway, Ste. 207
Denver, CO 80209
877-266-8722, 877-CONTRACTOR, 303-480-0992,
fax 303-480-9042
www.contractors.com
Search for prescreened contractors by trade or keyword

Handyman Online
handymanonline.com
*Free estimates from a network of pre-screened contractors
in your area*

ImproveNet
www.improvenet.com
*Free online estimates and help finding a contractor
in your area*

National Contractors Referral and License Bureau
PO Box 23123
Pleasant Hill, CA 94523
e-mail: info@contractorreferral.com
www.contractorreferral.com

ServiceMagic
www.servicemagic.com
Locate prescreened contractors in your area

ELECTRICAL

Electrical Contractor Network
e-mail: Info@Electrical-Contractor.net
www.electrical-contractor.net
Electrician finder, code information, forums

Sutton Designs, Inc.
Ithaca, NY 14850
800-326-8119 or 607-277-4301
e-mail: sales@netsaverscenter.com
www.suttondesigns.com/fred3.html
Outlet tester

FENESTRATION
(WINDOWS, DOORS, SKYLIGHTS)

AG-CO Products
PO Box 126
St. Johns, MI 48879
800-522-2426, fax 800-831-0869
e-mail: stall@ag-coproducts.com
www.ag-coproducts.com
Windows, cupolas

CertainTeed Corp. *(see* Building Materials)
Windows

Commercial Door and Hardware
4100 N. Powerline Rd., Ste. C4
Pompano Beach, FL 33073
954-917-9332, fax 954-917-9335
e-mail: commdoor@netdor.com
www.commdoor.com
Heavy duty hinges

Daro Industries, Inc.
3905 California St., NE
Minneapolis, MN 55421
763-789-0054, fax 763-789-0064
e-mail: Mail@Daro-Ind.com
www.daro-ind.com
Heavy duty hinges

Garage Door Hardware Association
3950 Lake Shore Dr., Ste. 502-A
Chicago, IL 60613-3434
312-525-2644

Handi-Klasp *(see* Builders)

Innovative Equine Systems *(see* Architects)

Leatherneck Hardware
PO Box 1142
Danville, IL 61832
888-442-4572
e-mail: doorhdwe@soltec.net
www.doorhdwe.com
Heavy duty strap hinges, sliding door hardware

National Association of Garage Door Manufacturers
1300 Sumner St.
Cleveland, OH 44115-2851
216-241-7333

National Fenestration Rating Council
1300 Spring St., Ste. 500
Silver Spring, MD 20910
301-589-6372, fax 301-588-6342
e-mail: nfrcusa@aol.com
www.nfrc.org

National Horse Stalls *(see* Stalls)

Rockin J Horse Stalls *(see* Stalls)

Woodstar Products *(see* Stalls)

FIRE PROTECTION

American Wood Council (*see* Building Codes)
Fire wall information

Fire Sprinkler Network
12959 Jupiter Rd., Ste. 142
Dallas, TX 75238-3200
214-349-5965, fax 214-343-8898
e-mail: afsainfo@firesprinkler.org
www.sprinklernet.org
Sprinkler system information

Flame Seal Products Inc.
4025 Willowbend Blvd., # 310
Houston, TX 77025
713-668 4291, fax 713-668-1724
e-mail: homefire@homefiresafetykit.com
www.homefiresafetykit.com
www.flameseal.com
Liquid spray-on fire retardant kit

Hickson Corp.
1955 Lake Park Dr., Ste. 250
Smyrna, GA 30080
404-362-3970, fax 404-363-858
e-mail: info@Dricon.com
www.dricon.com
DRICON® FRT fire retardant treated wood

International Fire Resistant Systems, Inc.
580 Irwin St., #100
San Rafael, CA 94901
888-990-FF88, fax 415-459-7365
e-mail: info@firefree.com
www.firefree.com
Fire-free 88 fire resistant paint product

National Fire Protection Association (NFPA)
1 Batterymarch Park
PO Box 9101
Quincy, MA 02269-9101
800-344-3555, 617-770-3000, fax 617-770-0700
e-mail: custserv@nfpa.org
www.nfpa.org

National Fire Sprinkler Association
PO Box 1000
Patterson, NY 12563
845-878-4200 ext. 133, 845-878-4215
e-mail: Info@nfsa.org
www.nfsa.org
Sprinkler system information

PYROLOGISTIX Inc.
1645 Howe Island Dr.
Howe Island, Ontario Canada, K7G 2V6
888-588-4538, fax: 613-545-1582
e-mail: mail@pyrologistix.com
www.pyrologistix.com
Liquid fire retardants and barriers for wood shingles, walls

FLY MISTING SYSTEMS

Farnam Companies, Inc. (*see* Anti-Chew Liquids)

Innovative Equine Systems
(*see* Architects and Barn Plans)

Pro-Tech Systems
PO Box 1450
Tomball, TX 77377
800-776-5005, 281-351-8134
e-mail: CustomerService@protech-control.com
www.protech-control.com

United Spray Systems
PO Box 86
Le Sueur, MN 56058
800-950-4883
e-mail: plonske@bugpage.com
www.bugpage.com

U-Spray, Inc.
4653 Hwy. 78
Lilburn, Georgia 30047
800-877-7290
e-mail: jonathan@bugspray.com
www.bugspray.com

HEATING AND COOLING

American Society of Heating, Refrigerating
and Air-Conditioning Engineers, Inc.
1791 Tullie Circle, NE
Atlanta, GA 30329
800-527-4723, 404-636-8400, fax 404-321-5478
www.ashrae.org

Enerco
2685 East 79th St.
Cleveland, OH 44104
800-2511-0001, 216-881-5500
e-mail: process@enerco-mrheater.com
www.enerco.com
Infrared heaters

Innovative Cooling
3849 Hidden Acres Circle
North Ft. Myers, FL 33903
877-929-2655, 941-656-1111, fax 941-656-0566
e-mail: waycool@ix.netcom.com
www.waycoolfans.com

JE Adams Industries
1025 63rd Ave., SW
Cedar Rapids, IA 52406
800-553-8861, fax 319-363-3867
e-mail: sales@jeadams.com
www.jeadams.com
Aqua Breeze Cooling System

Kalglo Electronics Co., Inc.
5911 Colony Dr.
Bethlehem, PA 1807-9348
610-837-0700, 888-452-5456, fax 610-837-7978
e-mail: kalglo@kalglo.com
www.kalglo.com
Infrared heaters

Schaefer Fan Co.
PO Box 647
Waite Park, MN 56387
800-779-3267
www.schaeferfan.com
Fans, coolers, radiant heaters

Solaronics, Inc.
704 Woodward Ave.
Rochester, MI 48307
800-223-5335, fax 248-651-0357
e-mail: Sales@SolaronicsUSA.com
www.solaronicsusa.com
Gas-fired infrared heaters

HELP AND INFORMATION ON THE WEB

American Society of Home Inspectors
85 W. Algonquin Rd.
Arlington Heights, IL 60005
708-290-1919
www.ashi.com

B4Ubuild.com
www.b4ubuild.com
Information on all aspects of construction

Builders' Booksource
1817 Fourth St.
Berkeley, CA 94710
510-845-6874, fax 510-845-7051
e-mail: service@buildersbooksite.com
www.buildersbooksite.com
Extensive selection of books on all types of building

Buildscape
www.buildscape.com
Bulletin board, product reviews, articles

Calculator
www.calculator.com
Calculators for beams, spans, conversions, and more

Calculators
www.cyberyard.com/calculators
Calculators: concrete estimator, board footage calculator, drywall calculator, rise and rafter length calculator, insulation calculator, paint coverage calculator, span information, roofing square footage calculator

DoItYourSelf.com
www.doityourself.com
Help and forums on all aspects of building and remodeling, contractor locator and estimates

Dunn-Edwards Paints
www.dunnedwards.com/specs/t111.htm
Charts to help you find a paint for a particular material and application

Electrical Contractor Network
e-mail: Info@Electrical-Contractor.net
www.electrical-contractor.net
Electrician finder, code information, forums

Family Handyman.com
www.familyhandyman.com
How-to and fix-it articles and tips

Handymanwire
www.handymanwire.com/forum.html
Canadian forum on all building topics with resident experts on plumbing, electricity, masonry; extensive collection of Q & As

Home Inspection and Construction Information
www.inspect-ny.com

Hometime.com
www.hometime.com
Remodeling, repairs, product information project advice from electrical to framing to installing a garage door

Horsekeeping.com
www.horsekeeping.com
Horse care and facilities information

ImproveNet
www.improvenet.com
Message boards with more than a dozen experts, contractors, architects

Phone Man
www.geocities.com/SiliconValley/Pines/4116
Phone wiring tips and information
Plbg.com
www.plbg.com
Help forum frequented by plumbing manufacturers, master plumbers, kitchen and bath designers, architects, engineers, home owners

Plumbnet
www.plumbnet.com
Plumbers, plumbing engineers, plumbing designers, architects, interior designers, and homeowners sharing information and resources for new construction, remodeling, renovation, and restoration

Septic Information Website
www.inspect-ny.com/septbook
Inspecting, designing, maintaining septic systems

State and County Extension Specialists
www.reeusda.gov/1700/statepartners/usa.htm

Western Wood Products Association
Design tables

Today's Home Owner
www.todayshomeowner.com/forums
How-to tips, Q & A groups on all aspects of building including electrical and plumbing

Women in Woodworking
www.womeninwoodworking.com
A site designed especially for women woodworkers

INDOOR ARENA FOOTING

Equestrian Surfaces
10940 S. Parker Rd., #417
Parker, CO 80134
303-617-3598, fax 303-841-8685
e-mail: info@equestriansurfaces.com
www.equestriansurfaces.com

Equi-tread
2347 Hamm Rd.
Black Creek, BC, Canada V9J 1B4
250-337-8265, fax 250-337-2220
e-mail: equitred@island.net
www.equi-tread.com

TIREC Corporation (Perma-Flex)
PO Box 5258
1245 Delsea Dr.
Deptford, NJ 08096-0258
800-993-9411, fax 856-845-2445
e-mail: info@perma-flex1.com
www.perma-flex1.com

INSULATION

Celotex Corporation
PO Box 31602
Tampa, Florida 33631
1-800-CELOTEX
www.celotex.com/products/commercial/insulation/thermaxfinish.htm
Rigid insulation finish board

CertainTeed Corporation (*see* Building Materials)
Fiberglass batts and rolls

Energy Conservation Technologies
8095 South Lake Circle
Granite Bay, CA 95746
800-426-6200, 916-791-4372, fax 916-797-3022
e-mail: rwp@quiknet.com
www.polar-ply.com
Polar ply radiant barrier sheathing

Heartland Insulation Supply
1440 W. Douglas Ave.
PO Box 2846
Wichita, KS 67201
316-265-6712, fax 316-269-3299
e-mail: insulate@astrofoil.net
www.innovativebldgproducts.com
Radiant barrier

ICAA – Insulation Contractors Association of America
703-739-0356
e-mail: ICAA@insulate.org
www.insulate.org
Information, contractor locator

Innovative Insulation, Inc.
6200 W. Pioneer Pky.
Arlington, TX 76013
800-825-0123, 817-446-6200, fax 817-446-6222
e-mail: insulation@earthlink.net
www.radiantbarrier.com
Radiant barrier

Insulation Corporation of America
2571 Mitchell Ave.
Allentown, PA 18103
800-523-9366, 610-791-4200, fax 610-791-9984
e-mail: ICAsales@insulationcorp.com
www.insulationcorp.com/index.html
All types and forms of insulation

NAIMA (North American Insulation Manufacturers)
44 Canal Center Plaza, Ste. 310
Alexandria, VA 22314
703-684-0084, fax 703-684-0427
e-mail: insulation@naima.org
www.naima.org
Information

Polyisocyanurate Insulation Manufacturers Association
1331 F St., NW, Ste. 975
Washington, DC 20004
202-628-6558, fax 202-628-3856
e-mail: pima@pima.org
www.pima.org

Spray Polyurethane Foam Alliance
1300 Wilson Blvd., Ste. 800
Arlington, VA 22209
800-523-6154, fax 703-253-0664
e-mail: feedback@sprayfoam.org
www.sprayfoam.org
Information and list of spray foam companies

United Tape Company
2545 Ivy St., East
Cumming, GA 30041
800-233-1455, 770-889-4276
www.unitedtape.com
Foil tape and contractor's tape

LIGHTENING PROTECTION INFORMATION

American Fire Sprinkler Association
12959 Jupiter Rd., Ste. 142
Dallas, TX 75238-3200
214-349-5965, fax 214-343-8898
e-mail: afsainfo@firesprinkler.org
www.firesprinkler.org

Home Inspection and Construction
Information Website
www.inspect-ny.com/lightning/lightnin.htm

Lightning Protection Institute
3335 N. Arlington Heights Rd., Ste. E
Arlington Heights, IL 60004
800-488-6864, 847-577-7200, fax 847-577-7276
e-mail: strike@lightning.org
www.lightning.org

National Lightning Safety Institute
891 N. Hoover Ave.
Louisville, CO 80027
e-mail: rich@lightningsafety.com
www.lightningsafety.com

NFPA's Lightning Protection Code, NFPA #78
(*see* Fire Protection)

Underwriter's Laboratories Follow-up Services
Departments (*see* Safety)

Wisconsin Public Service Corporation
PO Box 19001
Green Bay, WI 54307-9001
800-450-7260
www.wisconsinpublicservice.com/farm/lightning.asp

LIGHTENING PROTECTION PRODUCTS

Automatic Lightning Protection
7548 West Bluefield Ave.
Glendale, AZ 85308
800-532-0990, fax 602-548-0351
e-mail: mheiberg@aol.com
www.lightningrods.com

Crosswinds Gallery
29 Buttonwood St.
Bristol, RI 02809
401-253-0344, fax 401-253-2830
e-mail: wvanes@aol.com
www.crosswinds-gallery.com

LIGHTS AND SKYLIGHTS

Daylite Company
Energy Efficient Systems
1560 Eastman Ave.
Ventura, CA 93003
888-DAYLITE, 805-642-6557, fax 805-642-4544
e-mail: lyndam@dayliteco.com
www.dayliteco.com

Kennies Plumbing, Heating, and Air Conditioning
319 Jessie St.
Hanford, CA 93230
888-WE DO AIR
e-mail: webmaster@kennies.com
www.kennies.com
The Sky Pipe

Lighting Research Center
21 Union St.
Troy, NY 12180-3352
518-687-7100, fax 518-687-7120
e-mail: lrc@rpi.edu
www.lrc.rpi.edu

Lighting Resource
PO Box 48345
Minneapolis, MN 55448-0345
952-939-1717, fax 952-939-1742
e-mail: lightsrc@lightresource.com
www.lightresource.com
Articles, resources, product information

Orion West Lighting
2524 E. Becker Lane
Phoenix, AZ 85028
602-788-4343, fax 602-788-9528
www.equinelighting.com
Waterproof fluorescent fixtures

Solar Bright Corp.
836 Deville Dr.
Largo, FL 33771
800-780-1759
e-mail: Solar@Solarbright.com
www.solarbright.com

Solatube International, Inc.
2210 Oak Ridge Way
Vista, CA 92083
800-966-7652
e-mail: info@solatube.com
www.solatube.com

X10 Wireless Technology, Inc.
15200 52nd Ave., South
Seattle, WA 98188
800-675-3044, 206-241-3283, fax 206-242-4644
e-mail: info@x10.com
www.x10.com
Wireless switches

ROOFING

AEP SPAN
5100 East Grand Ave.
PO Box 150449
Dallas, TX 75223
800-527-2503, 214-827-1740, fax 214-828-1394
www.aep-span.com
Metal roofing

Asphalt Roofing Manufacturers Association
4041 Power Mill Rd., Ste. 404
Calverton, MD 20705
301-348-2002, fax 301-348-2020
www.asphaltroofing.org

Atlas Roofing Corporation
1775 The Exchange, Ste. 160
Atlanta, GA 30339
800-933-1476
www.atlasroofing.com

Benjamin Obdyke
65 Steamboat Dr.
Warminster, PA 18974
800-523-5261
www.obdyke.com
Roof vents and gutter guards

Cedar Shake & Shingle Bureau
PO Box 1178
Sumas, WA 98295-1178
604-820-7700, fax 604-820-0266
e-mail: info@cedarbureau.com
www.cedarbureau.org

CertainTeed Corporation (*see* Building Materials)
Fiberglass and organic shingles, roofing felt, ceramic slate, clay tiles

Columbia Concrete Products Limited
8650 130 St.
Surrey, B.C., Canada V3W 1G1
877-388-8453, 604-596-3388, fax 604-599-5972
e-mail: rooftile@crooftile.com
www.crooftile.com

Echo Star
230 Center Dr., #201
Vernon Hills, IL 60061
800-211-7170, fax 888-780-9870
e-mail: shari@echostarinc.com
www.ecostarinc.com
Rubber slate roofing products

Englert Inc.
1200 Amboy Ave.
PO Box 149
Perth Amboy, NJ 08862
800 638-2507, -732-826-8614, fax 732-826-8865
e-mail: info@englertinc.com
www.englertinc.com
Metal roofing, gutter, Leaf Guard gutter protector

Englert Leaf Guard
1200 Amboy Ave.
PO Box 149
Perth Amboy, NJ 08862
800-Leaf Guard
e-mail: info@leafguard.com
Seamless gutter system

Evergreen Slate Co.
68 E. Potter Ave.
Granville, NY 12832
518-642-2530, fax 518-642-9313
e-mail: slate@evergreenslate.com
www.evergreenslate.com
Roofing slate

GAF Building Materials Corporation
1361 Alps Rd.
Wayne, NJ 07470
201-628-3536
e-mail: ResidentialSales@gaf.com
www.gafmc.com
Roofing products

GutterTop Solutions, Ltd.
PO Box 293124
Dayton, OH 45429
937-298-6630, fax 937-293-5389
e-mail: info@gutterguard.com
www.gutterguard.com
Vinyl gutter guard

National Roofing Contractors Association
0255 W. Higgins Rd., Ste. 600
Rosemont, IL 60018
847-299-9070, fax 847-299-1183
e-mail: nrca@nrca.net
www.nrca.net

Roof Tile Institute
PO Box 40337
Eugene, OR 97404-0049
541-689-0366, fax 541-689-5530
e-mail: info@rooftile.org
www.ntrma.org

Roofing Industry Educational Institute (RIEI)
2305 E. Arapahoe Rd., Ste. 135
Littleton, CO 80122
303-703-9870, fax 303-703-9712
www.nrca.net/riei

Tasman Roofing, Inc.
1230 Railroad St.
Corona, CA 91720
909-272-8180, fax 909-272-4476
e-mail: marketing@decraroofing.com
www.decratile.com
Metal roofing

Unicrete Products Ltd.
PO Box 246, Station "T"
Calgary, Alberta, Canada T2H 2G
403-279-8321, fax 403-279-0251
www.unicrete.com
Concrete roof tiles

SAFETY

Equi-Master, Inc. (*see* Architects)
Giant floor magnets

OSHA
U.S. Department of Labor
Occupational Safety & Health Administration
Office of Public Affairs - Room N3647
200 Constitution Ave.
Washington, DC 20210
800-321-OSHA (6742)
www.osha.gov

Underspace®
The WEB Home of Underground Focus Magazine
www.underspace.com/index.htm
Excavation safety issues

Underwriters Laboratories (UL)
e-mail: info@us.ul.com
www.ul.com
UL Follow-up Services Departments:

- 333 Pfingsten Rd., Northbrook, IL 60062
  (708) 272-8800

- 1285 Walt Whitman Rd., Melville, NY 11747
  (516) 271-6200

- 1655 Scott Blvd., Santa Clara, CA 95050
  (408) 985-2400

- 12 Laboratory Dr., Research Triangle Park, NC
  27709, (919) 549-1400

- 2600 N.W. Lake Rd., Camas, WA 98607
  (360) 817-5500

SECURITY
(CLOSED CIRCUIT TV, INTERCOMS)

Keepsafer Easy Do-It-Yourself Home Security
1525 North Hayden Rd. Ste. #4
Scottsdale, AZ 85257
800-221-9362, 800-835-2680, 480-994-0808
fax 480-946-6385
e-mail: csr@easyhomesecurity.com
www.keepsafer.com
Video monitoring systems, wireless intercoms, smoke detectors

Riverwind Surveillance Supply
888-409-7665
e-mail: riverwind-surveillance@att.net
home.att.net/~riverwind-surveillance/index.htm
Video monitoring systems

Hunter Creek Video Systems
403 W. Pine Lodge Rd.
Roswell, NM 88201
888-626-7911
e-mail: huntercreekfarm@usa.net
www.huntercreekvideo.com

X10 Wireless Technology, Inc. (*see* Lights)
Surveillance cameras, remote light switches, motion and heat sensor switches

STALLS AND COMPONENTS

AG-CO Products (*see* Fenestration)
Stalls, feeders

Alternate Solutions
103 S. Walters
Poteau, OK 74953
800-451-4660, 918-649-3785, fax 918-649-3790
e-mail: info@alternate-solutions.com
www.buytack.com
Miniature horse stalls

America's Acres, Inc.
PO Box 2153
New Preston, CT 06777
888-250-5151
e-mail: info@americasacres.com
www.americasacres.com
Anti-cast stall strips

Armour Gates
1101 E. 25th St.
Sanford, FL 32771
800-876-7706, fax 407-74-9763
e-mail: info@armourgates.com
www.armourgates.com
Aluminum stall components

C & P Eng & Mfg Co, Inc.
5650 Industrial Ave., South
Connersville, IN 47331-7715
800-783-4283, 765-825-4293, fax 765-825-4292
e-mail: candpgates@aol.com
www.aceofgates.com
Window guards, stall gates

Classic Equine Equipment
RR #2, Box 681
Ironton, MO 63650
800-444-7430, fax 573-546-6700
e-mail: info@classic-equine.com
www.classic-equine.com

Country Manufacturing
PO Box 104
333 Salem Ave.
Fredericktown, OH 43019
740-694-9926, fax 740-694-5088
e-mail: info@countrymfg.com
www.countrymfg.com
Stalls and accessories

Equi-Master, Inc. (*see* Architects and Plans)
Stalls, waterers

Handi-Klasp (*see* Builders)
Cupolas, Dutch doors, stalls, mats, waterers

Innovative Equine Systems (*see* Architects)
Stall fronts, exterior doors

JW Hall
PO Box 68
Santa Fe, TX 77517
800-475 8158, fax 409-925 4782
e-mail: jimhall@maillandinternet.net
www.jwhall.com
Stall assemblies

National Horse Stalls
PO Box 153
Raphine, VA 24472
800-903-8908, fax 540-337-5973
e-mail: info@nationalhorsestalls.com
www.nationalhorsestalls.com
Dutch doors, window doors, stalls, aisle doors

Northern Light Stalls
1438 Country Rd., G
New Richmond, WI 54017
800-246-3190, (715) 246-3190, fax 715-246-9629
e-mail: nlstalls@pressenter.com
www.nlstalls.com
Stalls, feeders, grilles, edging, steel channel

Priefert Manufacturing Co., Inc.
PO Box 1540
Mt. Pleasant, TX 75456
800-527-8616, fax 903-572-2798
e-mail: sales@priefert.com
www.priefert.com
Stalls and accessories

Richard Klimesh
PO Box 140
Livermore, CO 80536
fax 815 366 8793
e-mail: rklimesh@horsekeeping.com
www.horsekeeping.com
Tie rings, blanket rods, door handles

Rockin J Horse Stalls
Box 869
Mannford, OK 74044
800-765-7229, 918-865-2781, fax 918-865-4191
e-mail: info@rockinjhorsestalls.com
www.rockinjhorsestalls.com
Custom stalls, grilles, rolling doors, full grill doors, drop panels, feed doors, swing feeders, waterers, doors, hinged blanket bars

Silk Tree Manufacturing
Rte. 1, Box 3430
Dillwyn, VA 23936-8730
804-983-1941, 800-297-SILK (7455), fax 804-983-1910
e-mail: silktree@juno.com
www.silktree.com
Chew guard edging, shatterproof mirrors, bucket heaters

Woodstar Products
PO Box 444
Delavan, WI 53115
800-648-3415, 262-728-8460, fax 262-728-1813
e-mail: woodstar@idcnet.com
www.wdstar.com
Stalls, Dutch doors, cupolas, waterers, feeders, grilles, steel channel, mats, weathervanes, accessories

STALL FLOORING

Caple-Shaw Industries, Inc.
1112 NE. 29th St.
Fort Worth, TX 76106
800-969-3234
Black Beauty Mats

A.C.F., Inc.
2831 Cardwell Dr.
Richmond, VA 23234
800-788-6223, fax 804-271-3074
e-mail: ACF100@sales.com
www.equustall.com
Equustall permeable flooring for protecting French drain and drywell

Groundmaster Products, Inc.
HC4, Box 169P
Gainesville, MO 65655
800-411-2530, fax 417-679-3015
e-mail: bjpqh@hotmail.com
www.eqwi.com/groundmaster
Permeable flooring for protecting French drain and drywell

Humane Manufacturing Co.
805 Moore St.
Baraboo, WI 53913-2796
800-369-6263
Lok Tuff Mats

Innovative Equine Systems
3550 Calistoga Rd.
Santa Rosa, CA 95404
800-888-9921, 707-538-4153, fax 707-538-4069
www.equinesystems.com

Linear Rubber Products, Inc.
5525 19th Ave.
Kenosha, WI 53140
800-558-4040
e-mail: info@rubbermats.com
www.rubbermats.com

North West Rubber Mats Ltd.
33850 Industrial Ave.
Abbotsford, BC. Canada V2S 7T9
800-663-8724
Red Barn Mats

RB Rubber Products, Inc.
904 E. 10th Ave.
McMinnville, OR 97128
800-525-5530, 503-472-4691;
fax 800-888-1183, 503-434-4455
www.rbrubber.com
Tenderfoot Mats

Southwest Animal Products
3052 Industry St., Ste. 107
Oceanside, CA 92054
800-400-3165, fax 760-754-9692
e-mail: info@stallskins.com
www.stallskins.com
Cover for French drains

Summit Rubber Products, Ltd.
4820 Old LaGrange Rd.
Buckner, KY 40010
800-782-5628
www.summitflex.com
Rubber bricks and tiles, Protector Mats

WeatherBusters
PO Box 2270
Alpine, CA 91903
877-228-7837, 619-390-2420, fax 619-390-2425
e-mail: info@weatherbusters.com
www.weatherbusters.com
Geotextile fabric

TREATED WOOD

American Wood Preservers Institute
2750 Prosperity Ave., Ste. 550
Fairfax, VA 22031-4312
800-356-AWPI, 703-204-0500, fax 703-204-4610
e-mail: Info@awpi.org
www.awpi.org

American Wood-Preservers' Association
3246 Fall Creek Hwy., Ste. 190
Granbury, TX 76049
817-326-6300
www.cssinfo.com/info/awpa.html

AWPI's Consumer Safety Information
www.ccasafetyinfo.com

Caribbean Lumber Company
P O Box 2687
Savannah, GA 31498-2687
912-748-7800
Borate pressure-treated lumber

CSI, Chemical Specialties, Inc.
One Woodlawn Green, Ste. 250
200 East Woodlawn Rd.
Charlotte, NC 2821
800-421-8661, fax 704-527-8232
www.treatedwood.com
Search for treated wood by use and brand

Louisiana-Pacific Corporation
10115 Kincey Ave., Ste. 150
Huntersville, NC 28078-6479
800-580-4296, 704-875-2131, fax 704-875-1680
www.smartguard.lpcorp.com

Nisus Corporation
Cherokee Place
101 Concord St.
North Knoxville, TN 37919
615-637-1226, 800-264-0870
www.nisuscorp.com
Borate preservatives

Osmose, Inc.
980 Ellicott St.
Buffalo, NY 14209-2398
800-877-POLE, fax 716-882-7822
www.osmose.com

U.S. Borax Inc.
26877 Tourney Rd.
Valencia, CA 91355
1-800-USBORAX (872-6729), 661-287-5400
fax 661-287-5495
www.borax.com
Borate preservatives

VENTS AND SCREENS

A.S. WebSales Corp.
103 S. Walters St.
Poteau, OK 74953
800-451-4660, 918-649-3785
e-mail: info@buytack.com
www.buytack.com
Weathervanes and cupolas

Benjamin Obdyke (*see* Roofing)
Ridge vents

CertainTeed Corporation (*see* Building Materials)
Ridge vents

Cor-A-Vent, Inc.
PO Box 428
Mishawaka, IN 46546-0428
800-837-8368, fax 800-645-6162
e-mail: info@cor-a-vent.com
www.cor-a-vent.com
Ridge and soffit vents

Farm Tek's TekSupply
(*see* Building Materials)
Humidistat, vents

Fly Away AgriProducts
1550 Industrial Dr.
Blue Earth, MN 56013
888-285-7454
e-mail: flyaway@bevcomm.net
www.flyawayagri.com/screens.htm
Weatherscreens

Home Ventilating Institute
30 West University Dr.
Arlington Heights, IL 60004
847-394-0150, fax 847-253-0088
e-mail: general@hvi.org
www.hvi.org
Tests and rates ventilation products

Kace International
300 Big Town Mall
Mesquite, TX 75149
888-827-7789, fax 214-320-3737
e-mail: kaceintl@msn.com
www.kaceintl.com
Weatherscreens

MWI Components
1015 32nd Ave., West
Spencer, IA 5130
800-360-6467, fax 800-361-3452
e-mail: contactsales@mwicomponents.com
www.mwicomponents.com
Roof vents, cupolas

WATER

AG-CO Products (*see* Fenestration)
Insulated bucket holders

Allied Precision Industries
705 E. North St.
Elburn, IL 60119
800-627-6179, 708-365-0340, fax: 630-365-0241
www.alliedprecision.com
Heated bucket holder

American Tank Co., Inc.
PO Box 340
Windsor, CA 9549
877-655-1100, 707-535-1400, fax 707-535-1450
e-mail: sales@americantank.com
www.watertanks.com
All types of steel and plastic water tanks

America's Acres, Inc. (*see* Stalls and Components)
Tankless water heaters

Bar Bar A Equipment Company
230 East 1700, South
Farmington, UT 84025
800-451-2230
e-mail: johnk@synergyplastics.net
www.synergyplastics.net
Non-freeze horse waterer

Behlen Mfg. Co.
PO Box 569
4025 E. 23rd St.
Columbus, NE 68601
402-564-3111, 402-563-7405
e-mail: behlen@behlenmfg.com
www.behlenmfg.com/ind.htm
Freedom Fountain automatic waterer

Controlled Energy Corporation
340 Mad River Park
Waitsfield, VT 05673
802 496-4357, fax 802 496-6924
e-mail: sales@controlledenergy.com
Tankless water heaters

Field Controls
2630 Airport Rd.
Kinston, NC 28504
252-522-3031, fax 252-522-0214
e-mail: sales@fieldcontrols.com
www.fieldcontrols.com
Water Sentry™ automatic water shutoff for leaks or burst pipes

Handi-Klasp (*see* Builders and Contractors)
Automatic waterers

National Well Owners Association
601 Dempsey Rd.
Westerville, OH 43081
800-551-7379, 614-898-7791, fax 614-898-7786
e-mail: customerservice@ngwa.org
www.wellowner.org

Nelson Manufacturing Company
3049 12th St., SW
Cedar Rapids, IA
888-844-6606, 319-363-2607, fax 319-363-3601
e-mail: nelsonmfg@uswest.net
www.nelsonmfg.com
Automatic waterers
OK Water, Inc.
3824 E. 6th Ave.
Stillwater, OK 74074
800-750-2837
www.Okwater.com
Heated bucket holder

Ritchie Industries, Inc.
PO Box 730
Conrad, IA 50621
800-747-0222, fax 641-366-2551
e-mail: info@ritchiefount.com
www.ritchiefount.com
Automatic waterers

INDEX

Page references in *italic* indicate photographs, those in **bold** indicate measured plans.